'Quite unlike some high profile UK Muslims to date ... Dr Bari carries the weight of the community with him ... He is not afraid to challenge the elders or the angry voices of young people. His words and advice in this book will be an uncomfortable challenge for all who wish to stay in their comfort zones and blame others for their plight.'

– **Neil Jameson CBE,**
Executive Director of Citizens UK

'The subject of Muslim engagement in Britain is a fraught one. In this book we hear first hand one man's journey and hopes for the future.'

– **Shelina Janmohamed, author of**
Generation M: Young Muslims Changing the World.

'Instrumental in creating a successful multicultural, multi-ethnic London Olympic Games Muhammad worked tirelessly to unite faiths, nationalities and communities to ensure the delivery of the most cosmopolitan Olympic Games ever seen.'

– **Lord Colin Moynihan, Chairman of the**
British Olympic Association London 2012 and former Minister for Sport.

'I have had the privilege of knowing Dr Muhammad Abdul Bari for many years. He is a figure of great compassion and integrity, and has played an enormous role in representing the British Muslim communities. This book is a deeply moving personal story about how one British Muslim has dealt with courage and patience with very complex and sensitive issues for over three decades.'

– **Peter Oborne, Columnist for the Daily Mail and Middle East Eye**

'In this memoir, Muhammad Abdul Bari provides a unique perspective on the evolution of the Muslim community in the UK, through his role as a community activist. His personal account offers an insight into the multitude of community projects and initiatives, and the challenges faced in light of key events and policy developments for the Muslim community as it has continued to mature over the last few decades. Dr Bari's efforts to cultivate relationships within and beyond the Muslim community to contribute towards a better understanding and foster positive relations is a great example of how Muslims can play a positive role in society.'

– **Shaykh Akram Nadwi, Islamic scholar,**
Dean of Cambridge College and author of *The Women Scholars in Islam*

T0273594

A LONG JIHAD

My Quest for
the Middle Way

MUHAMMAD ABDUL BARI

A Long Jihad. My Quest for the Middle Way

First published in England by
Kube Publishing Ltd
Markfield Conference Centre
Ratby Lane Markfield Leicestershire
LE67 9SY United Kingdom
Tel: +44 (0) 1530 249230 Fax: +44 (0) 1530 249656
Email: info@kubepublishing.com
Website: www.kubepublishing.com

Cataloguing-in-Publication Data is available from the British library

ISBN 978-1-84774-118-9 Hardback
ISBN 978-1-84774-117-2 Paperback
ISBN 978-1-84774-119-6 ebook

Initial Concept Cover Design: Inspiral Design
Cover Design: Nasir Cadir
Typesetting: Nasir Cadir

Printed by: Mega Printing in Turkey

Contents

Acknowledgements

OVER THE COURSE of an eventful life I have worked alongside many groups and individuals and this book is the outcome of the ideas, discussions and debate that arose with many of them. I am hugely indebted to each and every one from all these groups and no amount of gratitude will suffice; acknowledging them individually will be an impossible task and I beg forgiveness from all those who have helped me during this process but whose names I have failed to mention.

However, there are a few who have energetically helped me with their support during the preparation of this manuscript. In particular, I would like to mention Rumman Ahmed, Dr Jamil Sherif, Musleh Faradi, Neil Jameson, Nick Ryan and Sir Stephen O'Brien. Among them, Rumman and Jamil devoted their invaluable time with ideas, suggestions and painstaking critical analysis at various stages of the draft, and I am grateful to Nick for his editing. I am also grateful for Usaama Azami's very helpful comments on various issues discussed in the book, as well as his invaluable editorial support. May God almighty reward them all for their efforts.

I am where I am today because of the parenting I received from my own mother and father in my childhood years. They are no more in this world, but continue to be my guide in life, may God bless their souls. Our four children: Rima, Raiyan, Labib and Adib – who are now all adults and professionals – have been my companions in life. Raiyan spent a huge amount of time, in spite of his demanding job, going through most of the chapters, and I am indebted to all of them for their direct and indirect help through all the phases of the book.

However, my indebtedness to Sayeda, my life partner and confidant, knows no bound. As the main pillar of our blessed family, she has encouraged and supported me ever since we first formed a family, and her liveliness, resilience and wisdom have always kept me in high spirits.

At the end of the day, this book is written by me and I take full responsibility for its contents. I am grateful to God almighty for guiding me in every stage of my life, and I seek His forgiveness for my errors and shortcomings.

Foreword

I AM WRITING THIS as the repercussions of President Trump's blanket ban on refugees and residents from several Muslim countries in the Middle East and Africa entering the USA are being felt across the world. The President says the ban is temporary and denies it is aimed at Muslims, and although it has been somewhat modified with a new Executive Order, since Trump also says it is intended to challenge Islamic terrorism and to 'keep America safe' the message is pretty clear to all and resonates with what he said many times on the campaign trail: It's all the 'Muslims' fault'!

The tragic consequences of this ban at a human level – families forced apart, loved ones stranded, the Syrian refugee programme suspended indefinitely – have yet to be counted, but they will be tragic for the thousands of individuals affected and desperate stories will continue to be told and amplified across the web and news channels. Yet again, 'Muslims' and 'tragic stories' will be linked and the negative narrative associated with the world's second largest religious group of 1.6 billion adherents, or 23 per cent of the world's population, will be compounded.

In the UK, this negative image (often portrayed and exaggerated by the media) is in spite of the UK's Muslim community being the most generous, most family focused, most self-sufficient and most proud of being British (Britain being seen as the most Muslim-friendly of many Western countries). So, those of us who are not Muslim but know and love Islam and seek to be good neighbours to all (just as Prophet Muhammad and Jesus Christ instructed) must work harder to challenge the negative narrative and promote the good. That's why this book and the life and example of Dr Muhammad Abdul Bari is so important and his resilience, in the face of hostility from all sides, is so impressive.

I have had the privilege of knowing and working alongside Dr Bari for the last twenty years, mainly in east London. I live in Stepney and he has worked and done most of his community work in Tower Hamlets. We have shared both the good and the not so good moments of this journey together. He is too young to talk of legacy, since that usually happens when people die, but Dr Bari's legacy is already clear to me; not only in the bricks and mortar of the outstanding London Muslim Centre and East London Mosque but, equally significantly, in the thousands of young people he has mentored, encouraged and supported on their own journey as British Muslims or Britons who happen to be Muslim. If these are not enough for a legacy, then there will be the thousands of families who have read and relied on his books on parenting and his blogs on youth identity, parenting and public life.

My vocation to revive the tradition of community organizing in the UK started properly in 1989, when I helped set up Citizens UK to be the home of community organizing. Initially, I organized in Bristol and managed to build a Citizens Alliance of twenty-seven institutions – churches, schools, voluntary associations, three Sikh and one Hindu Temple. Together we campaigned for better housing, more sensitive policing, business accountability, and general issues surrounding the 'common good'. In 1994, I was invited to take this model to east London and see if it was possible to organize across the four east London boroughs of Newham, Waltham Forest, Hackney and Tower Hamlets (twenty years later, The East London Citizens Organization [TELCO] now includes civil society groups from Redbridge and Barking and Dagenham, too).

In November 1996, leaders and members of forty-seven civil society groups across the four boroughs gathered at York Hall in Bethnal Green for the Founding Assembly of TELCO (now part of London Citizens with over 200 institutions in membership). More than 1,200 citizens packed the historic Hall and were encouraged and endorsed by the late Cardinal Hume, the BBC presenter and former *Independent* editor Andrew Marr, Sir Stephen O'Brien (of London First), local politicians and other religious leaders. The largest and most disciplined turnout was the delegation from the East London Mosque (ELM) in Whitechapel. Siraj Salekin from the ELM co-chaired the Assembly, and made it clear that he was a proud East Ender and that we were all in this together, as did the diverse and youthful delegation from his Mosque community. This was the beginning of what has been a mutually beneficial relationship between what is now the London Muslim Centre, its neighbours in TELCO/London Citizens, and Dr Bari and myself. Citizens UK organizes around the broad and common interests of the member groups.

At the end of the 1990s, apart from promoting Islam and providing services for the growing body of worshippers, the self-interest of the East London Mosque was growth and expansion. Consequently, in 1998 TELCO and the mosque joined hands in an ambitious campaign to protect the plot of land adjacent to the building for mosque expansion against the alternative threat of expensive private flats for City workers. The story of this successful struggle will be told elsewhere, but the tactic we decided on was for the Christian clergy of

TELCO to lead the campaign for the land and the ELM team to stand back but oversee developments and support large public actions to attract media and public attention. The outcome of this 'jihad' (in its true meaning, as 'struggle') was that the East London Mosque acquired the land in 1999 and HRH Prince Charles and HRH Prince Mohammed al-Faisal launched the fundraising for the London Muslim Centre in 2001, which was opened in 2004.

Dr Bari became Chair of the ELM in 2002, so much of this tremendous effort of both internal and external politics, negotiation and fundraising was led by him and his Committee, and their many willing volunteers. In 2003, Dr Bari was awarded the MBE for services to the community. This growth and commitment to service within the local community was extended for women in 2013, with the opening of the Maryam Centre.

On 6 July 2005, I and about 100 young people and staff from Norlington School for Boys in Leyton (an active member of TELCO) were standing with thousands of others in London's Trafalgar Square to hear the Chair of the International Olympic Committee announce that the city had won the privilege of hosting the 2012 Olympic Games. When, to everyone's surprise, the Chair announced that London had won, we cheered louder than most. We knew in 2004 that TELCO (including some of the students present) had struck a historic deal with the London Olympic Bid Committee to include a series of economic deals which would benefit east Londoners if London won! It was a day of celebration. The sun shone and all was well with the world.

Early on 7 July 2005, I went to the Citizens UK office in Whitechapel to meet the fifteen student interns that were training as student organizers during our Summer Academy training month. They were unusually late arriving, and a passer-by said there was a problem on the Tube. I then checked the news and saw that there had been an explosion at Kings Cross and another at nearby Aldgate. I tried to phone the students and realized that the mobile networks were either down or so busy there was no service. Fortunately, all of the students were unharmed, but London was not. Fifty-six people died and many others were injured as a result of four young men leaving bombs on London transport. This has come to be known as the 7/7 bombings, and though it did not match in devastation and deaths the horror of New York's terrible atrocity in September 2001, the consequences for the Muslim community and across the world have been dramatic.

Although TELCO and the London Muslim Centre immediately mobilized support and solidarity – by noon that day we had issued joint press statements and a major interfaith witness and walk by hundreds of our members to Aldgate Tube – by the following day the shock waves and implications of this act of mindless violence and terror had already set back community relations very significantly. In the longer term this led to the 'Prevent' anti-extremism programme, a major investment by the government in the surveillance powers of the State. Leading individuals and institutions of Islam came under an all pervasive spotlight, including the Muslim Council of Britain (MCB), which was launched in 1997, as well as the East London Mosque and anyone connected to it.

Despite a hostile press and the growing power and presence of far-right street movements like the English Defence League (EDL) and British National Party (BNP), Dr Bari was persuaded to stand as the MCB's Secretary-General in 2006, and once elected served loyally and effectively in the post for four very tough and challenging years. His contribution to public life continued after this as a member of the London Organising Committee of the Olympic and Paralympic Games (LOCOG), which delivered one of the most glorious Olympics in history in London in July and August 2012. He describes the summer of 2012 as the world as it should be – London smiled, the sun shone and the rich diversity of London was celebrated and relished by the thousands of tourists who flocked to the Olympic site in east London. Although much of the Games was held during Ramadan, Dr Bari and Tower Hamlets mosques worked with TELCO to put on the UK's largest *iftar* (daily breaking of the Ramadan fast after sunset), hosting competitors from all over the world, including delegates from Israel and Palestine sitting together.

* * *

As the focus on radicalisation continues and anti-Muslim prejudice swells, Dr Bari has chosen one of the most difficult journeys: forging a common consensus between the fragmenting British Muslim communities – including young people and elders, Shia and Sunni, literalists and secularists – and the rest of British society. All at a time of unprecedented tension and change. I commend this book to you and challenge the reader to put yourself in Dr Bari's shoes and think how you would have coped living and leading through these very turbulent years.

This book presents a vision, or blueprint, for 'getting on' and the 'common good', including both social and political as well as spiritual dimensions. Setting out his stall, Dr Bari reflects on lessons from his own life: growing up in rural Bangladesh, inspired by a primary and then secondary teacher, drawn from mysticism; joining the Bangladesh Air Force; coming to the UK to study for a PhD and working as a science teacher, and later a special needs teacher in inner city east London. And then he reflects on his journey and shares observations from close to the heart of British Muslim life and the many lessons from the communities he represents and respects. All the time influenced by the tremendous commitment to public life and service of his father, and his respect for his mother's own unique leadership and ability to nurture the best in her children and the people she met.

Uniquely, Dr Bari bridges two distinct worlds: the old guard Muslim first generation elders, and the newer generation. He is a mild-mannered family man, but bold, straight and determined when it comes to standing up for social justice and community interests. He is a passionate supporter of helping young people to understand power and how vital it is for anyone seeking to be a leader to play a responsible part in public life. Yet he also respects the key role played by the first generation of Bangladeshis and British Muslims, who came to the UK in the 1960s and 1970s and sometimes struggle to understand the paths chosen by their children and grandchildren. He argues that these 'elders' are the heroes who built the Muslim community infrastructure – the 'hardware', as he calls it. He believes it is now time for the younger generations to pick up the baton and create the effective 'software' to professionally run these institutions and open them up to ensure that all the community can fully engage with wider society and their neighbours.

Unlike some high profile UK Muslims – often ex-radicals who have chosen to leave the middle way or been shunned by mainstream Muslims – Dr Bari carries the weight of the community with him, along with his credentials as a peace maker. He is not afraid to challenge the elders or the angry voices of young people, and his words and advice in this book will be an uncomfortable challenge for those who wish to stay in their comfort zones and blame others for their plight. To quote Dr Bari: 'Islam demands from Muslims to continuously read, re-read, re-interpret and renew their faith with the context of time and space through the power of *ijtihad* (or reasoning).'

> Jihad (striving or struggling) ... comes from the root word *jahada* – meaning endeavour, exertion, effort, diligence, etc. Jihad also means a personal commitment of self-purification through pure intention, patience and determination to achieve

one's personal best. Confronting one's own weaknesses in the best possible manner is also jihad. So, any individual effort to bring good to oneself, family and community can be termed as 'jihad'.

To use the maximum effort of striving and struggling – to continuously improve oneself and the environment in the family, community and public life – is an obligation, as well as a civic responsibility to a Muslim. Dr Bari's life and service is a great example of this in practice.

Since 2010, the East London Citizens Organization and its parent body, Citizens UK (CUK), has been blessed by his active involvement in our work and practice as a delegate from the London Muslim Centre. He has been an active member of CUK's Council and has visited Downing Street and City Hall to meet the prime minister and two London mayors. He has joined with non-Muslim neighbours to support the Real Living Wage campaign, welcomed refugees and actioned pilot projects for genuinely affordable housing in east London. He has consistently encouraged other members of his network and the London Muslim Centre to follow his example and has argued that we are all so much better and wiser together.

I hope that another likely legacy for Dr Bari will be the unique Citizens Commission on Islam, Participation and Public Life, which was primarily his idea (with Sir Stephen O'Brien and Sir Trevor Chinn) and initiated by the trustees of Citizens UK in September 2015. The Commission is unique in many ways, one of which is that it is not primarily addressed to the State. There are only four Muslim Commissioners, and it has significant support from public figures in the business, academia, media and military worlds, The Commission has spent over a year visiting most major cities across the UK and listening to hundreds of Muslim and non-Muslim citizens. It has been very lucky to have Rt Hon Dominic Grieve QC, MP and former Conservative Attorney General, as the Chair, and Jenny Watson, the then Chair of the Electoral Commission, as Vice Chair. After reporting to the CUK Trustees, in summer 2017 the Commission published a report: 'The Missing Muslims: Unlocking British Muslim Potential for the Benefit of All', with a series of recommendations aimed primarily at civil society, including the Muslim community, the State and the business community. Dr Bari was an adviser to the Commission, supported by the Scholars Groups and Young Leaders Group which has run parallel to the Commission and both supported and critiqued its work.

I am confident that the Commission Report will initiate a series of practical actions and some policy changes aiming to honour the central role that a healthy and integrated civil society has to make in public life. The ambitious aim which Dr Bari and I hope for (along with the Commissioners and CUK Trustees, of course) is that the changes the Citizens Commission have recommended, and CUK will initiate, will lead to the UK's Muslim community taking a proud and positive role in public life, alongside their neighbours.

Inshallah (God willing), this Commission and its works will be another fitting tribute to the vision and persistence of this quiet and unassuming, but determined and courageous, civil society leader (who happens to also be a Muslim): Dr Muhammad Abdul Bari. His lifetime's work for conciliation and understanding within and between communities has played an outstanding part in making the UK that bit safer and its communities more at peace with one another. It has also led to Dr Bari's substantial following of young people being ready, keen and able to join with others in the struggle to make the world a much better place.

That cannot be a bad legacy.

Neil Jameson CBE
Executive Director of Citizens UK

Introduction

IN 2010, after stepping down as Secretary-General of the Muslim Council of Britain, I contemplated writing a book on my community activism from the 1980s onwards. But before I could begin, I felt I needed some quiet time to rekindle the reading habit that I had developed during my school years. As I started to write blogs for various media outlets, I found a way to marry my activism with my lifelong hobby of reading. My early retirement from teaching, in March 2011, had also given me an opportunity to invest more time with the London Organising Committee of the Olympic and Paralympic Games (LOCOG), and my rejuvenated interactions with young people and increased involvement with the Citizens UK community allowed me to remain connected with the dynamics and complexities of Britain's civil society.

But the horrific murder of Lee Rigby in 2013, Birmingham's 'Trojan Horse' affair and the meteoric rise of Daesh (ISIS) in 2014, and the Charlie Hebdo killings in 2015, put Muslims under further scrutiny. CUK felt the need to form a Citizens Commission on Islam, Participation and Public Life; to get to the bottom of the realities – the challenges and opportunities – of Muslim participation in wider society. Since its launch in September 2015, I have had the privilege of travelling with the Commission to many cities across the UK and to listen to Muslim and non-Muslim voices on this issue. The Commission published its Report, 'The Missing Muslims', on 3 July 2017 in Westminster Cathedral Hall.

This book is a story of my observations of contemporary British society, vis-à-vis the diverse Muslim community. It presents an intimate and revealing portrait of the challenges and struggles faced by Muslims before and during the years of the 'War on Terror'. It offers my vision of a shared future for both Britain's Muslims as well as non-Muslim communities, a template for a bold rethinking of 'the middle way' through my own personal jihad (quest and effort), and I hope will go some way to healing the widening divisions between (and within) Muslims and the rest of society. This is also, to my understanding, Islam's middle way, or treading the middle path – be it through the individual journey of life or working for the good of society as active human beings and citizens.

Here I need to say a little about some core Islamic vocabulary that is often misunderstood and misused by many, including Muslims. Due to a lack of inspirational and deeply knowledgeable religious leadership over the last few centuries, combined with political failure and socio-economic decline, the capacity of reasoning among Muslims has sadly weakened over time. As a result, many Muslims find themselves unfamiliar even with the basics of their own scripture and history; they are not clear about the proper meaning of certain religious terms that could help shape (or reshape) their life. These terms are not just words; they encapsulate the spirit and message of Islam. Rooted in classical Arabic, they were taught and exemplified by the first generations of successful Muslims who were equipped with deep knowledge and spirituality.

A striking example of how an Islamic term has lost its comprehensive sense is 'jihad' (striving or struggling) that comes from the root word *jahada* – meaning endeavour, exertion, effort, diligence, etc. Jihad also means a personal commitment of self-purification through pure intention, patience and a determination to achieve one's personal best. Confronting one's own weaknesses in the best possible manner is also jihad. So, any individual effort to bring good to oneself, family and community can be termed as 'jihad'. Most importantly, individual effort to continuously remain in the middle way of life is a very important jihad, as this is known to be very difficult in real life.

Jihad is also a collective effort to fight against inequality, injustice and oppression in a civil way and within the established laws of the land. On the other hand, large-scale jihad by a nation is to defend life, land and religion in a legitimate war (a morally justifiable 'just war') with established rules and ethics of engagement such as using minimum necessary force, humane treatment towards non-combatants, bringing no harm even to trees, etc. The terminology 'violent' jihad is a misnomer in Islam. Glamourized violence or terrorism can never be called a jihad, and it is a far cry from the popular understanding of jihad as a religious war! There is no question that killing innocents in the name of jihad has absolutely no place in Islam.

Because of the atrocities in New York in September 2001 ('9/11'), London in 2005 ('7/7'), and others, the debate and discussion surrounding Muslims and Islamic terms such as jihad, Shariah, caliphate, and Salafism have become banal and politicized. As the Arab and Muslim world fell behind, and the connection of ordinary Muslims with the Arabic language became weaker, these Islamic terms encapsulated deep-rooted messages that have gradually lost their original meaning. This is unfortunate and dangerous, and Muslims, via deeper scholarship and positive bridge-building, have a duty to reclaim Islam and Islamic terminology from extremists and opportunists.

By nature and upbringing, I have always tried to maintain moderation in the affairs of life. Community interest and social justice are at my heart, and since adolescence I have also been conscious of the need for a spiritual anchor in attaining personal peace and resolving human issues. I have been fortunate in having a good number of close and trusted friends who have given me honest opinions and advice when needed. I have learnt from all of them, as well as from hundreds of other friends from all backgrounds – faith or no faith – from colleagues that I have worked with, in various voluntary groups and organizations, or people that I have only met briefly.

I have always been passionate about watching young talent flourish through education and participation in civic engagement. In my childhood I learnt to give respect to my elders, thanks to the guidance of my parents and the community in the beloved village where I grew up, and I have kept this value alive in my respect for the first generation of immigrants who struggled to survive yet managed to build the infrastructure and institutions for future generations. But, I am also aware that without the involvement and dedication of the dynamic and professional younger generations in various institutions, such as mosques, our diverse communities cannot fully engage with wider society across all areas of life.

As a teacher in the classroom, a behaviour support specialist, a parenting consultant and as a community activist, I have encountered many young people who became my friends; I developed empathy with them and they showed their warmth to me. In recent years I have been working with dozens of professional young Muslim men and women who are dedicated to 'give something back to their communities'. This book aims to inspire the young and old, men and women, from Muslim communities as well people from other faith and non-faith backgrounds, to live a harmonious life by working in balanced ways for the common good.

I have endeavoured to bridge two worlds all my life: between the 'old guard' Muslim elders and the newer generations, between factions within communities as well as between ethnic and religious communities. At a time of unprecedented tensions and changes, as well as the occasional personal attacks that I have faced from hardliners from both ends, my motto has always been 'drowning hate through reason and love'. I have tried to present this vision in the form of a blueprint for 'getting on', including both social and political as well as spiritual dimensions. In this book, *A Long Jihad: My Quest for the Middle Way*, I have shared my own story and expanded upon the stories of my fellow Muslims. The title of the book may also remind non-Muslim readers of the Buddhist concept of the 'Middle Way', though this idea is a very well developed one in Islamic thought too, as my reflections in the succeeding pages will testify.

Prologue

Joy and Despair

Wednesday, 6 July 2005

'We've won, we've won!'

The boy looked up, his eyes meeting mine. He frowned, his beetle-brows drawing together, then his curiosity sank without a ripple.

'What's happened?' I called out to the corridor. It was nearly lunchtime and my stomach grumbled loudly.

'We've won, Muhammad. We've won!' shouted Andrew, a thirty-something, crumpled-looking English teacher, 'we've beaten Paris – I've just heard it on the BBC!' He was in a state of near-ecstasy and looked like he was ready to jump into the air, or collapse – or perhaps both. Other teachers began crowding round.

London ... Paris: the fog broke. The Olympics. We'd won the Olympic bid. 'Wow ... wow, well done London!' I shouted with glee. This was something we'd fought for years to achieve: Londoners, and many of us in Muslim organizations, had fought hard to bring the Olympics to our city. Paris had been the front runner but had been pipped at the post. It was hard to believe: the Olympics was actually going to happen right here in London. Not only that, but in the heart of the famous East End, where I had spent so much of my life. I suddenly remembered my student and stumbled back into the classroom with a dazed smile.

'What's happened, sir?' the boy asked, his curiosity piqued again. I gave him the big news. It was almost one o'clock so I finished as quickly as I could and hurried to the staff room. The news had spread like wildfire: the TV showed crowds going wild in Trafalgar Square and the talk on everyone's lips was about our victory. We had won against all the odds, it was a great story indeed.

Defeating front runner Paris by fifty-four to fifty votes had been sweet. Jacques Rogge, the International Olympics Committee president, had made the dramatic announcement at 12.49pm the day before. No city had ever hosted the Games three times (London's last two Games were in 1908 and 1948). My colleagues at the MCB – the Muslim Council of Britain, the body representing 500 Muslim organizations – had used their influence in swinging the votes of several Muslim countries. The Secretary-General, Sir Iqbal Sacranie, and Chair of the London Affairs Committee, Tanzim Wasti, were appointed as Olympic Bid Ambassadors; they spoke with several key Muslim ambassadors in London, arguing with them for Muslim member countries to support the London bid. The MCB also wrote to the Secretary-General of the Organization of the Islamic Conference (OIC) on 5 July urging that Muslim member countries back London in its bid to host the 2012 Olympics because of 'London's vibrant multiculturalism and its positive and active engagement with the city's many different ethnic, racial and religious communities'.

We sent each other excited text messages and calls that evening, congratulating ourselves on our efforts. The MCB congratulated London's bid leader, former Olympic champion Sebastian (Lord) Coe, London Mayor Ken Livingstone and the entire bid team for their historic achievement. 'I send my warmest congratulations to you and every member of the London 2012 team for winning the bid for the UK,' the Queen told Lord Coe.

* * *

Thursday, 7 July 2005
My routine began pretty much the same way every day: Wake up early, do my Fajr (pre-sunrise) prayer, a bit of short exercise, eat breakfast, spend some time with the kids before school and college, then kiss my wife and head off into the East End of London. This day was no different and the morning air was hazy and warm as the rush-hour traffic inched slowly forward. Once I had finally reached the borough of Tower Hamlets, I drove through familiar streets – streets which had once rang to Yiddish calls, and before that to the dialects of Kerry and Donegal – a place which was my 'home from home' when I first settled in the UK.

Tower Hamlets and the East End are a million things to a million different people – 'the Awful East', as Jack London called it – a ghetto beloved of writers, complete with Cockneys who still loved their pie and mash, but also homeless beggars, drug addicts and prostitutes. Yet it was also home to tens of thousands of Bangladeshis, my countrymen and women. As the situation in war-torn Somalia was turning from bad to worse, many Somalis had also made the long journey to the UK and now made Tower Hamlets their home. Soon they were being joined by those from other European countries also attracted to our country: Polish plumbers, Latvian builders, Estonian and Russian IT contractors, and more. The continuous wave of new immigrants and their transient presence – sooner or later they moved on to other parts of London – had been the defining feature in this part of the city for centuries. Nowadays, these new people and the white working-class Cockneys jostled with the City wealth and yuppies that were now crowding in.

Passing through this landscape, I was a roving special needs teacher engaged in behavioural support throughout the borough's inner city schools; a slim figure, middle-aged, often dressed in a suit (which had seen better days), my greying hair dyed to its once-natural brown. Some of the pupils I dealt with were in gangs and came from problem families: boys who had lost fathers, mothers who had lost husbands to addiction, or with other wives 'back home'. They were bright kids who just needed a bit of time to get on their feet – before drugs or prison got hold of them. Today, with the news of the Olympics and optimism charging the air, perhaps that world was now going to change. Even the dust-filled classrooms of the crumbling Victorian school where I was teaching couldn't hide the hope we all suddenly felt. I was still light-headed as I made my way to Tower Hamlets' Special Educational Needs department. It was housed in a rather dilapidated three-storey building near Queen Mary University, but was widely regarded as one of the top such units in the country.

At 10.00am my phone chirped and I looked at the text message on the screen, which was from a close friend. I had to read and re-read it again, willing the words to focus. I stood up and read it a third time: 'News about a few explosions/collisions in the London Underground, British Transport Police has shut down the entire Underground system.' I was confused. Collisions on the Tube …? But why more than one? The thought flashed through the back of my mind – not a terrorist attack, surely? But who …? Without warning, I had a flashback to the afternoon panic at my office nearly four years before; 11 September 2001 was etched into our collective memory. Those attacks had changed the world forever, particularly for Muslims: two Muslim countries were now under US occupation and Muslims in the West had been put under increasing scrutiny. I looked over at my colleague, blankly; she was as puzzled as I was, clearly having seen or heard something too. Before she opened her mouth I read her the text message in a dry monotone. She shot bolt upright and yelled, 'Oh My God!' I flinched, startled, as others looked from across the room. The news began to spread quickly across all floors.

I called home to check that my daughter, Rima, and son, Raiyan, were still there: they were undergraduates and might be up for lectures or still sleeping – I wasn't sure. I was relieved to hear Rima's voice, telling me she had the day off and Raiyan would go into the university in the afternoon. My wife, Sayeda, was working in a local nursery and my other two children were at school, so the family was safe. Sayeda gasped and stifled a scream when I called and told her about the explosions.

I then quickly phoned the executive director of the East London Mosque, Dilowar Khan, in Whitechapel to find out if he knew anything. I was the mosque's Honorary Chairman and had been there when Prince Charles and a Saudi prince visited together in November 2001. In fact, although I was from a different part of Bangladesh than most East End Bangladeshis (who usually hailed from Greater Sylhet) and didn't live in the area, I had adopted the community and they me for many years: during my PhD in the mid-1980s, I had volunteered to teach some young community members science and mathematics; they were now becoming the community's elders. Dilowar's number was busy, so I left a message.

I was walking back to my desk when the phone chirped again: Dilowar was on the other end. He was well-liked in the community, a man who until recently had lived in the same council house for over twenty years, a stocky, kind figure who was familiar to everyone around. He told me breathlessly that there had been an explosion near Aldgate tube station. This was grim news: Aldgate was less than half a mile from the mosque. I told him to get in touch with the local police and other key people in the community. He asked me whether I could get down to the mosque – quickly.

By now there was clear panic in our office. I headed downstairs to Liz Vickerie, our manager and director, and asked if she had heard the news and whether she had any briefing for us. She was famously calm, but right now you could see she was battling fear; she fixed a smile and said she had just heard the news and was discussing the situation with other managers. With a dry voice I asked whether I could visit my mosque. She knew about my role in the big Muslim religious centre nearby but asked whether I could wait – she needed further instructions. I ran back upstairs and tried, without success, to work; the texts and calls kept coming in. Finally Liz called and told me I was free to go.

Sirens and smoke filled the air and the roads were full of confusion; people were standing around and talking, looking furtively at each other, as if to guess whether their neighbour was somehow involved in this chaos. It was not far off noon by the time I reached the East London Mosque. Dilowar was in the London Muslim Centre, the huge glass and steel community complex that loomed over the mosque next door. When we had opened it, on 11 June the previous year, thousands had carpeted the roads outside, praying. With Dilowar was Alan Green, an unshakeable, balding vicar who was head of the Tower Hamlets Inter Faith Forum. Other senior community leaders were crowding around them, anxiety and concern growing as they shuffled nervously. I'd never seen them like this; I guessed my own face probably reflected theirs.

There had been four explosions now and the collision theory had gone out of the window; London was under attack. Three bombs had exploded on the Underground and one on a bus in Tavistock Square, close to the headquarters of the British Medical Association. Explosions had taken place on underground lines between Liverpool Street and Aldgate; King's Cross and Russell Square; and at Edgware Road tube station. The Metropolitan Police Commissioner, Sir Ian Blair, confirmed that these were coordinated 'terrorist attacks'. The number of casualties was not yet known. The phrase 'terrorist attack' was very startling. Who would do this and why?

Dilowar took me through to the Centre's foyer, where a number of walking wounded were sitting or standing with shocked, dazed looks. They were visibly traumatized: ashen-faced, soot or burn marks on their clothes; faces, heads and hands often streaked with blood. Volunteers were talking to them, calming them, giving them tea, biscuits and water. It was not much, but it seemed to help. Some were then getting up and walking home; others were being escorted to the famous Royal London Hospital, just a few hundred yards away. I did my best to reassure the wounded.

We came back to the office to discuss what to do. Huddled around the radio and TV set, we listening attentively to the midday news. Facts were dribbling in frustratingly slowly and we were desperate to know more; the number of casualties was still unclear. Sirens continued to wail outside and a helicopter droned overhead. The Prime Minister, Tony Blair, was hosting a G8 summit in Glencagles, Scotland, and he broke from the summit to issue a statement, calling the bombings a coordinated series of 'barbaric terrorist attacks'.

In the meantime, Alan Green told us that the Bishop of Stepney, Stephen Oliver, was on his way to our mosque. It was a wonderful gesture from a senior bishop and very timely. He came and we sat with him, trying to work out what we should do. Everyone feared that if it was terrorism, this could be 'our 9/11'. We swiftly agreed a public statement, should we need one, saying that: 'We Muslims, Christians and other faith groups stand in solidarity with one another. Whoever perpetrated these heinous acts – they do not represent any community and cannot divide us. Terrorists are terrorists and they do not have any religion.' But would it be enough? I swapped messages with Sir Iqbal Sacranie, the Secretary-General of the MCB, and we voluntarily divided our tasks:

Iqbal would coordinate our responses nationally and I would handle London.

The lunchtime prayer at 1.30pm was approaching. But, instead of worshippers, journalists were starting to pour into the foyer and I could see camera crews pointing their lenses up and down the streets outside. I was nervous and tried to convince myself that their interest was purely linked to geography, as one of the bombs had gone off nearby. Or were they sensing that Muslims were behind this? I tried to bury that thought. I was out of my depth, I was just a normal, middle-aged guy who had volunteered for a small but growing band of Bangladeshi people, and was now leading a diverse and expanding Muslim community in the largest city in the country. I prayed silently that Muslims were not involved. If they were, as a community we would start paying for their crimes.

I had quick words with the bishop and we decided to visit the wounded at the Royal London Hospital. It was the least we could do, I suggested. After walking to the hospital, we weren't allowed in to meet the patients, so we talked with the Christian and Muslim chaplains who had been serving them. As we did so, someone came up and whispered to me that there was a large number of journalists waiting outside who wanted to hear from us. I was struck by fear, I had no media training nor any media exposure before. I was just a silent community activist and teacher and at that moment I desperately wanted to be somewhere else. Sensing my trepidation, the bishop laid his hand on my shoulder and said: 'Muhammad, now is not the time for hesitation.' He encouraged me with an assuring smile. He was right.

I made up my mind, asked him to speak first, and walked out into the glare of the spotlights and camera flashes. On that bright summer afternoon, Stephen and I stood side by side in front of dozens of microphones in the open space at the western corner of the hospital. They were journalists from our national news media, TV stations and print media; TV crews from a few overseas countries such as Australia and Japan were there as well. Stephen introduced himself and said how as a bishop of the three boroughs he had been working closely with all the communities, including Muslims, how he valued his friendship with Muslims in the area and how the East London Mosque was contributing towards the social fabric of the ever-changing East End. With a determined voice he concluded: 'We don't yet know what the casualty figure is, but whoever carried out these heinous acts in the transport network of our beloved city today cannot divide our communities. We, as people of faith and no faith, must now multiply our efforts to make sure we remain united.'

Then it was my turn and by that time I had decided what I was going to say. I introduced myself and briefly mentioned how the East London Mosque had been serving all communities and working for a better understanding between the peoples of the East End, where people of diverse backgrounds lived side-by-side and had enriched the area for generations. 'Terrorism is a depraved act of criminality,' I said. 'It has no religion, no nationality. Terrorists are none but terrorists. As proud Londoners and East Enders our job is now to collectively keep peace in our communities.'

There were a few questions on who we thought the perpetrators might be and whether we feared any backlash. I took the questions and expressed my confidence in our police and security services that they would soon find the perpetrators behind the attacks. Whatever the cause or motivation, the carnage in London would fail to frighten or divide us. Stephen added by assuring that London, especially the people in the East End, had always been united against race hate. 'Sanity will prevail,' he said confidently. Stephen thanked me for my performance, though I didn't then realize that this would be the beginning of a new journey – and the start of a very public life for me.

I returned to the mosque and spent the rest of the day talking with people and gathering more information as to the number of casualties and possible implications for Londoners and the rest of the country. The journalists were gradually leaving the ELM complex and the mosque management turned to discussing how best to reassure the local community. I was also constantly in touch with the Muslim Council of Britain office. The Secretary-General had issued a statement that the MCB: '... utterly condemns today's indiscriminate acts of terror in London. These evil deeds make victims of us all. It is our humanity that must bring us shoulder to shoulder to condemn, to oppose and to overcome those who would spread fear, hatred and death.' A Joint Statement from the Muslim Council of Britain and Churches Together in Britain and Ireland declared: 'The scriptures and the traditions of both the Muslim and Christian communities repudiate the use of such violence. Religious precepts cannot be used to justify such crimes, which are completely contrary to our teaching and practice.'

There was one more shock that day. In the late afternoon, one of our very regular mosque worshippers, a very respectable Bangladeshi in his eighties, Jamshed Ali, who was always to be seen in the front row during the congregational prayer, told us that his granddaughter, Shahara Islam, had been missing since morning. The family had been desperately looking for her since she had left for work on the Tube. Neither she, nor the police or any hospital, had contacted the family yet and they were hoping against hope that she was fine somewhere, but as time passed that hope was fading. The news quickly spread among the close-knit Bangladeshi community in the East End. She was later confirmed as the first Muslim victim of what would soon become known as '7/7'. Some of us visited Shahara's house in the early evening to meet the family. They were in a state of shock and the father wouldn't talk with us. We said a prayer for her safety.

By the time I returned home it was about midnight. All of the family were still awake; the normally boisterous children were very quiet. Sayeda and I sat with them for a brief discussion and assured them that everything would be alright, Inshallah. We advised them not to worry, but just to remain a bit more alert. I went to bed with thoughts churning around in my head, but could not imagine what the next day would bring for us.

Chapter 1

On My Way to Britain

ON A CLEAR LONDON afternoon in early September 1978, two young officers of the Bangladesh Air Force (BAF) landed at Heathrow airport in a Bangladesh Biman (BB) jet. With the severely short haircuts typical of most armed forces servicemen, they looked pale but carried themselves confidently. As they approached passport control, they handed their passports and documents to the customs official, who stamped them and wished them, 'a nice time in the UK, officers'. Thanking her in return, they strode off with their characteristic military stride and headed in the direction of luggage reclaim. This is the brief story of my first arrival in Britain, one of humanities' great melting pots.

I grew up in rural Bangladesh, where a broad minded Hindu teacher in my village primary school had inspired me, with tough love and care, to discover faith in God. In my small village there existed only Muslims and Hindus, and during my secondary school education a saintly Muslim teacher influenced me to become a 'bookworm' and nurtured an enthusiasm for the spiritual dimension of Islam. My parents, especially my spiritually-rich father, and these two teachers, helped shape my childhood with thoughtfulness, respect for others and broader horizons. But I was only exposed to South Asian people during my college and university life.

In London, for the first time in my life, I suddenly encountered a mosaic of humanity from my very arrival at Heathrow. I was both amazed and exhilarated by the experience, I had never seen such diversity, with people of all colours and languages around me. I looked at Mostafa, my fellow officer, and exclaimed: 'Did you ever see so many types of people, Mostafa?' He shook his head. We both were amazed and uplifted, despite the long tiring journey. From that day onward it became my personal article of faith that God's human garden is all the better for being multi-coloured.

Outside, a junior staff member from the Bangladesh High Commission was waiting to receive us. He led us to the underground station to catch a Piccadilly Line train towards central London. It was a totally a new experience, travelling underground for the first time. I had heard and learnt about riding on 'the Tube' from reading and talking with others, but 'seeing was believing'. Feeling bemused as the train broke out of the tunnel, I could see London's clear blue skies, cars moving around and children playing. Realizing we were new to London, our host tried to run a mini-commentary whilst we kept quiet and soaked it all in. My train of thought was travelling just as fast as the Piccadilly Line train.

It was only a year before that I was unsure I would even join the Air Force, as I prepared to become a physicist. But failing to secure a teaching or research job in either Bangladesh or abroad I had to think of other avenues. Some of my friends, who had been trying hard to move to America for higher education with teaching assistantships, had already left. I was probably too complacent, thinking I would easily get a job and could then secure a scholarship to go abroad. But one day I suddenly realized that I was jobless and would not be able to pursue my academic ambition. So I decided to join the Bangladesh Air Force … and now here I was in London.

My job in the BAF was something of an accident. When I kick-started my search for a commissioned career in any of the three services, I caught sight of an advertisement by the BAF for two commissioned officers in the Armament Wing; and they were looking for graduates with a Physics or Engineering background! There was an additional incentive: the advert mentioned that after a short basic training the two successful officers would have to attend an overseas course in the UK. I decided to test my luck.

I was well aware of the need for both physical fitness and mental agility for any commissioned post. A hyperactive childhood and a rather free-thinking nature gave me confidence in both. The selection process was long and arduous, and as I made my way through the selection stages I found myself uplifted and growing in determination. After a gruelling final few weeks – the long oral, IQ and personality tests as well as physical tests by the 'Inter Services Selection Board' (ISSB) – two of us had crossed the final hurdle. Once the news of my success was announced I felt ecstatic, and so did Munshi Golam Mostafa, the other candidate and by that time my new-found friend.

We were given two weeks of basic physical training before our commissioned officer status could be approved and so the two of us travelled to the officer cadet mess in Dhaka on 20 August 1978. The short training was as gruelling as it could be and my physical agility was tested to extremes. The thought of a secure job in the Air Force, and also the course in the UK, kept us going. Two long weeks finally passed and we received our Pilot Officer's insignia on 5 September. We became proud officers of the BAF and were reminded of our status and obligation to the country.

As the train reached our final destination in Gloucester Road and we were led to a nearby hotel, my mind jumped back to the present. Here we were, in London now, I thought, but I never had the slightest idea that one day I would settle in London and call it my home.

* * *

The following day we took a train from King's Cross to Sleaford in Lincolnshire. A taxi was waiting for us at the station to take us to the big airfield at Cranwell, around five miles away. Cranwell was essentially a training base, and we were allocated rooms in Trenchard Hall Officers' Mess (THOM), which for about a year would be our home in this new land. We organized the room, settled in and relaxed for the rest of the day. In the late afternoon, we went to an ante-room for tea. A Bengali-looking officer in uniform entered, and although we had not met before we immediately realized he was Flight Lieutenant Mahbub Malik from the BAF. He had arrived some months previously for another course. We stood up, straightened and gave him a BAF salute along with the Muslim greeting of peace, *Assalamualaikum* (peace be upon you). With a broad smile he embraced us, but advised us not to be that animated with senior officers in the officers' mess! We had a good chat and learned some basic tips for life at Cranwell. Over the next few months, until he left, he was to be a great help and friend to us.

Life followed a strict routine at Cranwell. There was no physical training, and there were designated batmen for individual officers who would bring morning tea to the room and help them organize their uniform and polish their shoes, prior to starting academic classes or practical training. After the day-long lessons, life in the officers' mess was pretty relaxing. We were provided with high tea in the big ante-room after office hours, which was an opportunity to meet other officers, chat or read papers and journals. There were quite a few designated rooms for indoor games or watching TV, and dinner was served early. During the late 1970s halal food was not easily available, but this was not an issue, as some of us easily became vegetarians or pescatarians; egg and fish were often available, too. There was a reasonable-sized gym, with squash facilities. Squash was new to me, but I enjoyed it and within a few weeks it became my favourite game.

There was plenty to learn during our training. Each full day supplied us with the basic technical skills needed for an officer in ground engineering and relevant to military personnel. Handling and firing weapons, workshop experience in repairing and dismantling equipment, and various aspects of aircraft engineering were all part of the course that gave us a broad knowledge for the job of an Armament Engineer. The effective functioning of ejection seats for pilots to use during emergencies occupied a large chunk of the course. The training was geared to connect us with the world of high-tech air warfare. We were both amazed at the availability of better technologies and a positive environment to learn in.

Our training was run by civilian instructors as well as commissioned and non-commissioned officers. Sergeant Davies, from Wales, became very popular with us for his warmth, style and professionalism. We had a few junior Nigerian Air Force officers on our course, as well as several from the Gulf and a British-born Bangladeshi officer on other related courses. To my surprise, I found life in the officers' mess very relaxed. Everyone was respectful to one another, senior and junior officers behaved like friends and the relationship with the civilian service staff was very cordial. There was no formality and no inhibition.

We also had the opportunity to visit other Air Force bases across the country, and with plenty of notes to hand all the BAF officers managed to pass the final exams with flying colours. There was a need for a theoretical knowledge of physics, which allowed me to relax on that front, so I used my time to read contemporary journals and publications on defence matters and other areas of life.

* * *

Here I was in Britain, once upon a time a world super power where the sun would not set. A land that had produced Newton, Shakespeare, Darwin, Churchill and was an intellectual leader of the world. However, Britain has its dark history as well. In 1757, the East India Company (also the British East India Company that received a Royal Charter from Queen Elizabeth I in December 1600), defeated the ruler (Nawab) of Bengal, Siraj ud-Daulah, who ruled the-then provinces of Bengal, Bihar and Orissa. But Siraj ud-Daulah's defeat was through deception, due to the treachery of his commander-in-chief Mir Jafar. Within a few decades, 'Golden Bengal' was reduced by colonial plunder and depredation to an impoverished land: from being one of history's fabled lands of riches to a vast rural slum.

Britain ruled its empire with an imperial 'divide and rule' policy. It was also once part of the transatlantic slavery trade which dehumanized African people. However, it also redressed some of its wrongs, such as the abolition of slavery throughout the British Empire via an 1833 Act of Parliament (there were a few exceptions, but they were eliminated in 1843). In the early twentieth century, around one-quarter of the world's population was a subject of the British Empire, and until the end of the Second World War it directly ruled many countries; many are now part of the Commonwealth. Britain may have lost its imperial glamour, but it still punches above its weight in the international arena with intellectual dominance and diplomatic skills.

What made Britain great and how she rose so high in the world community often occupied my thoughts. Feelings of envy and amazement reigned at the beginning of my Cranwell period. As a keen reader of history, I knew something about Britain. But I wanted to know more and directly 'from the horse's mouth'. I wanted to see it from the inside. How could a small island country, with a population far smaller than Bangladesh, rise so high? What was the catch? The answer to me was in its people: their vision, ambition, hard work, resilience and sense of pride. In its heyday, the British nation manifested this enterprise, adventure, determination and courage to catapult it to the farthest corners of the planet. It was the quality of leadership in all walks of life; professionalism, adaptability and the ability to create institutions and their sustainability that helped them to direct the course of human history. Far-placed lands like India, Australia, and America became nearer. With English as the lingua franca, and world class institutions such as the BBC and Oxbridge, it became a diplomatic super power; Britain's soft power is still the envy of many nations.

On my free weekends I would travel across this England. Away from my family I had plenty of time to write poems in Bengali, some of which were later published as a book. There is a joke about Bangladeshis that everyone has some poetic juice. 'Why should I be an exception?' I thought. I would make the 135 mile journey to London to see the seat of what had once been the world's first global super power. Apart from visiting Westminster, the popular London shopping areas and higher educational institutions and museums, I also spent time in London's East End: especially along Brick Lane and Whitechapel High Street, where many Bangladeshis had started to live.

The East London Mosque (ELM) in Whitechapel, which was already known to many people back in Bangladesh, was just a small pre-fabricated prayer place at the time, perched on a patch of scrubland adjacent to the Fieldgate Street Great Synagogue and near the Whitechapel Bell Foundry. The ELM's history started in 1910, when it was founded by an Indian émigré in the Ritz Hotel, and so it was the oldest mosque in London. One weekend I came to the mosque and tried to find someone I might recognize (I knew a couple of individuals from Bangladesh who later settled in east London). One, Aziz Rahman (Aziz Bhai), did his MPhil in Physics at Imperial College.

In the mosque I met a few people who were slightly younger than me. They were very hospitable, especially when they learned that I was in England for training, and after the midday prayer invited me to a nearby youth club opposite a multi-storey hospice. The 'club' turned out to be in a basement flat, with an arrangement of table tennis tables. Towards the end of our chat I asked if anyone wanted to play. We kept on talking and started a friendly match. By the time I finished the games I realized it was time for me to leave London. This was the start of my relationship with the group. We exchanged telephone numbers and they invited me to come whenever I was free.

I quickly learned that sport brings people closer together, and from then on the youth club became a focal point of my visits to London. I became close with several of these East End Bangladeshis; they would take me sightseeing in London during my weekend visits. Through this interaction I learned that most of them had come to Britain in their childhood with their parents, mainly from the Sylhet region of north-eastern Bangladesh. They were either working in factories or restaurants. During my stay in 1978–1979, and later on in 1981, I would often spend time with these new friends. This sowed the seeds of my future youth and community work over the coming decades.

A quarter of a mile from the ELM, not far from London's economic heartland, was the Brick Lane mosque (Brick Lane Jamme Masjid, or Brick Lane Great Mosque). During the 1970s, the whole area was subject to heavy immigration from Sylhet, many of whom then attended either the ELM or the

Brick Lane Mosque, depending in part on their political and religious affiliations back home. Those who founded the mosque on Brick Lane bought and refurbished a synagogue (which had been a Huguenot church before that) as the area's once-dominant Jews continued to move on and out of the area. Brick Lane today is synonymous with diversity and modern London; it is Britain's Banglatown and London's curry centre. Back then it was still poor, and would later suffer from National Front violence.

* * *

Soon the British autumn was ushering in winter, and watching trees shed their leaves was a whole new phenomenon to me. The days were getting shorter and the chilly air forced us to adopt more suitable clothing. The first day of snowfall was hugely exciting. Even with my thick clothes I was shivering in the classroom. But I still loved the look of the trees, now enveloped by snow. When I got back to my warm room, I spent quite a long time watching the beauty of snowfall from my window.

As 1979 began, the weather took a turn for the worse. There were blizzards and deep snow and we were told it was the coldest winter since 1962–1963. The weather had an impact on consumer spending and hit the economy badly, but it was not the cold or faltering economy that surprised me, but the 'Winter of Discontent' that paralysed almost all of Britain, with widespread strikes by public sector employees demanding larger pay rises. The ongoing pay cap by Jim Callaghan's Labour government was challenged by the powerful Trades Union Congress (TUC), but no agreement could be reached. The situation took a turn for the worst when cemetery gravediggers also took industrial action; this left 150 bodies unburied at one point, with twenty-five being added each day. This caused huge public concern, then to add insult to injury, many bin men (the local authority waste collectors) went on strike and local authorities up and down the country ran out of waste storage space and were forced to use local parks. Reports of rat infestations and bad smells were splashed across the news headlines. The Labour government's inability to handle the situation was one of the main reasons for its defeat to the Conservative party in the following May national election (that brought Margaret Thatcher to power).

Elsewhere, the Iranian Islamic Revolution in February 1979 had reverberations that shook the world. Iranians were already unhappy with the ruling Pahlavi dynasty, but a new phase of the uprising started against Mohammad Reza Shah Pahlavi in October 1977, with persistent demonstrations by various leftist and Islamic organizations, as well as Iranian student movements. This developed into a civil resistance that intensified in January 1978. From August onwards, coordinated massive strikes paralysed the country. The Shah left Iran for exile on 16 January 1979 and Ayatollah Ruhollah Khomeini, who had been in exile in Iraq and France since 1964, was invited back to Iran by the government. He was greeted by millions of Iranians in the capital Tehran. On 11 February, guerrillas and rebel troops took control of Tehran, bringing Khomeini to power.

The UK general election of 1979, held on 3 May, was another event that caught the world's attention. For the first time a woman, Margaret Thatcher, leader of the Conservative party, became prime minister of the British government; the first of four consecutive election victories. As Margaret Thatcher stepped up to power, our time in Britain was coming to an end. One more BAF Officer, Flight Lieutenant Bashir, had joined us at Cranwell, and Mostafa and I were occasionally travelling to other cities in the north of England. I still harboured ambitions of going back to my physics research, although I did not have any clue how this would ever materialize.

Mostafa eventually became one of my closest friends. His integrity, sense of humour and wisdom were enviable. Even after I had left the BAF in 1982, we remained in close touch. His personality reminded me of a beautiful saying of Prophet Muhammad, may Allah bless him and grant him peace: 'The example of a good and a bad companion is like that of a perfume seller and a blacksmith. The perfume seller either puts the perfume on you or tries to sell it to you, but in the blacksmith's workshop you will either burn your clothes or you'll be blackened by the soot'. I have been blessed with quite a few trustworthy friends like him.

We finished our final exams and completed our course by the end of July 1979, with excellent results. The Base Commander threw a party for all the departing overseas officers, and officers from some other branches joined us. We shared our addresses and promised to keep in touch with one another. Our friendship with the Nigerian officers was deep, though we never knew if we would ever meet again. Overall, it was a jovial atmosphere. We had a few free days before we would catch a flight from London, so Mostafa and I decided to spend a couple of days visiting some nearby seaside towns and a few more days in London. We took a taxi to Sleaford with our luggage and were on our way to London once again. After few busy days of shopping and meeting friends, we were on a Bangladesh Biman plane once again, returning to Dhaka, which when we got there was soaked with summer monsoon rain. After a couple of weeks break with family and friends, the two of us arrived at Jessore Air Base, in western Bangladesh, for our main physical training.

* * *

We were kept busy with over six months of gruelling physical training, but we were not using any of the skills that we had learned at our valuable course in Cranwell. It was frustrating and our knowledge was getting rusty; we should have attended the course after basic military training, we thought. In any case, life continued: Mostafa got married and my father was also reminding me to do the same. I could find no reason to disagree with him and began inquiring about potential spouses. Our training finished towards the middle of 1980 and both of us were posted to Dhaka Air Base.

It was in the officers mess in Dhaka that I became somewhat settled, with time again to think and reflect about my life and do some forward planning. But life as a junior officer was regimented, with unexciting office work in the morning, lunch at the mess, a games session in the afternoon and then occasional formal events in the evening. It was a stable but boring experience, there were few contemporary books or journals, so I tried to build connections with some of my army and navy friends by visiting them occasionally.

As I was not far away from my village, I tried to visit home more frequently to see my elderly father. My older brother was now deeply entrenched in various community projects; he was running a secondary school that he had helped establish, plus a religious school (madrasah) for children to memorize the Qur'an, and a bazaar was also springing up nearby. He was the main man behind all this! His wife and my father lamented one day that he was doing all this at the cost of his own health and his children's education. I was younger than him by ten years, but I chatted with him one night and implored with him not to ignore his health and family. He was loud and boisterous, and with an infectious smile he laughed off my suggestion as if it was coming from a little boy. After quietening down he asked me in a combative mood: 'Who's going to do all this then? Find me someone.' I thought it was beyond my ability to convince him, and I just ended by saying: 'Please, do not ignore your children at least'. He loved his work, and used to spend hour after hour every day helping others, particularly poor lower-caste Hindus. He continued this for another two decades when he was diagnosed with a killer disease, late-stage bowel cancer. When I went to see him he was the undisputed leader of the region, both Muslims and the Hindu minority, and it was painful to see him suffering. He urged me to support his children when he would not be there. Sadly, he passed away within a month of my return to London.

Apart from the initial charm of living in the officers' mess in a posh area of Dhaka, the capital city of Bangladesh, there was little opportunity to learn and develop oneself further. Some of my friends had already got married, some had left for America and one or two had left their Air Force jobs and were making money in industry or by setting up their own businesses. Without informing the Air Force Board, I began exploring a future in the academic world. Gaining admission to any western university for a PhD in, say, physics was not that difficult, but securing funding was the main obstacle. I asked a few of my friends in Britain to see whether they could help me, and Aziz Bhai worked hard to put me in touch with the physics departments of some London universities. In the meantime, early in 1981 Mostafa and I were promoted to Flying Officers.

During this uncertainty, one afternoon my maternal uncle (Nuru mama) came to see me in the officers' mess. He had a thick envelope in his hand and I remembered I had used his home as my postal address before joining the Air Force. I opened it and saw it was from the King Faisal Foundation (KFF) in Saudi Arabia. I quickly read it, then paused and read it again. Nuru mama observed my facial expression and asked: 'What's in it, dear Bhagne (nephew)?'

I abruptly stood up and hugged him. He was perplexed. 'What's the matter, my nephew?' he asked again.

With excitement and a loud voice, I said: 'Mamma (uncle), I've been awarded a scholarship from the King Faisal Foundation to do a PhD!' He sat silent for a few seconds, then stood up and hugged me tightly. A worrying thought arose and

I said: 'But, I'm in the Air Force now and have just been trained in the UK. Will I be allowed to take up this opportunity?'

He advised me to work it out and left me with a positive comment: 'Don't worry, there'll be a way out, inshallah (God willing).'

My mind was buzzing, how could I avail this opportunity? But first I realized that I needed a PhD enrolment from a British university, and so I informed Aziz Bhai of the news and requested his continued help. I also consulted Mostafa and a few close friends on what to do next. We were all junior officers, and we came up with a plan that I ought to talk with the head of the Armament Branch. As I was setting this plan in motion, another surprise was waiting for me: I received an official memo from Air HQ that I was selected to attend a six-week British Army course at Chattenden in Kent, England, which would start in a few weeks. I agreed to attend the course in England and asked the KFF if they could place a hold on my scholarship offer.

Soon, I was back in London again.

* * *

My six-week stay in Kent was memorable not only for its tough training and long fasts, since Ramadan fell that July, but also for finding my life partner, Sayeda. Fasting was a challenge for two reasons: sleep deprivation, given I had to wake up and eat before dawn (*suhur*); and day-long physical training during the summer months. As my stay there was longer than fifteen days, I could not call myself a traveller (*musafir*), which allowed observant Muslims to excuse themselves from fasting. However, with intention and determination, and with God's mercy, I survived. It was a once-in-a-lifetime experience.

I met Sayeda's older brother by accident, but it was a meeting that was to change my life forever. As the journey to London was just over an hour by train, I would visit Whitechapel for a couple of weekends to relax and meet the friends I had made last time. One weekend, I bumped into a well-dressed gentleman in the East London Mosque, which was then still just a hut. I recognized his face as someone I had met in Dhaka, at a mutual friend's house. Firdaws was a few years older than me, but was very sociable and we had a good chat. I discovered that he had come to London two years earlier to do a course leading to chartered accountancy. When he learned that I was living near Rochester, he offered to visit me at the officers' mess, as he often came to Rochester to help his brother-in-law in running a restaurant.

He arrived the following weekend. He told me he hailed from Bangladesh's southern district of Faridpur, but had settled further south in Barisal. We talked on many issues, including our future plans in life, and in that relaxed conversation the issue of marriage naturally came up. He was married with a little daughter and by that time I had also been thinking of getting married myself, and had always been fairly straightforward. So without much thought, I said: 'Firdaws bhai (respected brother), you've now learned something about me. If you come across a suitable girl for me, please let me know.' It was normal at that time to seek assistance about marriage from friends. He thought for a while: 'Yes, I may know someone who you might like!' he warmly replied. 'This girl I'm talking about,' he said, 'has been brilliant since her primary years; she recently sat her final economics exam from Dhaka University and is waiting for the result. Her father is a senior education officer, and her brothers and sisters are all settled in their life after higher education. Most importantly, she's been brought up in an honest family with good religious practice.'

He gave me some more information, before adding: 'If you feel positive and want to know more about this girl, I can inform her family but they will want to know about your background as well.' I gave him some brief details about me and my family. Before parting, he said: 'If you are really serious about the girl please let me know before you return to Bangladesh and I can inform her family.'

'I'll definitely let you know, inshallah', I said.

A few days later I got a call from Firdaws: 'Bari bhai, I thought I would visit you again, but cannot due to my work pressure. I didn't disclose on that day that the girl I mentioned is my younger sister, Sayeda. I discussed with Sayeda and my family about you and they want to see you. From my side, I think you two would probably be a good match. After your return, if you want to see her then just contact my family directly.' I thought it was very positive news.

Once back in Bangladesh, I had two immediately personal jobs in hand: to find someone who could give reliable information on Sayeda, and to kick-start the process of applying for my PhD. Through one of my friends I came to know a college lecturer, of about my age, in Dhaka's Maghbazar area who knew Firdaws. He was from a district in western Bangladesh, but had recently got married in the city of Barisal. I called him one evening and asked how much he knew of Firdaws' family. He responded: 'I know them well; my wife also knows Sayeda very well.' I visited him the next evening and learnt more about Sayeda and her family. It was all very positive and I asked if he would become an intermediary for us. I then went home and informed my father and family of my course of action. Everyone was delighted and I was given the go-ahead to proceed.

What followed from then on was simple: Sayeda and I exchanged pictures, she must have heard plenty about me from her brother, and I asked if she could come to Dhaka and stay in a relative's house. My auntie in Azimpur (in old Dhaka) spent plenty of time with her and gave me a favourable description of Sayeda and her personality. The following day I went to see her and we 'connected' straight away. I felt an immediate bond as we shared information about our lives, our likes, dislikes and ambitions for life. We spoke for hours and both felt we should agree to tie the knot – and straight away, I said. It was a momentous decision and I couldn't sleep that night. The thought of not being alone anymore and a sudden sense of responsibility weighed on my mind. I later learned that Sayeda had spent a similar few nights thinking the same. The rest was a formality that would be sorted out between the families. I informed my father and brother of my choice and asked my father to visit Barisal and meet Sayeda himself. He stayed for couple of days in their house and came back with a smile. We were married on 10 October 1981.

Marriage in Islam is seen as a blessing. Husbands and wives are mentioned as a 'pair' or 'garments to each other' in the Qur'an. When a man and a woman, with their unique and complementary features, join in union it brings two families together. Our marriage has indeed been a blessed one ever since.

* * *

As I was arranging my marriage, I was also continuing my efforts to enrol for a PhD in the UK. In early September 1981, as I was getting ready for my wedding in October, I received an offer letter from Chelsea College (which became part of King's College a few years later). I consulted my Air Force friends and wrote directly to the Chief of Air Staff (CoAS) pleading for a three year leave, with a firm pledge that on completion of the PhD I would return to complete my service in the BAF. His response came after my short honeymoon was over: my application was rejected. The CoAS was forthright in his response, saying that he was personally willing to give me the opportunity but had to take into account the opinion of my Branch head, who disapproved on the grounds that I was 'indispensable' to the Armament Branch. I was heartbroken, but remembered my father's teachings of reliance on God.

Sayeda was calm; she was confident that some good would come from this.

About a week later, at an informal event in the officers' mess, I managed to get near the CoAS and briefly (and politely) raised the issue with him. My Branch head was around and I could see the annoyance on his face. I was still a junior officer, but the CoAS remembered my case, although he could only express his sadness. I realized I would be chastised for this break in protocol and within the week I was told that I would be posted to Chittagong Air Base, about 165 miles from Dhaka on Bangladesh's south east coast, from New Year's Day, 1982. My hopes were dashed and I left for Chittagong with a broken spirit. Sayeda moved in with her parents in Barisal while I tried to keep myself busy: working in the office by day, doing sports in the late afternoon and studying in the evening. On the weekends I would visit Barisal to see Sayeda, or spend time in the city, as I had plenty of friends there having studied at Chittagong University.

Being a hyperactive sportsman I came to the attention of the Base commander, a senior Group Captain. He was very sociable and one evening I raised the subject of my PhD with him. He appeared sympathetic, thought for a while and told me that he would write to the Air Secretary directly to hear my case. I did not expect he would actually do this, but soon after I received an invitation for a meeting in Dhaka. I flew by BAF transport aircraft and appeared before the Air Secretary. To my trepidation, the meeting started with a verbal assault: 'How dare you talk with the Base Commander once the CoAS had already written to you!' I politely explained how important this was to my life, but he did not budge and with a stern tone advised me not to do raise it again. I returned to Chittagong downhearted and briefed the Base commander. He kept quiet; I did not know what to say either.

Within a few weeks, towards the end of April, I was called to Dhaka again. I was surprised when the Base commander told me that he had written to the Air Secretary again and asked me to try my luck. This time I flew to Dhaka with some apprehension and again the meeting started with some tough language. I remained quiet, remembering his earlier command, when he suddenly lowered his voice, looked into my eyes and said: 'We cannot give you such a long leave. You should be grateful that we have trained you twice in the UK, but you are stubborn and breaking protocol. This could easily be a disciplinary issue, but we can't punish you for your ambition. At the same time, it cannot go on like this. The only option is for you to take voluntary retirement and leave us.'

This was music to my ears, but I controlled myself and looked at him puzzled. He continued: 'I'm going to give you until tomorrow to think about it and consult your family; let me know your decision.' I thought for a while and politely said: 'Thank you sir! I'll let you know tomorrow.' I stayed at the officer's mess overnight and called Sayeda. She was calm as usual and simply said: 'I had a feeling something like this would happen; I was praying all along for a good outcome from this saga.' I expressed my gratitude to her, then informed my family and close friends. They couldn't believe it was going to happen!

The following day I went to Air HQ and informed them of my decision to resign. This had never happened before in the Bangladesh Air Force – and I had signed up for at least ten years! Soon the news broke in the officers' circle. I went back to Chittagong and gave massive thanks to the Base commander. The release order was issued and in early May I left the BAF and returned to Dhaka.

* * *

It took nearly a year to sort out all the arrangements for travel to London. I lost my first scholarship offer, but luckily managed an alternative: in life, when one door closes another opens. I flew into Heathrow on 23 April 1983, and Aziz Bhai had already arranged a meeting with my supervisor, Professor A.K. Jonscher, the following day. The two of us reached the campus near Fulham Broadway in south-west London, and with a broad smile, a full hearty beard and thick glasses, Professor Jonscher welcomed us. We settled in his room and he initiated the conversation with a light joke: 'Bari, thanks, you've now arrived. But why did it take so long? Were you travelling by a bullock cart?' He laughed and so did we. I enjoyed his joke and felt it was a warm welcome; humour really brings people together.

Professor Jonscher was to be my PhD supervisor. He showed us the campus and the laboratory where I would be working; a large room used mainly for postgraduate research in solid state physics. We arrived at the lab during lunch time and about a dozen researchers and couple of technicians, all from diverse backgrounds, joined us around a big table. He introduced me to my new colleagues and with a smile repeated the bullock-cart joke. Everyone started laughing and I was relieved that the elderly academic was so full of life with a good persona, and that the environment there was so informal. After about an hour they all went back to their tables. Jonscher and I agreed to meet on another date and we left the campus for the day.

During our next meeting, when I briefed him about the long gap in my physics career because of my life in the Air Force, Jonscher looked at me sympathetically and said: 'Bari, you have to work hard now. You must quickly revisit the world of physics'.

'You are right, Professor!' I replied, earnestly. 'Please give me couple of months to prepare myself before I start my research.'

He agreed and advised me to talk with a few overseas researchers who would be able to help me. I visited the lab again and talked to a PhD student from Karachi University,

Ashraf Choudhury. He gave me a brotherly embrace and took me to his table. He briefed me about the nature of research under Jonscher and our other physicist, Professor Robert Hill. I explained my situation and the need to recover gaps in my knowledge. He assured me that he would help in any way he could and advised me to go through a few books and journals as well as occasional reports published by the Chelsea's Dielectric Group. On my way home I bought a few relevant books and was determined I would start my research on a par with my colleagues in no more than three months. Ashraf kept his promise and helped me as and when I needed in the first few months.

Sayeda joined me towards the end of June; she was in the middle of her pregnancy with our first child, Rima, and I was renting a small flat above an Indian restaurant in South Wimbledon. In the meantime, I had begun my research on the dielectric interface between electrodes and electrolytes in batteries. After spending a few days with Sayeda, and making sure she felt safe at home, I became busier than ever in the lab. My grant was only for three years and I had to finish on time!

Soon the research was becoming increasingly intensive and I felt sorry for Sayeda, as I would leave her at home alone in the morning and return late at night. I even started working in the lab most weekends as well. No doubt it was tough for her, but she proved to be resilient and built up friendships with people from the area and spent time mostly reading; like both her parents she was a bookworm. I could only apologize and call her as often as I could from the laboratory for little chats. She held on to her nerve and prepared for the arrival of our child in late September.

Rima was born on 21 September, a tiny little angel with all her sweetness, innocence and vulnerability. The first touch was ecstatic and she quickly became the centre of our life. The arrival of a child brings a total change to a family: 'The jewel of the sky is the sun, the jewel of the house is the child,' goes a Chinese saying. In Islam, children are gifts of God; according to the Prophet, a woman herself is blessed if her first child is a daughter. A mother in a family is, of course, special to any child. But the role of a father is similarly vital, especially to a daughter. He is the first man in her life and his character, behaviour and humanity in the family subconsciously shapes her self-worth in life. As single-parent families are often a reality in modern times, the burden of parenthood falls on one parent who has to act to fill the gap of another. Rima was special to us, particularly to me, as I was longing for a daughter (a 'little mum!') ever since I had lost my own mother when I was sixteen. Rima radiated joy and happiness in our small world, and it was a unique experience to see a totally dependent little life growing in our arms with her own unique features. Sadly, my father and the rest of our families in Bangladesh could not share our happiness.

It was not easy for Sayeda to look after a baby virtually on her own. I tried to change my routine slightly so that I could spend some quality time at home looking after Rima, and give Sayeda some rest. But she was a woman of steel, and how Sayeda quickly learnt to efficiently multi-task – first raising Rima and then our other three children later on – was inspiring and amazing. If leadership is about vision and imparting that vision to people around you, especially growing children, then mothers are the primordial leaders in human society. Sadly very few societies recognize this treasure within them.

Financially, Sayeda and I had to live within our means, my scholarship funds just about covered our living expenses and I was not allowed any public money, neither was Sayeda. She was a brilliant student and wanted to pursue a higher degree in economics or a relevant subject. But even if I were allowed to work, or Sayeda to attend a course, we could not do so because of my research pressures and her 24/7 role in looking after Rima. It was a big career sacrifice on her part.

Professor Jonscher, who I learnt was a practising Polish Catholic, was delighted to discover that I had a baby girl. When I informed him of the good news he looked at me and said: 'You are very lucky Bari. The start of your research is blessed with a daughter.'

I could not have agreed more.

* * *

The atmosphere in our laboratory was buzzing every day, it was highly academic but still informal. We all felt like and behaved as family members, and with researchers from many backgrounds – overseas and domestic, with faith and non-faith backgrounds – it was a microcosm of the world of physics. The permanent members of the research staff were highly professional: John Pugh, with his bushy beard, was a computer whiz and an excellent programmer; Dr Len Dissado was the brains and a theorist in his area of theoretical physics; Terry Ramdeen was always available to help. Professor Jonscher's PA, the always smiling Josephine Woropay, was motherly and a wizard with her typing and organizing of the whole team. There were often lively discussions around the table, especially during lunch hour, and professors Jonscher and Hill, as well as some guests, would often participate. There were also occasional seminars on our research, and we would take turns to present our findings. It felt frightening in the beginning, but gave us confidence and a good grounding on what we were doing. The Dielectrics Group, led by Jonscher, was well known in the world of physics research and we all felt proud to be a part of the group.

Life was moving fast. In order to finish my PhD by summer 1986 I led a ruthlessly disciplined life. I was on course with my progress and Professor Jonscher was happy as well. During the second and third years I co-authored with him a few papers that were published in international journals, and began writing my PhD thesis at the beginning of my third year. In 1985, the New Year started with huge discussions and concerns within London University about the merger of smaller colleges with big ones to save costs. We learned that Chelsea and Queen Elizabeth Colleges were merging with King's College, and our links with King's Physics Department, in its Strand campus, started growing.

All the while I was studying for my PhD I continued to visit east London, by this time my favourite part of the city. Aziz Bhai and I were helping some young Bangladeshi boys with their GCSE and A-level mathematics and science examinations, and most of them later performed very well in life. A few were involved with a group known as the Young Muslim Organization (YMO), which was originally founded in 1978. As most other members of YMO were Bengali-speaking, this small group was struggling to blend in with the majority. Our time spent voluntary tutoring both the English-speaking boys and interacting with the Bengali-speaking YMO youngsters kept me in touch with the East End and its Bangladeshi people, particularly the East London Mosque. By 1985, the ELM was no longer just a shed, and the first phase of the multi-purpose mosque that stands today had been completed. Through this group I gradually entered deeper into the world of youth and community work in Tower Hamlets. Although I lived in south London, I had quickly become part and parcel of east London, an East Ender-by-proxy, you might say.

I was coming towards the end of my thesis, and submitted the completed work in mid-May 1986. My oral examination date was fixed for July 1986 and I was preparing for the PhD 'viva voce', or defence of my thesis. On 26 May we were blessed with another child, this time our first boy, Raiyan. We were overjoyed and I informed Jonscher of the good news. With a huge smile, he said: 'Congratulations! Now you are completing one PhD with two children!' After some chat about the viva, he looked into my eyes and said: 'Bari, you know Chelsea has merged with King's, but I've decided to move to Royal Holloway College and set up a laboratory there. Would you like to join me?'

I realized that I had not seriously given much thought about what I would do after completing my PhD. I expressed my gratitude and said: 'I'll definitely go with you if you need me. But for how long?' He replied: 'I've funding for three years for two posts.' It was a great relief, I would not have to immediately plan about the future. I learned that the other person who was invited was Enapu Owede, my co-researcher from Nigeria.

In July I faced my viva, which was gruelling, to say the least. There was a natural tension, but I was confident that I would get through. Once the viva was finished, I was asked to wait. Within a few minutes the external examiner and Professor Jonscher came out smiling and congratulated me. 'Dr Bari, you've defended your work very well. We'll recommend your name to the university senate. It's just a formality. You will need to make small changes in some places.' They shook my hands and Professor Jonscher handed over couple of pages to me for amendment. I gave them massive thanks, ran to the telephone booth and called Sayeda to give her the great news. My dream was fulfilled! I gave thanks to God. For the rest of the day, Sayeda and I shared the news with our families in Bangladesh and close friends in London.

After about a month's rest, in August 1986 I started my work as a postdoctoral researcher at Royal Holloway College.

Chapter 2

Into The World of Community Activism

I T WAS EARLY 1987, and my postdoctoral research on semiconductor physics at the Royal Holloway College started in earnest. The campus was in a pleasant hilly location, just over a mile west from the village of Egham, not far from Heathrow Airport. Royal Holloway College was a public research university within the federal University of London.

Working at Royal Holloway College was my first full time job in the UK, albeit on a temporary work permit and an initial contract for three years. Professor Jonscher excelled at securing research funding from various British and American industries. Our laboratory was quiet, as there were only the two of us working there, but Professor Jonscher often came to our lab to oversee and discuss the progress of our work and A-level students from the Greater London area occasionally visited us. After a few weeks of separate journeys by car, Enapu and I decided to car pool to share the burden of cost, as well as the long drive to and from London.

As I settled into my research with a few more publications, Sayeda and I also went through some serious thinking about our future with our two young children. I had a burning desire to return to Bangladesh and serve my own country, a place that had given me so much. 'How could I give something back' was always in my mind. I sounded out with friends and extended family members in Bangladesh whether there were any suitable job opportunities in the capital, Dhaka. I preferred Dhaka because it was near my home and it would allow us to provide better education facilities for our children. But I didn't get much encouragement and some even questioned my desire to return.

In the summer of 1987, we decided to visit Bangladesh to explore the situation directly. We stayed for couple of weeks but surprisingly both extended families, as well as close friends, advised us to stay in the UK, or even move to the US; they honestly felt we would not be able to financially survive in Dhaka. Both Sayeda and I came from modest financial backgrounds, with no other sources of income except the earnings from our jobs; if we decided to settle down in Dhaka we would have had to find extra work to top up our income. I turned to other friends, some of whom were in high positions already. Most of them suggested I would do better in the UK. Only one friend, a few years older than me, instantly offered me a senior non-academic job in a new private university. I was aware of the new emerging universities in Dhaka, and as I knew there were no pure science departments in any of them, I politely rejected the offer. However, we seriously considered such a role: could I give up physics and take a senior management job just for more money? I could not reconcile myself to the idea. We returned to the UK undecided, but I had not given up the idea of going back to Bangladesh – I just could not be so sure about that move, either.

* * *

Life could have been relaxed if I had just stuck with my research, but I felt I should use my weekends and holidays to go to east London and extend my support to the young people there. I spent more and more time in the East London Mosque, which by now served a congregation of around 3,000 people, with a main prayer hall on the ground floor and a multi-purpose hall in the basement. My friend Aziz and I continued to expand our efforts to help GCSE and A-level students, and we saw huge potential in them. Some were now gravitating onto adult education courses, switching away from work in the garment trade and restaurant business. We decided to talk to the parents of some of the most promising boys, trying to encourage them to be more 'aspirational' with their children.

Most parents felt that a good knowledge of Islam was important; many also had a special attachment with their local mosque, and wanted their children to be well educated. We convinced some religious scholars to join our side, adding more weight to our initiative. We used reminders from Qur'anic verses, such as: 'My Lord, increase me in knowledge' (Ta Ha 20: 114), and the Prophetic hadith (teaching): 'Seeking knowledge is obligatory upon every Muslim' (Ibn Majah) to encourage parents to guide their children into more fulfilling career paths. There is another powerful hadith: 'Whoever travels a path seeking knowledge, God makes easy their path to Paradise.' (Muslim) The need for better education was paramount, since Bangladeshi children were underperforming in Tower Hamlets. School attendance and punctuality were often poor, and many families suffered economic hardship and lived in overcrowded housing. What they needed was increased confidence and skills in order to create higher expectations at home and generate higher aspirations in their offspring.

With our small efforts, a few young men left their monotonous, low-skilled jobs and enrolled on vocational technical courses. Some even chose new careers, away from a life of catering or sewing. A few went on to positions in business and others in academia, while some came back to work with the area's growing number of charities. The ELM management was very supportive of this effort.

We slowly started to see improvements. During the past two decades, the results of Bangladeshi schoolchildren have improved significantly; they are now achieving higher than the national average percentages of A* to C in GCSEs, including English and mathematics. The outcome is that there has been a significant increase in the numbers of British Bangladeshi children going to university, and the trend has been encouraging for other communities as well. Tower Hamlets, being the spiritual home of the British Bangladeshi diaspora, has always been looked up to by other Bangladeshis in Britain. What is most needed now is to translate this academic success into even better employment and economic opportunities to fully contribute to the wider society. We need improved social mobility.

* * *

Raising a community's educational as well as socio-economic standard has always been my passion. Those who find time beyond their regular daily job and make (often unnoticed) contributions to our social life are the unsung heroes of our society. In this age of egocentrism and greed, this service ethos (Arabic: *khidmah*) is vital to our society's wellbeing. For religious adherents this is also highly rewarding, and Britain's faith groups have always been pioneering in the voluntary and community sector. A community that is otherwise behind others in socio-economic factors needs intervention from some of its members to raise its standards. Those who have the vision to serve, and can find some free time to invest in their future generation, should not shy away. I gradually entered this world of community activism, perhaps through a latent push by my own family tradition, especially the work of my brother, or maybe drawn by my initial attachment to people from my own ethnic background in east London.

Physics research and the world of physics still brought me great pleasure. However, I gradually felt that my success in academia would be limited. As I was becoming drawn further towards youth work, I became less enamoured with research. I felt torn, yet only Sayeda really knew what was going through my mind. Until the end of the 1980s, I had been merely a volunteer at the ELM. I learned from various elders that before my involvement the mosque management had switched alignment from Tablighi Jamaat (a global Muslim missionary organization, born out of the South Asian Deobandi movement) towards Jamaat-e-Islami, the largest religious party in Bangladesh that sided with Pakistan against the country's breakup in 1971. Both these religious movements originated in British India during the British Raj, to educate Muslims in their own ways.

The primary aim of Tablighi Jamaat, created in India in 1927 by Maulana Ilyas al-Kandhlawi, was the spiritual reformation of Muslims at the grassroots level. Its 'Six Point' teachings are: Kalimah (Islam's declaration of faith); Salat (ritual prayer); Ilm (knowledge), Ikram-e-Muslim (respect for Muslims); Ikhlas-e-Niyat (purity of intention); and Dawat wa Tabligh (invitation and conveyance). Tablighi Jamaat claims it is apolitical and focuses on the Qur'an and Hadith.

Jamaat-e-Islami was founded by journalist-turned-Islamic theologian and socio-political reformist, Abul A'la Maududi (or Mawdudi) in 1941 in British India. Jamaat started as a socially conservative movement, but became an Islamic political organization in both Pakistan and Bangladesh. Maududi emerged as an Islamic revivalist and influential intellectual with a belief that politics was 'an integral, inseparable part of the Islamic faith'. Jamaat participated in the democratic movement in Pakistan during the Martial Law period in the 1960s, but when Bangladesh rose against the Pakistani military crackdown in 1971, due to its active support for a united Pakistan Jamaat was banned in Bangladesh after independence. It was, however, allowed to resume political activities in 1978; when Jamaat became a political force and joined with the country's two main political parties, Awami League (AL) and Bangladesh Nationalist party (BNP), in a coalition against military rule in the 1980s.

I respected the elders of both camps in east London, those who were Jamaat-oriented and those Tablighi-focused. I felt comfortable because they were dedicated individuals with a long-standing record of community service in the management committee, including Sulaiman Jetha (formerly of the Ismaili community) and Haji Taslim Ali, a Bangladeshi philanthropist and keen Tablighi.

In 1978, the better-organized leadership of the Jamaat group formed a community organization in the East End called Dawatul Islam UK & Eire (DI), meaning 'Call to Islam', attracting various Bangladeshi elders as well as some youths. These youth members also formed their own group, the Young Muslim Organization (YMO) in the same year. However, after the first purpose-built structure of the East London Mosque was completed in 1985, and the mosque began to gain influence and stature within the local community, tensions began to grow within the DI leadership over who would run the mosque. Having finished my PhD, I also got involved in the ELM as well as DI in the late 1980s.

It was painful to see the misunderstandings and recriminations arise, and I joined in the efforts of a few professionals to try and heal these rifts – but to no avail. During much of 1987, others within the wider Muslim community made attempts to sort out the differences, but could not make any headway. The recriminations were becoming embarrassingly public, and eventually the YMO decided enough was enough and withdrew their support from Dawatul Islam. Well-connected with many youth leaders in

A Long Jihad

Tower Hamlets' Bangladeshi community, they attempted to bring in changes to the composition of the ELM's management.

Meanwhile, some British-Bangladeshi professionals both within and outside DI, including some former members of the YMO leadership, felt it was time to build a professional network in the UK and across several other European countries to concentrate on future generations of the Bangladeshi diaspora. I was very unhappy with the nature of community politics from those with supposedly Islamic leanings. I wanted to contribute to the professional class of the Bangladeshi diaspora and their future generations. So I became involved in this process from the beginning, working with a few dozen like-minded people, and in March 1988 we formed an organization called the Islamic Forum Europe (IFE). The YMO became a partner organization of the IFE and I was elected its first president. Its main objective was to bring together Bangladeshi professionals settled in various UK cities and universities, as well as those who were newly arriving in Britain and other European countries, to harness the talents of professionals in order to build the community's capacity. We received support from an influential office bearer at the East London Mosque during the 1980s, Chowdhury Mueen-Uddin, although he was not part of the IFE leadership.

A natural link grew between the ELM, the IFE and the YMO. In Tower Hamlets' close-knit Bangladeshi community, where almost everyone knew one another, the three organizations shared volunteering responsibilities. This cooperation created a synergy later on, towards the end of 1990s, and helped the ELM grow immensely. I remained IFE's president during its early years, It was an exciting period of growth, and all membership and council positions were voluntary. There was a small executive body, with a few designated volunteers, to organize a database of supporters and put together occasional events in major cities with a Bangladeshi presence. I would use some weekends and evenings to meet relevant people and plan for the IFE's future, as well as spend time with young people and occasionally their families. The IFE's initial goals were simple: to harness the contribution of expatriate Bangladeshi professionals and improve the educational and socio-economic conditions of the Bangladeshi community in Britain, and in other European countries. For me, it was an ambitious collective effort to add what we had already been informally doing in the East End on a very limited scale since 1983 (with the mosque's more talented youth members).

* * *

In the summer of 1989, during Rima's school holiday, Sayeda and I decided to perform Hajj (the main Muslim pilgrimage to Makkah). We were both excited with the thought that we would be God's guests. Every able-bodied and financially solvent Muslim needs to undertake this spiritual as well as physical journey once in his or her life, to fulfil religious obligations and also to use the time in the holy places for deep personal reflection and introspection. In our case, the main stumbling block was where to leave our two young children, Rima and Raiyan, for two weeks. There were a few offers from close friends, but eventually we were assured by one nearby, and with full reliance on God we left the children in their house and took a flight from Heathrow.

Hajj, the fifth pillar of Islam, is the largest yearly human gathering for a divine purpose on Earth. It is the collective human expression of the Oneness of God, *tawhid*. It is also a manifestation of unity among believers; a physical, emotional, mental and spiritual journey by believers passionate and devoted to retrace some of the rituals of Prophet Ibrahim (or Abraham) and his wife Hagar. It is for those lovers of God who are in need of His closeness and acceptance. With the all-white, two-piece unstitched simple attire for men, *Ihram*, it brings pilgrims to the same level of equality and demolishes human artificiality and arrogance. Once pilgrims are in the holy precinct, in the midst of a sea of human beings of different colours, cultures and languages, they feel spiritually and emotionally uplifted and overwhelmed – no matter what their background is or where they come from. The few days in Makkah, Mina, Arafah and Muzdalifah are etched into pilgrims' minds and hearts. They have the opportunity to immerse themselves in the intense and irresistible love of God and levitate on His limitless mercy, forget their transient existence on Earth and to make a change for good.

From hard-core sinners to the elevated pious, if one comes to Hajj with pure intentions then the experience is similar. The African-American Muslim minister and human rights activist, Malcolm X, was one such pilgrim who wrote from Makkah about his own feelings during pilgrimage:

> Never have I witnessed such sincere hospitality and overwhelming spirit of true brotherhood as is practiced by people of all colors and races here in this ancient Holy Land, the home of Abraham, Muhammad and all the other Prophets of the Holy Scriptures. For the past week, I have been utterly speechless and spellbound by the graciousness I see displayed all around me by people of all colors.[1]

It was unusually hot in Makkah that summer, with temperatures rising as high as 48°C. The scorching sun above the clear skies made the hot air stifling and the pavements were difficult to walk on with sandals. But the feeling of closeness to God in the precinct of the Kaaba (house of God) gave us a spiritual lift that words could not express. The sight of the Kaaba itself with my own eyes was pure joy and literally made

---

1. Malcolm X, 'Letter from Mecca', April 1964.

me forget the world outside. It was an exceptional reminder of the willing submission and sacrifices that Ibrahim (Abraham), his wife and son made for God 4,000 years ago. Hajj is a journey towards God, and this global assembly of humanity brings believers of all backgrounds into one place, to purify them and cleanse them from the garbage of our base desires in life. Alas, once they return to their normal life the spirit and message of Hajj are soon forgotten by many Muslims. Sayeda and I prayed for goodness for ourselves, our children and parents, families, community and all the children of Adam.

After completing the rituals of Hajj in Makkah, we travelled to Madinah (where the Prophet Muhammad had once lived with his Companions) with Firdaws, Sayeda's elder brother, who had introduced us both and was at that time working in Jeddah. The Prophet's City, or City of Light, had a serene and soothing atmosphere; people were more hospitable and approachable. I had learned about this difference in Hajj literature and from people who had performed Hajj before, but it was a unique first-hand experience. After a couple of days in Madinah, we went to Jeddah for another couple of days and returned to the UK refreshed and energized. The reunion with our children was exceptionally memorable. For the next few weeks, the memory of Hajj often made me unmindful; though life gradually returned to normal.

After our return from Hajj, I felt more inclined than ever to stay in the UK, but the decision and practical steps towards this were not taken until towards the end of the year.

* * *

After these decisions and our Hajj experience, I was torn by two options: to find a teaching or research job in a university and move up the research ladder; or to secure a teaching job in a school or a further education college that would allow me to have a better connection with the community. Sayeda was insistent I took the first option, my extended contract at Royal Holloway College would come to an end early in 1990. I sounded out Professor Jonscher and was disappointed to learn that he could not secure any new funding. However, he agreed to extend my contract until July, and from then on I was on the lookout for a university research post. Most jobs were outside London, temporary and not particularly well-paid. By this time, a few of my close friends had just finished their PGCE (teacher training qualification) and had begun teaching in secondary schools. They advised me to follow the same path so I made up my mind to go for it and take a PGCE, but I had to do a lot of convincing with Sayeda. I sat with her and gave all my reasons, including my growing passion for community work, and thankfully she relented and gave her blessing.

In the summer of 1990 I returned to King's College, this time on the Waterloo campus, to start my PGCE (Secondary Science) teaching course. It was a new experience in the world of England's statutory education system. Many things were new to me – the admissions process, the examination systems, school governance, types of schools, pastoral care, relationship with parents and career advice. Educational philosophy and classroom management, especially in inner cities, were other areas that I had to quickly grasp. Just like starting my PhD, I had to learn things very quickly to be on par with others who had gone through British schooling. However, the course was enriching and very useful; I thoroughly enjoyed it. When it came to choosing a school for teaching practice, I ended up at Tiffin Grammar School for Boys in Kingston upon Thames, which was actually quite close to my home. I did not know the school, but one of my course friends remarked: 'Man, you're lucky! You've got one of the best schools in the country!' I felt happy and thanked the staff.

Founded in 1880, Tiffin was a selective boys' school that became a grammar school under the Education Act 1944. It then changed from being voluntary-controlled to being grant-maintained in 1992; today it is an Academy and educates more than 1,000 pupils each year. It had always been a high-achieving school and students were selected in year 7 through competitive exams. It had strong A-level teaching facilities, and once I started teaching I was really impressed with the high standards, the behaviour of the boys and the dedication of both teachers and parents. The head of Physics was particularly happy to have a senior physicist teaching in his department for a few months. He put me mostly in the upper school and A-level teaching. We became good friends and he taught me valuable skills to make learning physics easier, as well as fun for young people.

Despite my enjoyable time at Tiffin, I wanted to know how an inner city school worked. Through one of my research projects in the PGCE, I had the opportunity to observe some Bangladeshi pupils in a secondary mixed school in Elephant and Castle. I visited the school for a few days, observed how they behaved in classrooms and talked with them. There was a sharp contrast compared to the Tiffin experience, and I realized that education was far from uniform in British schools. Over the next few years, as I moved into teaching low-achieving children, I was keener than ever in helping the disadvantaged ones.

As the PGCE course came to an end, most of my peers received job offers in various schools. My stumbling block was that I needed a new work permit, as the one for my research job at London University was expiring. It was not an issue for my postdoctoral research at Royal Holloway College, as my salary did not come from public money. I applied to a few schools in South London as a matter of preference. They liked me but were reluctant to go through the hassle of applying to the Home Office for my work permit. Eventually, a school in Haringey's Broadwater Farm, The Langham School (which had a fairly negative image due to the civil disturbances between youths and police in the mid-1980s), offered me a job and the head teacher agreed to apply for my work permit. I had to remain unemployed and survive on the little we had saved for a few months. Eventually, the permit came through and I started as a science teacher; we soon became permanent residents and within a few years Sayeda and I had also become naturalized British citizens.

* * *

The Langham School on West Green Road in Haringey (today Park View School), was a mixed comprehensive which had a wide intake of students from many ethnicities and faiths. The catchment area was one of the most ethnically mixed and socio-economically deprived in London. Within a few weeks, I realized that many children of Turkish and Kurdish origin had English as their second language. I was determined to make an impact on my students by giving my best to their education. But, as expected, behaviour was an issue. I was aware that the area was tough and class discipline would be a major issue, which meant I would have to concentrate more on managing my classes than simply teaching. I would have to be tough but flexible at the same time. It was a test for me; I could not afford to give in to deliberate attempts by some children to disrupt my class and establishing a tough but fair image was vital. I realized that in our science department we had a few successful strong-willed teachers who appeared to fit into that category. I followed them and talked with them to gain some practical tips. They would not tolerate indiscipline in the corridors as well as the classroom – using techniques of remaining calm through tough love.

I decided to attend a few day-courses on assertive discipline and techniques of classroom management with mixed ability and often difficult children. One of my techniques was to build individual relationships with the students, especially those who would easily engage in low-level disruption, and empathize with them by getting to know their backgrounds; having a personal touch was always effective. I knew about a highly successful college principal in my home district in Bangladesh who had memorized all of his students' names. It would not be difficult for me to memorize the names of a couple of hundred students – so I thought! I developed a student-centred approach and established clear expectations from each of them. Difficult children are often creative, they develop mental images of their teachers as to whether they are soft or tough and consistent; they take advantage by testing a teacher's ability to handle difficult situations. Students become less disruptive if they are more engaged in their learning, with age-appropriate differentiated materials. Empathetic teachers can relate to students in a mutually and informally agreed understanding; when teachers show the way, students respond positively. I also learned some key words in the first languages of several students to make them feel valued. I felt I needed not only to survive but to succeed and make an impact as a teacher.

To me, teaching has always been a noble profession. Prophets, sages and philosophers are essentially teachers of humanity. Our beloved Prophet said: 'Verily, I have been sent as a teacher' (Ibn Majah). In most cultures, respect for teachers is next to one's parents. Through teaching we also keep on learning and sharing our experiences with others. I was blessed with a number of successful teachers in my primary and secondary school life that helped shape my future. One of my secondary teachers impressed me so much that by trying to emulate him in reading, I became a bookworm. Sayeda's family was also blessed with a number of teachers. I decided to invest in young people, the most dynamic and creative section of human progeny. My aim was not just to help them with their subject education but also to give them the values of life that would allow them to become a force for good in society.

According to Islam's holy book, the Qur'an, human beings are created with the dual ability to do good and bad. It is their environment that affects someone's behaviour. With this principle in the back of my mind, I tried to build a positive relationship with each individual student, concentrating on behaviour management techniques and attempting to reach out to difficult students. Classroom teaching was indeed exhausting. Even with plenty of energy, one has to have good rest and leisure time to recuperate and prepare for the next day's teaching. But rest was not easily available to me, my commitment with the newly-formed professional community of the IFE, as well as voluntary work in Tower Hamlets, was also demanding. However, the feeling that I was given the opportunity in life to help shape others' futures was a satisfaction that drove me.

I continued as a Science teacher until the end of 1996. During this period I became more involved with the Special Educational Needs (SEN) of some students in the school and I set out to learn more about this work. Whenever I encountered a SEN child in my class or corridor, or in the playground, my instinct was to help by trying to understand from the child's perspective. I asked myself what would I do if I was that child and how would I expect my teacher to deal with me. Or, how would I have behaved if, say, one of my own children needed SEN support. I felt strongly that my response as a teacher mattered in dealing with a difficult situation. There were a few tangible successes in the way I handled some students with behavioural difficulties, and some of my departmental colleagues also sought my help when they struggled with aggressive behaviour from some students. I started giving some extra time with the SEN department on occasions and offered my help when I had free time.

Being away from university-level physics for a few years, and having some practical experience in classroom teaching – which was getting more tiresome – I thought of moving further into the world of SEN. Special Educational Needs teaching deals with smaller numbers of children, focusing on individual challenges and opportunities. It would need extra patience and empathy to deal with an emotionally vulnerable young person with learning and other difficulties. I felt I had some strength in dealing with such young people, and my skills would be better used in that special area of educational support. I thought about moving to a job in south London, where I lived, or east London, where my community work lay (and I was becoming increasingly busy).

An opportunity arose from the Tower Hamlets Education Authority, and after a series of interviews I was offered a job in its well-resourced and well-known Support for Learning Service (SLS). Beyond teaching, I was also expanding my involvement within the community – not only to Muslims nationwide, but also in the world of interfaith bridging. The East London Mosque was beginning to attract all sorts of people, not only from the East End of London but from all parts of the city – and beyond. It brought me into contact with various groups across the country, including some well-known multi-faith and interfaith bodies.

* * *

At the beginning of 1994, a new phase was opening in my life. When some relatively young community leaders and professionals started discussing the creation of a new national umbrella body, I joined them in earnest. After over three years of consistent work, in 1997 the Muslim Council of Britain (MCB) was born, later to become Britain's largest and most diverse Muslim umbrella body. Its purpose was to help shape the future of British Muslims, meeting and raising the hopes and aspirations of this burgeoning community. The MCB and my involvement with the organization will be discussed more fully in a later chapter.

One day, in the mid-1990s, a well-dressed white man of my age came to visit the mosque to discuss a project he was planning to start in east London. A few of us in the ELM gathered around him curiously: 'Does he have any agenda?' some wondered. He introduced himself as Neil Jameson, and spoke about community organizing by citizens working together to improve life in our neighbourhood communities. We knew little about his background, but he appeared approachable and his smile and body language suggested a gentle, visionary and determined man.

Neil was brimming with ideas and passion as he expanded his vision of using community organizing as a vehicle for social and even political change for good, ideas which immediately chimed with me. It reminded me of the basic Islamic teachings of social justice, i.e., working for the common good of all in society, a crucial civic responsibility for any citizen. Our Prophet himself was involved in a 'League of the Virtuous' (Hilf al-Fudul) in his early adult life, which helped people in need in the very rough and tumble life of Makkah; the whole purpose was to spread the principles of justice as well as to intervene on behalf of the oppressed in the tribal Arab society.

We discussed these ideas and soon signed up to Neil's project. Hence the ELM became a founding member of The East London Communities Organization (TELCO). Various faith organizations from Abrahamic and other backgrounds, as well as non-faith groups, came together to unlock the potential of grassroots community activism on issues such as living wages for low-paid workers in London. It was the start of a bold new experiment that was to bear fruit in the coming years. TELCO gradually expanded London-wide to become London Citizens, an alliance of four chapters with a membership of over 200 institutions from an array of churches, synagogues and mosques as well as union branches, voluntary agencies and residents' associations. London Citizens premier works included a London Living Wage campaign, an urban Community Land Trust and CitySafe havens to tackle knife crime and violence.

At the time of writing the parent body, Citizens UK, has over 350 affiliates in major cities across the UK, and has embarked on many other projects under the leadership of Neil Jameson, now its executive director. With multiple activities involving communities and other bodies, such as educational and trade union groups, CUK has emerged as the premier grassroots civil society organization in the country. In its bid to foster 'change at the local and national level', CUK's unique training programme is the 'combination of theory, practical tools, stories and real action' covering areas including 'Power, Self-Interest, Negotiation, Building Relationships, Leadership, Developing Institutions, Culture, and The Case for Broad-Based Organising.'

Community activism or citizen organizing is vital in shaping a nation as well as giving it a moral anchor. Without individual moral anchoring and public ethics, a society cannot function effectively, and in civic regeneration no section of the society or community should be left out. A vibrant civil society, including a strong voluntary sector, is the eyes and ears of any country. A government alone, however efficient, cannot run a country effectively and harness all its potential. Grassroots participation and non-partisan power politics has been the essence of citizen organizations in several countries. The Industrial Areas Foundation (IAF) in the US has been doing this with religious congregations and civic organizations since the 1940s and has since spread to other continents.

In the midst of a growing 'me first' culture, a greater sense of communal solidarity and community spirit is needed more than ever. Half a century ago, the American civil rights leader Martin Luther King Jr made a remarkable observation of his time: 'Our scientific power has outrun our spiritual power. We have guided missiles and misguided men'. As technological progress is changing our lifestyles, how true are his comments today!

Over the decades, community activism in the Muslim community has taken various shapes and forms. With many educational and socio-economic bodies, as well as numerous charity organizations, British Muslims have been enriching the voluntary or so-called 'third sector'. But with the passage of time, challenges have multiplied and become more complex due to the rise of Islamophobia and other internal shortcomings.

* * *

Although the Church and the State were separated long ago, religion has always played an important role in the British national and local life: in our school education, cultural manifestations and political ceremonies. One third of Britain's state-funded schools are religious denominational, and while it is true that the number of churchgoers has been dwindling for some time, the emergence of non-Christian faiths, the vibrancy of black churches and the rise of interfaith organizations in the 1980s and 1990s have kept religion at the forefront of the public domain. Due to a concerted and united call from Britain's faith communities, a 'religious affiliation' question was incorporated in the 2001 census for the first time (although the nature of the question was optional).

The UK today is rich with many faith as well as interfaith organizations that bring together religious and non-religious groups to one table to work for the common good of society. The Prince of Wales himself has been an exemplary role model in showing public interest in other faiths. One premier national body, the Inter Faith Network (IFN), played a significant role in fostering good relations between religious communities and later had a personal impact on me. Since its inception in 1987, the IFN had been working locally, regionally and nationally, representing nine major faith communities in Britain: the Baha'i, Buddhist, Christian, Hindu, Jain, Jewish, Muslim, Sikh and Zoroastrians.

The IFN was among the first such national interfaith-linking organizations in the world. It committed itself to drawing existing faith communities into better interaction and closer dialogue. In order to promote mutual understanding and cooperation amongst faith groups, it adopted a variety of routes, with an active 'faith and public life' programme, information and advice service and supporting interfaith activities. The IFN handbook, *The Local Inter Faith Guide*, has been very influential in the development and works of local interfaith bodies, and the IFN has worked tirelessly with educational and academic bodies with an interfaith interest. In the meantime, a book by the University of Derby academic Paul Weller, *Religions in the UK: A Multi-faith Directory*, is also a very useful resource in Britain's interfaith work.

Under the dynamic leadership of Brian Pearce, then IFN's long-term director, the umbrella organization successfully navigated the new and often difficult terrain of interfaith work. As Britain's premier ambassador of interfaith work, Brian was seen in many places discussing complex issues, convincing people and helping them to develop closer relationships for society's greater good. He was also very good in convincing successive governments on the importance of faith in public life.

My involvement with the Inner Cities Religious Council (ICRC), an interfaith body set up in 1992 by the Tory government's Department for the Environment, Transport and the Regions (DETR), began as an observer and later as a full member of the IFN. The ICRC was instrumental in my better understanding and increased activism in the interfaith world at the national level. It also gave me the opportunity to work with a government department on issues of faith-related community works. The ICRC worked to help the Conservative government's 'Action for Cities' initiative on community regeneration through Neighbourhood Renewal and other similar projects. It consisted of five faiths – Christianity, Judaism, Islam, Hinduism and Sikhism. A Minister from the DETR would chair the ICRC and a Church of England (CoE) official was seconded to act as its Secretary. Officials from the Home Office and other departments attended the ICRC meetings as and when necessary.

After 1997, when the UK elected its first Labour government for 18 years, the ICRC continued its journey and was put under the auspices of the Deputy Prime Minister's Office (DPMO). Tony Blair's government established a regeneration programme for some of England's most deprived neighbourhoods, known as the New Deal for Communities (NDC), which was overseen by the Neighbourhood Renewal Unit (NRU) and which sought advice from the ICRC. The government established local NDC partnerships for each regeneration area. There were initially seventeen local partnerships in 1998 that later increased by another twenty-two in 1999. This community-led regeneration programme was aimed at social regeneration with interventions designed to reduce relative deprivations such as poor job prospects, high crime levels, educational underachievement, poor health and problems with housing and the environment. It was, to me, a unique government-community initiative.

Alongside IFN's Brian Pearce, the two CoE officials in the ICRC, Reverends David Randolph-Horn, a bearded energetic churchman, and his successor David Rayner, a very mild-natured gentleman, were instrumental in helping me understand the role of interfaith work in mainstream public life. Over the last few decades, Britain's rich interfaith activities have worked positively to build bridges between communities. Partnerships between a government and civil society work much better if there is good will from both sides.

* * *

I started my work at Tower Hamlets' Support for Learning Service (SLS) in January 1997 as a specialist teacher. The SLS was based in a Victorian building very near to Queen Mary College (now QMUL) and its aim has been 'to improve the attainment of children and young people by supporting schools in their inclusion of pupils with Special Educational Needs and Disabilities, including social, emotional and behaviour difficulties, through offering advice, training and support'. I had to visit various schools in the borough and work with a number pupils selected by schools' SEN departments.

The SLS grouped its teachers on the basis of their expertise in areas such as language and communication, behaviour support, sensory support, specific learning difficulties – including dyslexia and physical disabilities – and severe medical conditions. As Tower Hamlets had a higher number of pupils with a range of specific needs, the SLS had to employ a significant number of full-time and part time staff to cover all the schools. After working with the learning difficulties team for a few years, I moved to the behaviour support team.

Tower Hamlets, an ever-changing and overcrowded borough with many transient souls – firstly French Huguenots and Jews, both fleeing persecution, then Bangladeshis coming as immigrants and Somalis arriving as refugees – has a uniquely complex set of dynamics. Often, because of the waves of highly visible immigrants, the majority white working class population remained unnoticed. I had to deal with children from all backgrounds and be 'colour-blind'. Under the effective leadership of Liz Vickerie and her direction in the service, I quickly grounded myself in the borough's SEN work and discovered a passion for my job. I thought that with my previous role as a class teacher, and growing expertise as a specialist teacher, I could give something extra not only to Bangladeshis living there but to all in the borough's melting pot.

The demography of the school population was interesting. Although the Bangladeshi population was around one-third of its total population, the school intake for its children was over 50 per cent. The borough did not have enough specialist teachers from the local community in various areas of SEN, so it needed people like me who had a grasp of cultural understandings. Within a short time I found myself offering help and advice to some of my colleagues who came from middle-class suburban backgrounds.

Our service comprised of wonderful teachers full of professionalism, energy, humour, good will and dedication. There was such diversity that a designated half-day a week (every Friday afternoon) was needed to share our experiences, challenges and future plans in the service. These sessions within various teams, as well as with the whole service, were lively and informative. They were often followed by individual or group support on any issues in the SLS. There was a common recognition in the SLS that many of Tower Hamlets' students, while academically achieving, lacked aspiration and ambition, thus hampering social mobility in the job market. We realized this was an issue across the borough's main communities – the white working class, Bangladeshi and Somali groups. This was linked to a combination of many factors, including socio-economic deprivation, poor and often congested housing, and a lower level playing field for the recently-arriving minority communities. Structural shortcomings in the education sector was no less responsible. Apart from addressing the educational challenges of special needs children, we also had to keep in mind these social realities.

There was an increasing proportion of SEN children from the newly-arriving Somali community. Their country was being ravaged by war and many children were separated from their close families. Some had severe mental health issues as a result of the horrors back home and their needs were desperate. All these were live issues and we needed greater knowledge to more effectively deal with such children. The SLS included these elements in its training provision by inviting community experts to attend and shed light on their perspectives. Relevant classroom teachers from across the borough were often invited so that all teachers, specialist or mainstream, had a similar understanding of important issues that were affecting education.

I empathized with classroom teachers in their struggle to manage children with behavioural issues. They had to provide education to a mixed-ability class of 25–30 pupils, and some would almost certainly not have the specialism to handle unruly pupils. As trained teachers from the SLS with certain specialisms, we often had to gently step in and help classroom teachers who would struggle with managing the class, sometimes because of the difficult children, without, of course, undermining their authority.

My daily involvement was with some of the most challenging and needy students across the borough. The job was demanding to say the least. Many of the children were on the verge of exclusion due to their challenging behaviour, and most of my allocated students were known to have emotional and behavioural difficulties (EBD). However, it gave me a good opportunity to teach individual children in personalized learning, which a class teacher normally struggles with in the classroom setting. My job included individual or group intervention – sometimes out of the classroom but often within – to be able to monitor how they were coping or progressing in classrooms. Building relationships with class teachers, support staff and parents or carers was vital, and to make positive changes in the life of these children I had to build a trusting relationship with them and their families where possible. I also built lasting and trusting relationships with experts from social services and various education agencies, who were a source of current information and developments in the field. As a result, paperwork dealing with all of the issues that the SLS dealt with was daunting, and included daily record keeping, reporting and discussions in the weekly SLS team meetings. Writing progress reports every academic term became a matter of routine.

My work with the SLS was by far one of the most satisfying experiences of my working life, and I derived great satisfaction from helping a variety of disadvantaged young people from all backgrounds and walks of life. From my part, I was just doing my job, but clearly my contribution was being recognized, because in 2003 I was awarded an MBE by Her Majesty the Queen for my contribution towards community regeneration and Neighbourhood Renewal. I did not expect it, but naturally Sayeda and the children were delighted for me.

* * *

My SEN teaching in Tower Hamlets gave me an insight into the day-to-day struggle of many lives. The story of a boy from one secondary school, Mamun (not his real name), has been etched into my memory.

Mamun was on the verge of being permanently excluded from his secondary school, and the moment I started working with the apparently quiet 15-year-old boy I could see his frustration, anger and aggression. But when I got him to talk I found within him sweetness mixed with bitterness. He was full of sorrow; Mamun's father was erratic in his behaviour and was often absent, while his mother was schizophrenic. As the eldest child of three this had a particular impact on him, but somehow the family kept it together until his father suddenly went missing a few months earlier. His mother snapped, Social Services became involved and the three children were placed with three different foster families. Luckily, his own foster parents were distant relations, but being separated from his parents and two younger siblings, he was going through big emotional changes. He started missing school and bunking lessons and gradually came across some drug addicts. He became rude with his teachers and aggressive with fellow students, for which he was often sent home from school with temporary exclusions.

I decided to visit his foster family, and as I knocked on the door one late afternoon it was Mamun who opened it. He looked visibly uneasy, so I quickly held out my hand and shook his, gently guiding him to sit near me on the sofa in the family's living room, then started a conversation as if I was one of his family uncles. He was obviously feeling uncomfortable as his uncle, Mr Ali (not his real name), entered the room with the Islamic greeting, 'peace be upon you'. His face looked familiar, and while grabbing a chair to sit Mr Ali exclaimed: 'Bari bhai (brother), I saw you at a community event a few months ago. I didn't realize you were helping my nephew! Thank you for coming.'

The boy left the room and Mr Ali and I had a good discussion on Manun's overall situation. At some point, Mr Ali was nearly in tears and in a choking voice said: 'I am sad that I could not foster his other two siblings, because of a lack of space in my house. Mamun is otherwise such a nice boy and I see him as one of my own children. But I don't know how I can fill up his vacuum and help him. Please help me and the boy, my brother.' I reassured Mr Ali and suggested a few tips on 'tough love': a combination of consistent love, discipline and boundaries. I assured him that I would try my best to do the same. 'Together, let's give him the support he needs,' I said. Mr Ali left the room and sent Mamun back to me again. I put my hand on his back and in a fatherly voice asked him to meet me the following day. I was a little worried whether he would do so, but to my relief he turned up on time, looking slightly more relaxed. Having the broken the ice at Mamum's house the day before we had a much better discussion. My journey with him continued and slow progress was made; at times he would test my patience, but somehow he hung on.

At my request, the school decided to not to exclude him and allowed him more time. Mamun's behaviour improved and somehow he stayed at school and was able to receive a few good grades in his GCSEs, enough to take up a course at the local Tower Hamlets College.

* * *

Once I had settled in at the SLS and started working more directly with parents, I could see that some, especially from minority communities, were struggling to cope with their children once they reached adolescence. Many had poor communication with their children and in some cases a lack of confidence in handling teenagers; some just gave up. Others were struggling to make ends meet and were unable to give enough time to their children. However, I could also see a strong correlation between positive parenting and children's behaviour and educational achievements.

I decided to gain better parenting skills by going through the literature on this wide subject area, including from religious texts, and also by attending a whole series of lectures. This, I thought, would help me in raising my own children with better skills. An opportunity came through a group of professionals, mainly based in America, who set up a web-based online course on social issues, including teenage challenges, drugs and parenting. When one of them asked for my support, I decided to help them by working in the parenting area; 'this would help me in better dealing with my own children', I thought. I developed course materials for seventeen sessions on various areas of parenting. I ran this course for several years with hundreds of parents around the world and responded to numerous online questions on topical issues by parents and aspiring parents.

The SLS managers themselves were thinking about this vital area of parenting education for the borough. They came across a suitable course, spread over thirteen weeks for three hours each day, called 'Strengthening Families, Strengthening Communities (SFSC): An Inclusive Parent Programme'. In 2001, several of us were sent for training; for trainers (facilitators) like us it was a full week-long programme. The SFSC course was originally developed in 1990 in America by four professionals as 'Strengthening Multi-Ethnic Families and Communities: A Violence Prevention Parent Training Program'. In 1999, the Race Equality Foundation (known as Race Equality Unit then) adapted the course for UK participants with input from one of the original experts, Dr Marilyn Steele, a remarkable lady with a vision and passion to raise future generations, which was rolled out in 2000.

After completing the course and running a few thirteen-week workshops, I was trying to blend my parenting skills with my community work and SEN specialism. Each gave me a complementary insight into the larger world of raising children as good human beings and active citizens. In boroughs like Tower Hamlets, having a knowledge of parental perspectives and neighbourhood dynamics has always been advantageous for any professional working in the area. I felt really happy after seeing the positive impact of our parenting course.

I vividly remember the difficulty of one father in his mid-40s: he was struggling with his 15-year-old son's rough behaviour at home, particularly towards his 5-year-old brother, as well as increasing amounts of truancy. Altab Khan (not his real name) was one of only three Bangladeshi fathers in that course of fifteen parents. Mothers generally showed more interest and seriousness in attending our parenting courses, and in this case Mr Khan had been asked by the education welfare officer of his son's secondary school to attend our particular course.

On the first day, when all participants introduced themselves, Mr Khan said he had a secondary level of education in Bangladesh and was working on-and-off with a local taxi company. His wife had been ill for some time. We were two facilitators and after mutual introductions we explained the learning objectives of the course and its interactive nature. During discussion on the need for ground rules in the sessions, including adherence to Chatham House rules on confidentiality (that demanded the source of information may not be explicitly or implicitly identified), we sought participants' opinions and asked them to freely raise any issues they had in raising their children.

Mr Khan said meekly: 'My oldest son often beats his young brother for no reason and the young one is now very scared of him. How can I stop this?' Everyone gave their opinion and the discussion continued for some time. I then advised Mr Khan to spend at least one half-an-hour quiet one-to-one time with his older son to discuss why he beat his little brother; I asked him to inform us of the son's progress in the next session. The following week, before starting the themed discussion, we recapped on issues of the first week and enquired of Mr Khan on the progress with his son. He mumbled: 'I could not get my son to sit with me.' With some surprise, I asked: 'In the whole week?!' He lowered his head a little and said: 'Yes.' I suggested: 'OK, let's talk after the session today.' He agreed and I sat with him when everyone had left and realized from the conversation and his body language that he was literally lacking confidence in dealing with his own teenage son.

This was not uncommon for some parents, especially those of a first-generation and mild-natured background, with teenage children who suddenly found more freedom in secondary schools and were not subjected to appropriate boundaries at home. This was all about a weak parent-child relationship and lack of assertiveness in disciplining a child. I gave Mr Khan a mini-lecture on his status as a father in our religion, his obligation to lead his son until adulthood, and the importance – and some practical ways – of keeping and strengthening the parent-child bond; I also offered some handy age-appropriate techniques of how to introduce assertive discipline with sensible boundaries. I asked him to think through what else he could do to help his beloved son. He came up with couple of ideas of his own, which I liked. I then said: 'Please Mr Khan, now invest in your own son and implement the ideas you feel comfortable with, but be consistent. Let's talk after every session for the rest of the course.' I gave him my personal number, in case he wanted to contact me, though I had a feeling he would pull out.

I sat with him the following week and to my delight found a change in his face and tone. I encouraged him to continue and learnt there was some improvement every week in his relationship with the boy. Towards the end of the course, he said that his son was showing considerable improvement, and by the time we completed the course we found him more confident: a small victory in the considerable challenges facing Bangladeshis in Britain as they raised a new generation that now had to become British, as well as Bangladeshi, in identity.

Chapter 3

An Inclusive Muslim Identity

I WAS BORN in an idyllic village in Bangladesh and grew up with people of one ethnicity (Bengali) and two religions (Islam and Hinduism). My father, a socially active and highly spiritual man, alongside two of my teachers (one a devout middle-aged Hindu during the last couple of years of primary school, the other an elderly saint-like Muslim in secondary school), helped shape my childhood. They all instilled in me an ethos of hard work, love and respect for others, with broad horizons and a high level of ambition and motivation. Although we were conscious of our religious identity, there was little difference between Muslims and Hindus in terms of our concerns, hopes and aspirations, and we were completely at ease with one another. Bangladesh was part of Pakistan then, but I never saw a non-Bengali person before the Pakistani military crackdown on the people of East Pakistan, the Bengalis, in 1971, a nine-month long military conflict that pushed me to be aware of my ethnic identity.

Identity is the belief and expression that identifies an individual or group. One's early identity is shaped primarily through parents or the adults one encounters in a particular social environment. Human beings have multiple identities, but I did not seriously think about many aspects of my identity until I set foot in Heathrow airport that day in 1978, when I first visited Britain for military training. I was amazed to encounter people from so many backgrounds during my one year stay, and even after I had settled and worked in London from 1983 onwards, I have always felt like a global citizen. With over 300 spoken languages, London is indeed a global city and microcosm of humanity.

People are born with some immutable features – skin colour, certain physical characteristics, as well as ethnicity and ancestry – that cannot be changed. But our other features – such as way of life, religion or even nationality – are a matter of choice and thus changeable. Human diversity also accommodates and shapes individuals with unique personality and features. We are born with our parental genes and in the milieu of family, neighbourhood, geography and the surrounding cultures. As individuals we grow, become part of groups and choose professions or lifestyles, etc., identity becomes multiple and generally complementary. Individual identity gives self-image, self-esteem and individuality; group identity is the collective expression of its members. Some aspects of identity, such as ethnic identities, are irreversible; on the other hand, belief or religious identities can be changed.

Human beings are multi-dimensional and complex; 'one size fits all' is not in our nature. Confident people, with their inclusive and multiple identities, are respectful to themselves as well as to others in society. With many complementary identities, Muslims and others should be able to navigate through the demands of multiple loyalties – to family, community and wider society. A supporter of a football team is also a family member and citizen of a country at the same time. At various times people use their common sense and prioritize their choices. Every citizen has a role to play in enriching society: through active civic participation, devotion to a faith or belief, and duty to families and communities. Inclusive multiple identities help create active citizenship that can be harnessed for the good of all. In a positive social, economic and political environment, they create better synergy where people and communities feel comfortable to live with and help one another. They will not only tolerate others, as that is the minimum, but respect and celebrate others' good.

Human diversity is amazingly complementary. From a religious – particularly Islamic – point of view, diversity of the human race is not only something of beauty but a divine essence on Earth. Belief in the unity of diversity is liberating from egotism and the disease of conceited individualism. This reality is in tune with nature and is energizing, and we ignore this at our peril. We are better together.

Passive citizenship, religious or secular dogma or a 'me first' mentality creates selfishness, stagnation and social ills. A singular identity, at the cost of others, creates one-dimensional, culturally impoverished people who would potentially be more self-centred and of a closed mentality. Ghettoization or segregation attracts some people because of fear of others. The path of segregation is a cul de sac and in extreme cases has often ended in violence and ethnic cleansing because of ignorance and bottled-up hatred. On the other hand, attempts to forcibly assimilate people into the 'melting pot' of the majority do not help or can even be counter-productive. The current French model of seeing all people with a singular identity has not solved discrimination or the alienation of its immigrant population. People are not clones; they flourish better in an open positive environment with the ability to choose for themselves.

Whatever our backgrounds, we are the inheritors or stewards of the planet: 'citizens of the world'. Contrary to assertions that religious identity fosters hatred and sows discord, the essential message of major faiths is of harmony and cooperation. There are obviously natural differences in doctrine and rituals, but they are between an individual and God. The message and teachings pertaining to religious identity are about being good to others and good to the planet Earth.

* * *

In 1978–1979, during my temporary stay in England, I keenly followed an historic event in a Muslim country that shook the world and gave a huge boost to Muslim morale and sense of identity. For the first time since the decolonisation of Muslim lands, the Iranian Islamic revolution in February 1979 caused near-universal jubilation among both Shia and Sunni Muslims. The success of 'people power' in overthrowing a powerful monarch, under the leadership of an elderly cleric living thousands of miles away in France, was indeed a momentous event. With plenty of free time to hand, every day I watched how the Iranian nation became united under a common purpose and created its own destiny with its sacrifice.

Fast forward to a decade later, when I was settled in London. In September 1988, the publication of a literary work provoked a ferocious intellectual as well as political debate around the issue of religious sensitivity in secular liberal society. It was to spark global protests by Muslims and the unfortunate deaths of dozens of people. The commotion was about a fantasy novel, *The Satanic Verses*, by British-Asian author, Salman Rushdie.

Born to a Muslim family in 1947, the year of India's bloody partition, Rushdie moved to England as a teenager, where he became a gifted novelist. After winning the Booker Prize in 1981 for his novel *Midnight's Children*, his new work, *The Satanic Verses*, was a dream fiction based on the crash of a hijacked airliner, the Bostan, and the miraculous survival of two fictional individuals, Saladin and Gibreel. The title referred to an alleged incident when Prophet Muhammad is reported to have once praised three pagan goddesses and used 'Satanic Verses' in his prayers to win over pagan leaders for his noble cause, until Angel Gabriel replaced them with actual revelation. However, many Muslim historians rejected the story regarding the fifty-third Chapter of the Qur'an as a fabrication to cast doubt on the authenticity of the Qur'an itself.

In *The Satanic Verses*, Saladin, the fictional character, resembled Rushdie himself: torn with multiple identities and clashes of cultures, and some critics suggested the book was a thinly-disguised story of an anglophile Indian, torn with identity and cultural confusion. On the other hand, Gibreel's dream sequences were delusional. A number of characters in Gibreel's dream were the names and lives of those hallowed in Islam – the Prophet Muhammad, his wives and companions. Rushdie's depiction of these characters, as well as the title of the novel itself, were deemed sacrilegious by most Muslims and infuriated many at the time. However, Gibreel's dream reference to the name Mahound, a businessman turned prophet, was seen as the most perversely disguised depiction of Islam's Prophet Muhammad.

The name Mahound (which may have been created by the conflation of 'Mahomet' and 'hound') is the name used in certain medieval and later European literature to vilify Prophet Muhammad and indicate a satanic figure; an imposter or anti-Christ, and this hurt Muslims deeply. Part of the Islamic doctrine is to love Prophet Muhammad more than one's parents and oneself; this is a measure of a Muslim's faith. The Qur'an says: 'The Prophet is closer to the believers than their own selves, and his wives are their mothers ...'. (*al-Ahzab* 33: 6) A Prophetic Hadith says: 'None of you truly believes until I (the Prophet) am dearer to him than his children, his parents and all mankind.' (Hadith compiled by Bukhari and Muslim) The characterization of the 'mothers of believers' as prostitutes was also a literary assault that was seen as depraved by any Muslim who has love for Islam.

The core Muslim belief that the Qur'an, the word of God, was revealed to the Prophet Muhammad through the Archangel Gabriel and was recorded verbatim by the Prophet's scribes, was also assaulted in the novel. In one of Gibreel's dreams, a venerated companion named Salman (Farsi) was shown as untrustworthy: this is anathema to Muslims, as he was a renowned companion of Prophet Muhammad and has been a revered figure for his wisdom and spirituality. During this tense period, some in the community even stopped naming their boys 'Salman', otherwise a very popular name, for a few years. I know of at least one family in London that did this.

* * *

British Muslims were first informed of this publication by the Islamic Foundation in Leicester, a research institute established in 1973. There was genuine frustration in the Muslim community, and after the book came on the market in late September 1988, we discovered that it was published despite warnings by Viking-Penguin's own editorial consultant, Khushwant Singh, that it would cause offence to Muslims. The fiery debate that ensued in the aftermath of the publication resulted in a war of words between the evolving British Muslim community and the very established secular-liberal supporters of Rushdie.

Although it was a novel by a non-practising Muslim, reactions from Muslims were instantaneous and almost universally critical. This surprised those who took unconditional freedom of expression as sacrosanct, and who clearly lacked religious literacy, particularly of Islam. As calls for the book to be withdrawn fell on deaf ears, feelings grew deeper among Muslims. Some went further than peaceful protests – threatening the publisher, vandalizing or firebombing book stores, burning effigies, killings and attempted killings overseas for the next few years. Needless to say, all this was unacceptable and counterproductive.

Major Muslim organizations, mosques and scholars formed an umbrella organization, the UK Action Committee on Islamic Affairs (UKACIA), in London on 11 October 1988, to peacefully mobilize public opinion against the book. It formed a Steering Committee, led by Dr Mughram al-Ghamdi of London's Islamic Cultural Centre as Chair and Iqbal Sacranie, of Balham Mosque as Joint Convenor, and a National Committee consisting of over fifty national bodies. The aim was to engage with the British political establishment to convey and express Muslim frustration and how tension could be reduced. As part of a campaign for legislation on incitement to religious hatred, Muslim groups met government officials, MPs, ministers and Church officials. A group of scholars took a legal route against the publisher in the name of the Islamic Defence Council; some signed a petition calling for the book's withdrawal from the market. One of the main tasks of the National Committee was to make sure our young people's frustration was not misused, especially in places like Tower Hamlets. This was a tense period for the community. Vigils and demonstrations were held across the country and there were civil protests to express Muslim feelings and channel frustration.

Some Commonwealth countries understood the sensitivities and by December 1988 the book was banned in India, Bangladesh, Sudan, South Africa and Sri Lanka. Other countries, including Kenya, Thailand, Tanzania, Indonesia, Singapore and Venezuela followed suit. Protests against the book spread far and wide and a number of protesters were killed in India and Pakistan in February 1989. There was an impasse; emotion was running high on both sides – Muslims against the book; Rushdie and the western establishment in its defence. To add fuel to the fire, a demonstration in Bradford on 14 January 1989, attended by over 1,000 people, saw a few angry Muslims suddenly set a copy of the book alight. It was unacceptable, and the media portrayed this as a barbaric act and a clash between Muslim and western liberal values.

A month later, a fatwa (religious edict) from Iran's Ayatollah Khomeini called for the death of Rushdie and his publishers. It shocked the literary world and Rushdie went into hiding. The fatwa was condemned by Western governments and Britain severed relations with Iran. British Muslims overwhelmingly put aside the theology behind the fatwa with the view that it was not relevant in Britain. The immediate hullaballoo somewhat quietened, but the issue would not die down.

* * *

Most in the liberal west, with their age-old historical Eurocentric world view and frame of mind, were obviously uninformed of the place of the Qur'an and the Prophet at the heart of Islam. There was little empathy, it seemed, to understand Muslim frustrations. Many saw the protests as a sign of Muslim backwardness – the best they could think of was irrational religious passion. The book burning in Bradford, as well as the violent demonstrations and deaths in some parts of the world, were seen as unfathomable at best and fanaticism at worst. But for Muslims with some basic knowledge of religion, vilification of religious sanctity was insulting and unacceptable. To many, Rushdie knowingly struck his literary sword at the heart of Islam in the name of fantasy and freedom of expression. The novel appeared to aim at popularising the myth surrounding the Qur'an, the Prophet and his wives, companions and Muslim religious practices in a depraved way.

The saga, as expected, created ill-feeling and division between Muslims and non-Muslim liberals. Rushdie was supported by major literary bodies such as PEN (Poets,

Essayists and Novelists) International and the Association of American Publishers, along with some prominent figures. One of them, Christopher Hitchens, would later go on to write a polemic against religion, *God Is Not Great*. A small number of western scholars and politicians unexpectedly broke rank and criticized Rushdie. The former United States president, Jimmy Carter, said of Rushdie: 'we have tended to promote him and his book with little acknowledgment that it is a direct insult to those millions of Moslems whose sacred beliefs have been violated ... We should be sensitive to the concern and anger that prevails even among the more moderate Muslims.'[2] Author Roald Dahl called the book sensationalist and Rushdie 'a dangerous opportunist'. The *Washington Times* review wrote:

> Having discovered no literary reason why Mr Rushdie chose to portray Muhammad's wives as prostitutes, the Koran as the work of Satan and the founders of the faith as roughnecks and cheats, I had to admit to certain sympathy with the Islamic leaders' complaint. True or not, slander hurts the slandered, which makes *The Satanic Verses* not simply a rambling and trivial book, but a nasty one as well.[3]

The British media was unhelpful to Muslims, particularly when the Bradford book burning was broadcast in some media with comments comparing Muslims with Nazis. Did this single event by a handful of angry people bear any

---

2.   Jimmy Carter, 'Rushdie's Book Is an Insult' (*The New York Times*, 5 March 1989).

3.   Muhammad Menazir Ahsan and A.R. Kidwai (eds), *Sacrilege versus Civility: Muslim Perspectives on the Satanic Verses Affair*, revised and enlarged edition (Markfield, UK: The Islamic Foundation, 1993), p. 37.

resemblance to the Nazi burning of libraries and books at the height of their power? Lord Bhikhu Parekh, a noted political theorist, rightly put this as 'escalated step by even sillier step to a wholly mindless anger first against all *Bradford* Muslims, then against all *British* Muslims, then against *all* Muslims, and ultimately against *Islam* itself.'[4]

The Satanic Verses was seen by many Muslims as a continuation of the long tradition of anti-Muslim prejudice in the European psyche, its literature and academic culture. Unfortunately, this has often permeated in popular public discourse and political life. For centuries, Prophet Muhammad and Islam have been portrayed in a derogatory manner. Given the occasional intensity of anti-Muslim rhetoric on any Muslim-related issue, which would otherwise be ignored for others, even many secular and non-practising Muslims had come to believe that western chauvinism had not ceased with the end of colonialism. This led to an increased sense of a Muslim identity.

Furthermore, since the crisis many in mainstream society saw Muslim protests and their disagreements with government policies as part of Muslim 'identity politics', because it privileged religious affiliation over and above other ways in which individuals categorize themselves. Thus, Muslims were seen as making political arguments for narrow interests and perspectives – often by playing the 'victim card'. Well, like many ordinary Muslims, I was part of the civil protest as I felt deeply hurt by the book, but this did not have anything to do with abandoning my other identities as an educationalist, parent or aspiring writer!

Love of parents, especially mothers, is inherent in human nature. No civilized human being would try to test anothers' love for their mothers by public abuse. To Muslims, their

---

4.   Bhikhu C. Parekh, *Rethinking Multiculturalism: Cultural Diversity and Political Theory* (Harvard: Harvard University Press, 2002).

Prophet is dearer to them than their parents. I wonder how many in developed democracies would tolerate insults to past war heroes or hallowed national symbols! However, violence or aggression by some Muslims was also plainly wrong, and just as unjustified as the blatant ridicule of the sacred. Moreover, the *Satanic Verses* affair occurred at a time of demographic and socio-economic change within the British Muslim population. There were an increasing number of younger-generation Muslims with a British education who were establishing themselves in various professions. These factors played a part in increased Islam-inspired social activism during the 1990s. In the years to follow, Muslim expression in the public sphere became more nuanced and also pragmatic.

* * *

For Muslims in Europe, in fact for Europe itself, atrocities inflicted on Bosniak Muslims by Bosnian Serbs during the breakup of Yugoslavia (1992–1995) was the worst tragedy since the Second World War. This went against Europe's determined pledge of 'Never Again', after the inhuman Holocaust against European Jews only half a century before. This was a test case for European Muslim consciousness in its effort to retain an identity as Muslims – an inclusive religious identity in the modern world. No other atrocity since the horrors of the Second World War created so much soul searching as the forty-four month-long siege of Sarajevo and the butchery, ethnic cleansing and genocide of Bosniak Muslims by Bosnian Serb paramilitary forces, supported by the Serb military. The Bosniaks were subjected to a brutal ethnic cleansing through torture, murder, rape, unlawful confinement and deportation, destruction of homes and businesses and destruction of places of worship. Political leaders, intellectuals and professionals were callously targeted.

The Bosnian tragedy unfolded in full view of the international community. The European Union (EU) and the United Nations (UN) were fully aware of the situation as the Communist-run state of Yugoslavia began falling apart. Bosnia and Herzegovina (BiH) declared sovereignty in October 1991 and held a referendum for independence from Yugoslavia on 1 March 1992. In spite of most Serbs boycotting it, the turnout was 63.4 per cent and a stunning 99.7 per cent voted for independence. On 3 March 1992, BiH declared independence, received international recognition and was admitted as a member State of the United Nations on 22 May 1992. But when Bosnian Serbs, under the leadership of Radovan Karadžić and General Ratko Mladić, decided to go on a rampage with the support of the Serbian President, Slobodan Milošević, the EU and UN showed how impotent they were in their ability to protect BiH. As the Bosnian Serb paramilitary forces swarmed over BIH, acts of modern day savagery ensued without any restraint or regard for international law.

Combined with the unjust UN arms embargo on Bosnia, the Serb paramilitary effectively declared 'open season' on tens of thousands of innocent Bosniaks. In early July 1995, under the noses of the EU and UN, the emboldened Bosnian Serb forces carried out systematic mass executions of 8,000 Bosniak men and boys who had sought safety in Srebrenica under the protection of the United Nations Protection Force (UNPROFOR). Altogether 100,000 people were killed: the unthinkable was happening in modern Europe.

The tragedy in BiH reverberated across the world, and in Britain we watched the daily carnage and destruction on our TV screens with horror, impotence and pain. For disparate and relatively disorganized British Muslims, this was a wake-up call. British Muslims created various charities to provide humanitarian assistance to Bosnia, and the *ummah*, the global Muslim community, ran across national boundaries. A small number of Muslim youths were also reported to have joined the fight against the Serb paramilitary forces. As the ethnic cleansing of indigenous Bosniak Muslims was turning into genocide, the British Muslim community decided to better organize itself. Some felt that better coordination and more unity was the only option for Muslims to be counted, and in April 1994 the process of forming a broad-based umbrella body to 'serve the community' and 'work for the common good of all' started in earnest. The process of forming a national interim committee, and three years of strenuous effort to form the Muslim Council of Britain before its launch in November 1997 is discussed in Chapter 4.

It was also an inspiration that Bosnia, under the leadership of its philosopher-president Alija Izetbegović, chose not to perish. In spite of all the odds – including the arms embargo – the Bosniak Muslims resisted. With utmost sacrifice and ingenuity, the Bosniaks started pushing back their enemies and gaining some ground. There was a stalemate in the fighting, and only then did the world powers decided to step up their efforts to bring the suffering to an end. The Dayton Agreement, initialled on 21 November 1995 and formally signed in Paris on 14 December, stopped the killings but failed to solve the political problems and ethnic divisions. We were learning that Izetbegović's hands were tied during the negotiation, as the Dayton Agreement created a 'High Representative' with more power than the President and the Bosnian parliament.

In his memoir, *Inescapable Questions: Autobiographical Notes*, Izetbegović gave an account of his remarkable life as he stood by his people throughout the turbulent and terrifying times of the 1990s. He was both a true European as well as a Muslim. He signed the Dayton Peace Accord in November 1995 and was re-elected to a three-member collective presidency in 1996, but resigned his position in 2000 announcing that 'the international community was pushing things forward in a manner with which he could not live'. Sadly Izetbegović died in October 2003 of heart disease complicated by injuries suffered from a fall at home, but he was an inspiration for many as a principled and effective leader for European Muslims in public life.

* * *

Europe was apathetic towards the Bosnian genocide, and only recognized the Srebrenica genocide fourteen years later. On 15 January 2009, a resolution was overwhelmingly passed in the European Parliament, by a vote of 556 to nine, to declare 11 July as a 'day of [remembrance] of the Srebrenica genocide all over the EU, and to ... [bring] to justice those responsible for the massacres in and around Srebrenica'.[5]

I first visited Srebrencia on 11 July 2012, and saw the beautiful alpine valley which had been declared a UN 'Safe Haven' and where the genocide had taken place. The small enclave in eastern Bosnia and Herzegovina, with 40,000 mostly Muslim refugees, was defended by only a couple of thousand government soldiers who held out for three years against a siege by Serb separatist fighters. But the international military protection, one of six UN-designated 'safe areas' established throughout the country in 1993, proved meaningless when the Serbs launched an all-out assault in July 1995. Srebrenica came to symbolise an appalling brutality and the international community's colossal failure in preventing a genocide. Srebrenica was being filled with more and more graves every year as victims of the genocide were continually being discovered, and I chided myself for not having visited the country before. My only consolation was by that time the main perpetrators of the genocide, including Ratko Mladic and Radovan Karadžić, were being brought to the courts in The Hague to face charges of War Crimes.

---

5. Taken from the text of the 'European Parliament resolution of 15 January 2009 on Srebrenica'.

The Dayton Agreement was meant to heal ethnic tension, but it failed to solve the region's ethno-religious problems. The peace agreement gave half of Bosnia to the Serbs, for their Republika Srpska, and the other half as a Federation of Bosniaks and Croats. They were supposed to be citizens of the same country, but the Serbs were continuously seeking to undermine the Bosnian statehood from day one. The Croats were not much better, and the Bosniaks' hands were tied by the Agreement. With probably one of the highest youth unemployment rates in the world, despair was overtaking the country. As we travelled from Sarajevo to Srebrenica, we were told that the Serb-held areas were still virtually no-go territory for Bosniaks. I couldn't shake an eerie feeling as we passed through this area.

There were tens of thousands of Bosniak people in Srebrenica on that day; women weeping and men lamenting their loved ones lying in their graves. Hundreds of visitors from other countries also came that year, and in a deeply sombre atmosphere at Potočari Memorial Park I heard the Grand Mufti of Bosnia and Herzegovina, Dr Mustafa Cerić, lament with prayers for the grieving families. In that commemoration, he recited the following prayer:

> We pray to You,
> Almighty God, may grievance become hope,
> May revenge become justice,
> May mothers' tears become prayers,
> That Srebrenica never happens again,
> To no one and nowhere!

The event was attended by the New York Rabbi Arthur Schneier (who lost his entire family but himself to the Holocaust) of the Appeal of Conscience Foundation. Rabbi Schneier delivered a personal message from the US President, Barack Obama:

The name Srebrenica will forever be associated with some of the darkest acts of the 20th century. A measure of justice is finally being served for the victims in courts in The Hague and Bosnia and Herzegovina, as the perpetrators of this atrocity, including Ratko Mladić and Radovan Karadžić, are now being called to account for their actions. We know that Srebrenica's future, and that of Bosnia and Herzegovina, will not be held back by its painful recent history ... The United States stands with the people of Bosnia and Herzegovina and grieves again for the loss of so many loved ones. Our hearts and deepest sympathies are with them, and we pledge our enduring commitment to support their aspirations for a better tomorrow.[6]

Bosnia and Herzegovina is a beautiful country with mountainous terrain, deep gorges, turquoise rivers and lakes. Its religious landmarks, both Christian and Islamic, are themselves an attraction. Bosniaks are known for their richness in higher education with a rich intellectual and Sufi tradition. I found them very open-minded and sociable, but like many of the people I met I was also lamenting for their uncertain future.

* * *

The *Satanic Verses* affair and the Bosnian genocide indeed influenced many young Muslims to consider what their faith meant to them. It was impossible not to look at the game-changing events around me – the unfair attacks and invalid criticism on the faith I hold dear, the inhuman ethnic cleansing of a people who were of the soil, indigenous in their own land

---

6. Barack Obama, 'Statement by the President on the 17th Anniversary of the Srebrenica Genocide' (The White House Archive, 10 July 2012).

but only of a different Abrahamic faith, not immigrants like me – to become aware of the reality of my own place in a diverse society. Seeing images of badly malnourished Bosniak men in the media and on television, housed like cattle by Serb forces in camps, was something that still haunts me.

A number of other international events impacted on some young British Muslims during the 1990s, namely the post-Soviet Afghan civil war among various warlords, Chechnya's fight for self-determination from a Russian military onslaught, and the Iraqi aggression against Kuwait that led to the first Gulf War. Some zealous youths from the British Muslim community went to physically fight on the side of their Muslim brethren, and this transnational fighting, although initially greeted with ambivalence by the British establishment, created suspicion and problems of a 'global Jihad' once the fighters returned home.

During this time, some mainly youth-led Muslim groups increased their public activities with large conferences and several big events. This created some envy and competition among various Muslim organizations, and a sub-cultural identity, which had always existed within Muslims, started becoming more visible in public. Most active of the groups were Hizb ut-Tahrir (HT, a pan-Islamic political organization formed in 1953), JIMAS (Jamiat Ihyaa Minhaaj al-Sunnah, which started as a Salafi body in 1984 and is now a Muslim educational charity) and Young Muslims UK (YMUK, formed in 1984 and becoming a youth wing of the Islamic Society of Britain in 1990). Each group sought to become loyal representatives of one or other religious undercurrents of the Middle East or South Asia and to try to emulate this in a British context to attract supporters. Each group seemed to want to appeal more to educated young 'floating' Muslims, those who had not decided how to express their Muslim identity, rather than the traditional Deobandi or Barelwi constituencies.

The message from HT, that the establishment of a modern

caliphate was the answer to all contemporary Muslim problems, gained traction among a section of socially-active professional Muslims and university students. Their main competitor was YMUK, and as such there was occasional tension between these two groups on higher education campuses across Britain. On the other hand, JIMAS' scripturalist approach – with a view to purifying Muslim beliefs and practices from religious innovations (*bid'a*) – was also popular to some as it was seen as a good attempt to link modern Muslims with the early pious and respected generations after the Prophet.

Tensions rose in east London during the 1990s, when HT began increasing its activities. HT wanted to use the East London Mosque to bolster its presence and help recruit the East End's Bangladeshi boys. Conflict arose when it targeted young men from the locally powerful YMO UK, some of whom were also ELM volunteers. Those of us in the newly-formed IFE had to handle the issue sensitively, as YMO was seen as very important for IFE's future leadership. The YMO, although socially conservative (due to its community background), had always subscribed to the civil and democratic path of influencing or bringing change in the community. It had a strong structure and many members had close family ties with one another. In contrast, democracy was anathema to HT and it initiated a battle of polemics against YMO in an attempt to undermine it, creating ill feelings that lasted for some time. However, HT failed to make any major headway in recruiting young Bangladeshi's, and the ELM's London Muslim Centre (LMC) project, which started towards the end of 1990s, captured the imagination of the local community; there was little room for tension between Islamic groups in the area. After 9/11, and more specifically when prime minister Tony Blair wanted to ban HT post-7/7, the YMO and other groups defended HT's right to operate as long as it did not go against the law of the land.

* * *

There is an apprehension among some Muslims that they may be losing a battle to retain the 'purity' of their religion and want to keep away from the 'evils' of wider society. According to their misplaced understanding, religious practice may not be possible in a secularized and materialistic environment, as it always poses a distraction or challenge. So, to them, isolation – or living exclusively within a confined environment – is the safest way of protecting their religion. To such a mind-set, (wider) society contaminates their piety or conspires against them. As a result of their fear, or their lack of confidence in living amongst people who are not like themselves, they avoid interaction or engagement with others who may dilute their religiosity. Some even keep away from interacting with non-practising Muslims or someone from a different Islamic strand. They fail to see religion's universality and the unity of the human species, as well as Islam's resilience in time and space.

This is not uncommon in faith communities across the world, but this should be avoided at all costs for the sake of religion itself, since isolationism creates suspicion and intolerance of one another. Insular but active sections of the community may indulge in attempts to 'purify' the less purified, converting the converts, and in the process unnecessarily competing with one another. No one should cast doubt on other peoples' hearts: this is against Islamic teaching. Those who are otherwise sincere can unwittingly harm their own religion's image by such rash actions. We have to accept the reality that there will always be believers, non-believers, practising and non-practising people. It is also true that religious purity has various grades and people have different ranks. Muslims are always reminded to look at the examples of their Prophet and his companions, who lived in the most difficult environment. Then there are Muslims who may not care about their surroundings and give in to all sorts of cultural practices that are not only unacceptable in religion but may also be harmful for themselves and for society. Islam is a middle-of-the-road way of life; it advocates a balance in individual and communal affairs. God talks about the 'straight path' in the Qur'an (*al-Fatihah* 1: 5), and the Prophet advised believers: 'Make things easy for the people, and not difficult for them; cheer people up (with glad tidings) and do not repulse (them).'

Building bridges among people and communities and creating good community relations are at the heart of Islam's social life. Muslims are expected to excel in these qualities in order to create a safer and better neighbourhood and society. Despair, alienation and grievances should not lead them to adopt policies and actions that go against religious principles and also public interest. Muslims should remind themselves to rise above the challenges thrown at them, including demonization hurled at them or against their religion. They should be in the forefront of unilaterally serving all in society. That is what morally upright people always do.

Human beings are prone to doing right and wrong, but only a small fraction in a rule-based society would normally subscribe to violence. We all have a role to play in making sure life and society, are 'centred', and Islam's teaching is not to be judgmental. The Qur'an demands that believers 'repel evil with what is better'. (*al-Mu'minun* 23: 96) The Prophet, seen as the best role model by Muslims, asked believers to achieve the best of human character when he said: 'I have only been sent to perfect good moral character.' (Prophetic Hadith compiled by Musnad Ahmad) Inclusive identity demands Muslims better equip themselves with knowledge and action as the antidote to human and social problems. It is encouraging to note that young Muslims are increasingly becoming engaged in many elements of our diverse, multicultural society. With more confidence than their predecessors, they are in a better position to navigate between freedom of expression and religious conscience.

A unity of purpose is the only guarantee for sustained occupancy of this planet. It is a reality that diversity brings natural differences and dissension. Each of us has our own unique features, strengths and weaknesses, but together we are better. The big test for us is to prove whether our differences create synergy and bring with them peace, or pit one against another to make the planet unliveable. In a great society like Britain's, diversity is an asset that promotes positive integration and negates isolation, segregation or insularity. Pluralism paves the way for a richer culture that is open, non-combative and celebratory. An individual or a nation can, at times, suffer from identity crises, giving rise to violence or degeneration. According to Nobel laureate Amartya Sen: 'reductionism provided by a solitarist understanding of people, in terms exclusively of a belligerently religious identity, can be disastrously deployed by promoters of violent jihad to close all the other avenues Muslims can easily take.'[7]

* * *

Towards the end of the 1990s, a local but outward-looking progressive initiative in Whitechapel symbolized the confidence and synergy of Tower Hamlets' Bangladeshi community. The project that became the London Muslim Centre (LMC) aimed to offer 'something for everyone' and was to help take the East London Mosque closer to the vision of its original founders at the Ritz Hotel in 1910.

There were two phases to building what was to become a massive expansion to the mosque – first, a civic campaign to acquire the piece of land adjacent to the East London Mosque on its west side, which was being used as a car park; and second, a massive effort to raise over £10million in order to construct

---

7.   Amartya Sen, *Identity and Violence: The Illusion of Destiny* (New York: W.W. Norton & Co, 2006), p. 179.

the multi-storey community complex on the site. As the Muslim community had increased significantly in the area, the LMC was deemed a necessity by many local congregants, many of whom had come from Bangladesh's greater Sylhet region and were known for their higher religious observance.

When the owner of the adjacent plot of land decided to sell it, the ELM made an offer but was outbid by a large property group, Ballymore. At the time I was the ELM's Vice Chair, and worked voluntarily with a number of organizations. I had also recently joined the Tower Hamlets LEA as a specialist teacher. Once we discovered that Ballymore was planning to build luxury flats on the site, we decided to object on the grounds that it was needed for community use. We came to learn that Ballymore had a number of properties to develop in Tower Hamlets, and to get planning permission from the Council near our site they needed to give the Council some planning gains. So, we stepped up our efforts to convince the Council to help the community by acquiring the land from Ballymore and sell it to the ELM for community facilities; in return Ballymore could be asked to build luxury flats elsewhere.

To us this made complete sense, but the Council was not ready to listen at first. We consulted mosque members and our regular congregation, as well as local friends and partners in wider society, and with the help of a group of experts we drafted a sustainable business plan for the future LMC; a multi-purpose community complex with social and economic regeneration programmes for the local area. Simultaneously, we devised a strategy to lobby the Council, and as the news spread people in the area became energized for what was clearly a good cause. It became a talking point among old and young, male and female, scholars and ordinary folk alike. We had people who would talk with their ward councillors and others who came to us with offers of help. In order to convince the Planning Committee we needed strong support from our friends in wider society. Neil Jameson from TELCO and a few others came forward, and the Fieldgate Street Great Synagogue, our nearest neighbour, also gave its strong backing with a video message.

We took our case to the Planning Committee in the Council chamber. Dozens of community leaders filled the hall and hundreds of others staged a vigil outside the building in the cold evening air. We presented our arguments, in my view well-prepared, supported by an impassioned speech from Neil Jameson and the Synagogue's video message. But we realized the Committee could not decide so we escalated the pressure by bringing young people into positive action: they organized a number of peaceful vigils in strategic locations. On one occasion after Friday prayers, 3,000 young people assembled and peacefully made a human chain, holding one another's hands around the car park. This instantly became big news in east London.

While the struggle was going on, the Council appointed a new Chair of the Planning Committee. We heard he was fair-minded and straightforward and through one of the councillors arranged a meeting and visited him to explain our vision, objectives and plan. By the time we left, he was convinced and assured us of his weight in favour of the community. He kept his word and things progressed rapidly. A decision was made that the whole site would be for community use – one-third would be for the Council's social housing and the ELM had to buy the remaining two-thirds for LMC, its community complex. The price was negotiated at £600,000 with a 125-year lease, but with a contractual arrangement to make it freehold. It was a large sum of money for the mosque at that time, but the community came up with amazing support and the amount was raised within four months. The land was transferred to the ELM, as arranged.

Our ambition, as well as the demand from local people, especially the young people, was to build a large complex as a community hub with educational, social and economic facilities. But we had only a fraction of the money needed for such a project. We spent some time thoroughly planning a project to build the LMC on the basis of the funds available to us and potential sources. Raising money from the community and using the ELM assets to generate funds were our two main sources of income. The Council was fully supportive by then and affirmed its commitment to find some regeneration money from various sources, albeit with strict conditions. While we were struggling to give the plan a practical shape, we came across a uniquely sympathetic builder who was also a rich philanthropist. Mohammad Arif Zabadne offered to build the complex and take a minimum profit, and with the help of his architects we planned to build a multi-storey multi-purpose building, including a smaller business wing attached to the west side that would generate sustainable income and house local businesses and community enterprises. The total budget was a staggering £10.5million, and over half the amount had to be raised from community donations!

The congregation gave their full commitment, a large group of volunteers was assembled, and construction work started in early 2002. From day one we made sure everything was done with professionalism and absolute honesty and transparency – this was an Islamic obligation but was also according to regulatory guidelines issued by the Charity Commission. A massive box-collection effort was launched in the mosque, door-to-door collections were carried out, and those with good jobs were encouraged to donate through standing orders. Volunteers also came up with innovative ideas, including one who suggested asking people to buy a square metre of land and donate that amount to the LMC fund. Young boys and girls were donating their pocket money to the fund; others cleaned cars and donated the proceeds. It was an amazing and inspirational example of community activism.

Towards the end of 2002, I took over the Chairmanship of the ELM from our elderly and highly respected Chairman,

Maulana Abdul Awwal. By that time the construction work had already started and for the next two years the work progressed with an astonishing speed. We decided to formally open the LMC on Friday 11 June 2004, with the Imam of Masjid al-Haram, the sacred mosque in Makkah, leading the prayer, and HRH Prince Charles as the chief guest. On the day, 15,000 people converged on the complex; the police closed Whitechapel Road and Fieldgate Street as thousands spilled onto the streets outside to pray. Unfortunately, Prince Charles had to attend former US President Ronald Reagan's funeral on the day, but he sent a video message instead (and visited the LMC later on). There were dignitaries from political, interfaith and civil society backgrounds and the launch event was a great success.

The LMC promised to give 'something for everyone', and the first group to hold an event in the LMC was English Heritage. Within five years we launched a further expansion project, the nine-storey women-focused Maryam Centre that drew similar if not more energy and dedication from the community – particularly from young girls and women. New ideas for fundraising, particularly one with an Alhambra Wall (symbolizing the design of Alhambra Palace in southern Spain) on the ground floor, brought in millions of pounds from the community. The LMC and Maryam Centre initiatives reflected a positive contribution not only to Tower Hamlets Muslim communities but to the diversity of modern Britain.

* * *

Beyond internal Muslim community dynamics, a national venture in the late 1990s significantly added to the Muslim consciousness. It was the launch in early 1997 of a Commission on British Muslims and Islamophobia by the think-tank The Runnymede Trust, under the chairmanship of Professor Gordon Conway. A multi-ethnic and multi-religious committee was formed as a result of a growing realization that prejudice against Islam as well as anti-Muslim rhetoric was surfacing in a disturbing manner in Britain. Runnymede observed that the racism of the 1970s and 1980s was gradually mutating into something that was termed 'Islamophobia' – prejudice against, hatred of or fear about Islam or Muslims. A statement from the Commission said: 'We are anxious that our report should be a spur to timely action, by many people, in many places, of many kinds. Everyone, we stress, has a relevant and important part to play. Islamophobia is a challenge to us all.'

In February 1997, copies of the Commission's consultation paper, *Islamophobia: Its Features and Dangers*, were distributed to public bodies such as county councils and metropolitan authorities, police forces, government departments and race equality councils. They were also sent to a wide range of Muslim organizations and leading professional associations, universities and unions and think-tanks. The Commission members visited many institutions, mosques and youth centres across the country. We organized a workshop in the East London Mosque, with important stakeholders, for Professor Conway and his colleagues. The discussion concentrated on practical examples of Islamophobia faced by our mosque and the congregation in daily life. Needless to say there were plenty of examples, including verbal and physical assaults because of the look and dress of some worshippers, particularly women. For some participants it was their first opportunity to express their experiences and feelings on racism and the Islamophobia they encountered.

The Runnymede Trust was an authoritative think-tank and had published a very useful report on anti-Semitism in 1994. So, the Islamophobia Commission was taken seriously by the political class and media establishment. The final report, *Islamophobia: A Challenge for Us All*, was published in 1997. It identified Islamophobia as 'unfounded hostility towards

Islam' and equated it with people's closed views (as opposed to open views) on Islam. The religion of Islam, according to the report, was seen negatively by many: monolithic, not diverse; inferior, not different; enemy, not partner; manipulative, not sincere. The report's sixty recommendations were aimed at three broad target groups: a) government departments, bodies and agencies, b) local and regional statutory bodies, and c) voluntary and private bodies – on vital issues such as education, employment, health, housing and legislation, where necessary. The report asserted that Islamophobia must be explicitly recognized through legislation to make 'religious and racial violence' illegal. It was clear that the term 'racial violence' was no longer adequate on its own. Launched by the-then Home Secretary, Jack Straw, it attracted great interest. For the first time in modern Britain, Islamophobia was seen as a reality. The Runnymede Trust decided it would closely monitor the implementation of the recommendations. It had some positive impact on the Labour government, some policy makers and the general public. The New Labour government was supportive, initially, of fresh ideas and approved the state funding of voluntary-aided Muslim schools that had been denied by previous governments. The Commission was re-constituted a couple of years later to follow up the progress and came up with a progress report, *Addressing the Challenge of Islamophobia*, in 2001.

In addition, a national campaign to incorporate a question on religion in the 2001 UK Census, for the first time since the Census began, brought faith communities together towards the end of 1990s. This brought religion to the forefront of British public life. It was an uphill task to initially convince the Tory government, but solidarity among faith groups and persistent pressure on the government worked well. The campaign itself was energizing and gave people the confidence to express their inclusive religious identity. Prominent national faith-based groups, such as the Inter Faith Network

(IFN), the Inner Cities Religious Council (ICRC), Churches Working Together (CWT) and the UK Action Committee on Islamic Affairs (UKACIA) formed an alliance to work on the campaign. As part of the ICRC, which was then within the Conservative government's Department of the Environment, we discussed the campaign at its January 1996 meeting; I was delighted to see leaders from all of the five major faiths in the ICRC were in unison with their support.

Churches Working Together produced a powerful paper the following March, submitted to the Office for National Statistics (ONS), which showed the importance of religious affiliation in public policy. Initially the ONS was not enthusiastic, however, the alliance of faith groups lobbied hard and eventually a Religious Affiliation sub-group, led by Professor Leslie Francis, was formed to work on a test question. The sub-group discussed three aspects of religion to be in the question: belief, practice and affiliation. In the end, it agreed only on religious affiliation, on the basis that it related to social and public aspects of religion. Some government departments were not sure of the benefit of religious affiliation in the Census and so were ambivalent. The ONS decided to carry out a few pilot tests in 1997, all of which brought very positive outcomes.

The campaign received a boost with the emergence of the Muslim Council of Britain in 1997. The MCB sought help from one of its prominent volunteers and experts in data analysis, Dr Jamil Sherif, to work with other partners. The Census group was able to convince the Home Secretary of the new Labour government, Jack Straw, to support the religious affiliation question. When the Labour government published its White Paper, *The 2001 Census of Population*, it recommended including the religious question although it observed:

> The proposal ... to include a question on religion in England and Wales in the 2001 Census would require a change to the primary legislation ... Before deciding whether to take such a step however, the Government would want to be satisfied that the inclusion of such a question in a census commanded the necessary support of the general public.[8]

What was needed was public support, and faith groups of all persuasions worked hard to convince public figures to support the inclusion of the question; the MCB conducted a census awareness campaign to encourage Muslim support, for example. It was an interesting exercise for secular Britain, and to the delight of faith groups the religious affiliation question was finally included in the 2001 Census.

---

8. *The 2001 Census of Population* (London: The Stationery Office, 1999), p. 40.

Chapter 4

British Muslims and the 7/7 Maelstrom

O N SUNDAY 4 June 2006, at just after 4.30pm, I stood
on the podium in front of the packed ground floor
hall of the London Muslim Centre in East London's
Whitechapel. My name had just been announced by the
Election Commissioner as the new Secretary-General (SG) of
the Muslim Council of Britain. I had to deliver an acceptance
speech and briefly outline my vision for the MCB, the wider
Muslim community, and Britain. I had already jotted down
some points after I was declared SG upstairs some 10–15
minutes earlier by the MCB's Central Working Committee
(CWC), so I was not that worried about what I would say. But
I was having a weird feeling – of a colossal burden and sense
of responsibility towards the 500 or so affiliates of the MCB as
well as to the Muslim community that was still reverberating
from the shock of the London bombings about a year earlier.
It was a fear of unknown challenges facing not only me as an
individual, but my family and my community on the wider
stage.

It was a tiring day, and although I was known to most of
the people in the hall, and as Chair of the East London Mosque

(ELM) Trust I was used to talking to the large congregations, I still felt somewhat nervous. However, my adrenaline was flowing and I organized myself quickly, looked at the audience and started in the name of God, then addressed the hall with the common greeting of *Assalamualaikum* (peace be upon you). The whole gathering warmly responded with 'peace be upon you too'; this was enough to buoy my spirits straight away and I started talking.

After giving thanks to the election commission, the volunteers and delegates for their job as well as the London Muslim Centre (LMC) for hosting the annual general meeting, I talked about my predecessor Sir Iqbal Sacranie's immense contributions to the MCB, how since its inception the MCB had developed a model of collective leadership 'to serve the community' and work 'for the common good' of our nation. I said that the MCB's source of strength lay in grassroots community work, then spoke about the reality of Islamophobia and the presence of extremism in a small section of Muslim youth. Looking towards our hopes and aspirations as ordinary Britons, I spoke about how we as a team would be addressing the challenges facing our community and promoting harmony and attempting to build bridges with other members of society. I said that we must involve all sections of our community – the first generation who had built our basic community infrastructure, mosques, small businesses, and charities – and the need for increased capacity and professionalism in all those institutions in order to bring more coordination and effectiveness.

I then turned towards our youth; how we must invest in them by harnessing their talents and getting them fully involved in our civic, religious and communal bodies. They needed to become a force for good in wider society. Our young people were a significantly higher proportion of our community compared to many others: they should be a real asset for us, but they would be a liability if we ignored them.

I reminded the audience that I was nowhere near Sir Iqbal in terms of his vast experience and leadership qualities, so, I could only perform well with everyone's support. I ended with a passionate appeal to all:

> Britain is a land of opportunity for all, and in spite of the post-7/7 challenges definitely better than other European countries. We have our rights, but we have huge obligations; the most important thing to remember is our obligation is unilateral. Let's together bring a qualitative change to build a mature, forward-looking and confident Muslim Community. Let us participate, engage and work with all around us to build a better Britain.

As I finished, I felt somewhat relieved but aware of a new sense of responsibility enveloping me. As the head of the largest British Muslim representative group, I would be often seen as representing the voice of British Muslims. This was the beginning of my new journey in public life, and as post-7/7 attention zeroed in on us it was to be an uncharted and testing time.

* * *

The history of an established British Muslim community is not that old: many Muslims arrived here during the past century (with some historical exceptions), though these numbers increased markedly after the Second World War. However, Britain's relationship with Muslims goes back to the early period of Islam. The coins of King Offa of Mercia (died 796 CE), a powerful Anglo-Saxon king, were minted with the inscription of Islam's declaration of faith (*Kalimah*), indicating diplomatic and/or commercial ties with Muslims in France, Spain and North Africa. Since then, the mercantile and commercial links between Britain and the Muslim world have continued to grow.

Muslims began living, working and openly practising their faith in England from the sixteenth century onwards. Many came from North Africa, the Middle East and central Asia, finding work in London. However, because of the encounters during the Crusades, Islam was not seen positively by many and Muslims were often termed as 'Saracens' and 'Moors' (used pejoratively in Medieval Latin literature). The excommunication by Pope Pius V in 1570 pushed Queen Elizabeth I to create commercial and political alliances with various contemporary Muslim states, and the situation for Muslims began to change more positively.

The Universities of Oxford and Cambridge established Chairs of Arabic in the 1630s, and throughout the medieval period and the Renaissance scholars in Britain relied heavily on translations from Arabic in the fields of mathematics, astronomy and medicine. A rendering of the Qur'an in English, which went on to have two imprints, was produced by Alexander Ross in 1649. By the nineteenth century, many Muslim seafarers had also settled in ports across England, Wales and Scotland. The acceptance of Islam by two prominent individuals, historian Henry Edward John Stanley and Liverpool solicitor, Abdullah Quilliam, contributed significantly towards its introduction in England at the end of the nineteenth century. Stanley accepted Islam in 1862 and adopted the name Abdul Rahman. Later, as the third Baron Stanley of Alderley, he became the first Muslim member of the House of Lords. Abdullah Quilliam embraced Islam in 1887 at the age of thirty-one. He led a very active life and established the Liverpool Muslim Institute (with a mosque), founded a Muslim college and initiated a weekly Debating and Literary Society.

The privileged individuals and young aristocrats who embraced Islam in the late Victorian era were met with curiosity and bemusement: Lord Headley (Rowland Allanson-Winn, fifth Baron of Headley), was an Irish peer who spent many years in India and accepted Islam in 1913; renowned English scholar, Marmaduke Pickthall, a classmate and friend of Winston Churchill, became Muslim in 1917 and contributed immensely by rendering the Qur'an into English. Lady Evelyn Murray (later Zainab) Cobbold (1867–1963), was probably the first British woman to accept Islam. In 1933 at the age of sixty-five, she performed Hajj and authored a bestselling book, *Pilgrimage to Mecca*, on her Hajj experience. On these early converts, historian Professor Humayun Ansari commented: 'They had experienced what they saw as the peace, the spirituality and simplicity of Islamic societies, and it appealed greatly to them.'[9]

Organized Muslim activities in London owe much to an Indian Muslim Judge, Syed Ameer Ali, who came to live in England after his retirement in 1904. He was the first Muslim Privy Councillor, a position he would hold from 1909 until his death in 1928. Along with other prominent Muslim and non-Muslim personalities of the day, he founded the London Mosque Fund inside the august halls of the Ritz Hotel in 1910. The Aga Khan III, Sir Hassan Suhrawardy, and Qur'an exegetes Marmaduke Pickthall and Abdullah Yusuf Ali (the former Indian civil servant, barrister and Qur'anic scholar who settled in London in 1914) were also involved in its foundation. Renowned non-Muslim individuals from the British social and political establishment who were involved were Nathan Rothschild, Lord Lamington, and the historian T.W. Arnold. Until 1941, when the mosque committee bought three adjacent houses in Commercial Road, it had no physical building and the congregation met in various hired halls. Both Ameer Ali and Yusuf Ali effectively advocated British Muslim

9. Josef O'Shea, 'The Victorian Muslims of Britain' (*Al Jazeera*, 15 June 2016).

concerns at home and abroad. Alongside Ameer Ali, some of the prominent Muslim individuals of this time are now lying at rest in the Brookwood cemetery in Surrey.

A new phase of Muslim presence in Britain began after the Second World War, when immigrants from former colonies were invited to rebuild a shattered Britain. Following the partition of India in 1947, many South Asian Muslims began to arrive in Britain during the 1950s, and there were estimated to be 82,000 Muslims in Britain in 1961; this number rose to about one million by 1991. The numbers, however, were based on people's ethnicity rather than a specific query and it was not until the 2001 Census that an optional question on religious affiliation was included for the first time, when results from the Census showed the number of Muslims was found to be roughly 1.6 million. According to the UK Census returns of 2001 and 2011, Islam is the second largest religion, after Christianity. In 2011, the number of Muslims was 2.7 million, roughly 4.5 per cent of the total population, coming from all corners of the world. With about 100,000 indigenous Muslims, 66 per cent women, the British Muslim community is rich in diversity. Ethnically, the largest groups are of Pakistani origin, followed by the Bangladeshis, and the majority adhere to the Sunni tradition.

Muslim sacrifice for Britain during the two world wars was enormous. On the occasion of the 2009 Remembrance Day celebrations, the MCB published a booklet, *Remembering the Brave*, to highlight this. An estimated one million Indian soldiers fought for Britain on various fronts during the First World War; 400,000 of them were Muslims, with 47,000 killed and 65,000 wounded. During the Second World War, the numbers were much higher; 2.5 million Indian soldiers, a substantial number of them Muslims, fought for Britain; 36,092 were killed or reported missing, 64,354 were wounded and almost 80,000 held as prisoners of war (PoWs). Many who were also employed on British merchant ships during both wars also lost their lives, and only a small number of them were buried in Brookwood cemetery in Surrey.

* * *

During the early stages of immigration, the main concerns affecting Muslim immigrants were about addressing basic social, religious and cultural needs; e.g. prayer places and halal food. Many wanted to go back, but usually this did not happen, and as the community grew, so the community dynamics changed. In spite of socio-economic deprivation, the great majority of British Muslims went on to engage with wider society and made positive contributions to the economy, culture and politics of the country. The picture is mixed, of course, in some walks of life, such as the medical profession and business entrepreneurship, there are success stories. However, there are also areas of concern, such as the prison population. Overall, the British model of social integration has so far worked better than many other European countries.

Muslims, like other religious communities, are not a homogeneous block. They consist of groups with both conservative as well as liberal views and practices. There are also various theological, socio-cultural and political strands running through this multi-varied community, and the British Muslim community reflects the microcosm of the Muslim world. There are two main traditions: Sunni and Shia, and Muslims observably carry the hallmarks from where they originated. The visible Sunni groups are the Barelwis, Deobandis, Tablighi Jamaat, Salafis, Ahle Hadith and the Sufis. Groups like the politically active Hizb ut-Tahrir (The Liberation Party) and the movement-oriented bodies (such as Brotherhood and Jamaat) hail from the Sunni tradition. On the other hand, the main Shia groups are the Ithna Athari (Twelvers), Zaydis, Ismaili and Khoja Shia.

With no religious hierarchy, particularly in Sunni Islam, and without a centralized authority in the community, bringing about a level of coordination and agreement on a shared agenda has not been easy. Bringing British Muslims together on a single platform or under one umbrella has always been a desire and a religious yearning for many, but in the past it proved to be wishful thinking. However, a number of broad-based networks or umbrella groups have emerged since the 1960s. The oldest among them, the Federation of Students Islamic Societies (FOSIS), was founded as a national student body by expatriate students in July 1963, looking after the interests of Muslim students at British universities. FOSIS has since been actively supporting and representing Islamic societies at colleges and universities in the UK and Ireland, and is now run overwhelmingly by British-born students.

One well-organized community platform, the Union of Muslim Organizations (UMO) of UK & Ireland, was founded by Dr Syed Aziz Pasha in 1970, and has served the Muslim community in mainly social and educational areas for a long time. It used to organize successful youth camps and education seminars or workshops (I attended a number of its high quality education workshops in Cambridge in the late 1990s), and also persistently defended Muslim interests in areas such as Muslim family law. But it gradually lost ground, offering an absence of opportunities for new leaders to emerge, a lack of expertise in handling media and an inability to cope with the changing dynamics of Britain and its Muslim community.

The Muslim Parliament of Great Britain was set up in 1992 by Dr Kalim Siddiqui (a former journalist and director of the Muslim Institute) and attempted to highlight Muslim political aspirations and rights in the public domain, as well as working to establish the Halal Food Authority in 1994, to monitor and regulate the halal meat trade in Britain. It disappeared a few years after Dr Siddiqui's sudden death in

April 1996. There was also another particularly active national body in the 1980s, the Council of Mosques. I heard about it frequently while doing my physics research at Kings College, but it also disappeared without notice after a few years.

* * *

The early 1990s were a sombre time for British Muslims, Yugoslavia had descended into chaos, with the Bosnian Muslims among the worst affected by the crisis, and the *Satanic Verses* controversy had dented the confidence of European Muslims. Watching the horrors of the Balkans unfold, as British Muslims we felt a natural demand to better organize ourselves. A few of us from various backgrounds, some with experience in leading the UK Action Committee on Islamic Affairs (UKACIA), decided to initiate a process of consultation with the communities across Britain. We wanted this to be an inclusive national conversation for everyone – from both the Sunni and Shia traditions – to gauge opinions on the important issues that affected us, and the process had to be organic.

We wanted to go through a bottom-up approach and involve grass-root community organizations and national bodies, as well as individuals. The idea was to discuss our day-to-day practical issues, as well as wider concerns, hopes and long-term aspirations. After some to-and-fro exchanges, we called for a consultation meeting in Birmingham in April 1994. About fifty people attended, representing various Muslim groups, and we were encouraged to see a meeting of minds and a passion to take the discussion forward. We formed a National Interim Committee for Muslim Unity (NICMU) to 'conduct a consultation exercise within the community to establish the need for an umbrella body and seek views on its priorities and structure.' The ball started rolling.

The NICMU established a working group to carry out a postal survey across the country. A comprehensive survey questionnaire was prepared with the help of talented activist, Abdul Wahid Hamid, and circulated to over 2,000 Muslim organizations and prominent individuals. Abdul Wahid encouraged a data analyst, Jamil Sherif, to analyse the responses, which represented the views of a cross-section of Muslim civil society at the time and included detailed comments from individuals such as the writer and former diplomat Guy Eaton. The survey response rate was about 10 per cent, and showed an overwhelming grassroots desire for greater unity and coordination and the need for a representative body. Soon the NICMU established a sub-committee to examine the constitutions of other like-minded bodies and to propose a draft for discussion. Teams from NICMU also began a roadshow to present the survey findings and seek support from important community organizations and religious leaders, across all schools of thought.

The findings of the survey, presented in July 1995, showed that children's education were respondents' number one priority. However, a large number also strongly felt that it was time to form an umbrella body to bring better coordination within the Muslim community and to effectively represent Muslims in wider society. The NICMU discussed this idea thoroughly and agreed in principle to form a broad-based umbrella body; it created a sub-group of experts and gave it the task to prepare a draft constitution that catered to the reality of a diverse community within a pluralist democratic society. Over a long meeting in Birmingham, in January 1996, we had a detailed discussion on the draft constitution and then agreed on a final draft. The NICMU held its last meeting in May 1996 in Bradford, where delegates agreed in principle with the proposed constitution of the umbrella body. We then agreed to choose its name, the Muslim Council of Britain (or MCB), with the ethos of 'working for the common good' in line with the teachings of the Qur'an.

The agreed constitution catered for the diversity and dynamics of the Muslim community, with a clear recognition that the MCB would be a non-sectarian, non-partisan democratic and independent body consisting of mosques and Islamic associations. There would be three types of affiliates: national, regional and local or specialist bodies (i.e. mosques, Islamic centres, charities, schools and similar institutions at one location). Its decision-making authority would be the yearly General Assembly, comprised of delegates from affiliated bodies. Every two years, the General Assembly would elect an executive body named the Central Working Committee (CWC) that would on the same day elect the Secretary-General and three other office bearers.

The MCB's permanent aims and objectives were about promoting cooperation, consensus and unity on Muslim affairs in the UK; encouraging and strengthening existing efforts by groups such as the Union of Muslim Organizations in the Muslim community; and working for a more enlightened appreciation of Islam and Muslims in wider society. It would endeavour to establish a dignified position for the Muslim community that was fair and based on due rights, work towards the eradication of disadvantages and forms of discrimination faced by Muslims, foster better community relations and work for the good of society as a whole.

The Bradford meeting formed a preparatory committee to organize the launch event of the MCB; the committee members divided themselves into various groups and travelled across the country to invite mosques and institutions to formally join the umbrella body. Years of hard work culminated in the inauguration of the MCB at London's Brent Town Hall on 23 November 1997. It was indeed an historic occasion for Britain's Muslim community, where 250 affiliates from diverse backgrounds agreed to be represented by their newly-formed umbrella body. The headline of the MCB's first press release was: 'Umbrella Body Heralds New Era for British Muslims.'

On the basis of the approved constitution, the first General Assembly meeting was held on 1 March 1998, at which the MCB delegates elected the first CWC, consisting of twenty-five nationally elected and twelve regionally elected members. In accordance with the provision of the constitution, each national and regional affiliate nominated one representative as a CWC member. The CWC then elected four office-bearers: Iqbal Sacranie (who was later knighted for his services to the community) as Secretary-General, Dr Basil Mustafa as Deputy Secretary-General and Yusuf Islam as Treasurer. I was elected Assistant Secretary-General. After over a decade of operational experience, the CWC was renamed as the National Council (NC).

The arrival of a broad-based, non-sectarian representative body was generally welcomed by Muslims, other faith and civil society bodies, as well as by the political and media establishments. From its inception in 1997, the MCB made strenuous efforts to make it clear that it was a complementary, service-oriented umbrella body, joining the dots and giving issues of importance a national voice as and when needed. There was initial scepticism from a small segment that its leadership consisted of people that could be best compared as 'Dad's Army' (an unflattering reference to a popular BBC television situation comedy), though the first batch of office bearers were professionals in their mid-40s! The UMO also expressed its unhappiness to see the MCB emerging at all, as it thought the MCB might be a competitor organization. But, individuals who were once involved with the UMO and then joined the MCB project clarified their position and gave assurance that MCB would be complementing and enhancing the UMO's ongoing work. A few tangential comments were also made by some sceptics who alleged that the formation of the MCB was probably instigated by the Conservative Home Secretary, Michael Howard (1993–1997), or even by the-then opposition Labour Party. I was not aware of the veracity of this claim, as I was neither a member of a political party nor was I a senior leader of the community at that time.

The MCB was the first experiment of its kind in Muslim community organization on a national scale in any European country. It was an ambitious and visionary project for British Muslims and the start of a timely and worthwhile journey.

* * *

There were two other national events in 1997 that had a long-lasting impact on the British Muslim communities. The first was the Labour Party's massive election victory in May that year under Tony Blair, and the second was the publication of a historic report on tackling Islamophobia by think tank, The Runnymede Trust, in November. New Labour came to power with fresh ideas and an energy to change the British landscape after eighteen years of Tory rule. It seemed ready to listen to all sections of society and for the first time Muslims felt they were being given some chance to be heard by Britain's central government; the Whitehall mandarins also appeared to be in listening mode. The MCB was ready to work with various arms of the Labour administration, and Iqbal and a few others already had some connections with the political establishment.

By that time we had been working with prominent faith and civic leaders through the Interfaith Network and the government's Inner Cities Religious Council. One of the Muslim campaigns was in the financial sector, pushing for the acceptance of Shariah-compliant finance (interest free) from the Treasury and Bank of England (for example, by the removal of double stamp duties for purchases of Islamically financed-homes). The MCB put its weight behind this campaign and the result was positive. There were a few other areas where the MCB's enthusiastic volunteer leadership was able to work with other Muslims and civil society bodies to put pressure on the political establishment to treat all communities fairly. It decided to organize several high-profile public events with politicians, as well as religious and civic leaders, to bring home the reality that Muslims, like others, were an indispensable part of society. The first of these events was a reception at which the chief guest was the Foreign Secretary, Jack Straw, in December 1998 at the banqueting suite at the Lords cricket ground. The event was a notable success and was attended by many leaders from across the country, both Muslim and non-Muslims.

Five months later, on 5 May 1999, we organized a bolder event at the Commonwealth Institute in London's Kensington High Street. This time it was a reception for the Prime Minister, Tony Blair, who was then riding high in British politics. With the presence of many dignitaries, including some senior Muslim diplomats as well as many from the business sector, the event was an even bigger success. In his welcome address, the MCB Secretary-General said: 'In two years, we have seen the first Muslim appointments to the House of Lords; to hospital and prison chaplaincies; and greater consultation with government departments on a range of issues of community, national and international interest, including redemption of the debt of the world's poorest countries.'[10] The MCB's public image rose higher and people felt it was bringing rightful recognition for the Muslim community into British public life.

Faith and religion were gradually emerging into the forefront of British public life. In the past, minority communities were categorized by their ethnic or geographic origin: Asian, Black

10. Iqbal Sacranie, 'Secretary General's Address at Reception for Prime Minister' (Muslim Council of Britain, 5 May 1999).

or Pakistani. With the incorporation of people's religious affiliation in the 2001 Census, religious identity was given natural recognition. It became easier for local and central government to make sure that faith communities were not excluded from the provision of services that affected their lives, including halal or kosher food, or interest-free mortgages. One major symbolic, as well as practical, achievement was the acceptance by the Labour government of independent Muslim day-schools. Islamia Primary School, founded in 1983 by singer and songwriter Yusuf Islam (Cat Stevens), became the first Muslim school to be granted public funding by the Government in 1998, and gave a moral boost to the community.

The effort to secure legislation on religious discrimination and incitement to religious hatred was another important element that the MCB worked on. The Government attempted to introduce an offence of 'incitement to religious hatred' in November 2001 via its Anti-terrorism, Crime and Security Bill, which was defeated in the House of Lords. After a few more attempts, a watered-down version, called the Racial and Religious Hatred Bill, received Royal Assent in February 2006. The MCB also put its weight behind another important area: pushing the Foreign and Commonwealth Office (FCO) in Jeddah and Makkah in Saudi Arabia to give practical support to the thousands of British pilgrims during the Hajj period. Historically, Britain played an important role in facilitating the annual pilgrimage for its Muslim subjects, despite the political and logistical difficulties of the time. The MCB, the Association of British Hujjaj (Pilgrims) and other relevant institutions, as well as individuals, worked with the FCO and in 1999 the Labour government re-enacted the tradition by establishing a consular delegation in Makkah during the Hajj season. The range of support included advice on Hajj preparations, such as passport and documentation, helping hospitalized pilgrims, making necessary logistical and bureaucratic arrangements for bereaved families in the event of a death, and giving advice to British pilgrims who were the victims of unscrupulous tour operators.

* * *

The summer of 2001 posed an unusual challenge to the Muslim community as well as to the British political establishment. There was a sudden eruption of violence in several northern towns in England. Hundreds of South Asian (Pakistani and some Bangladeshi) youths took to the streets of Oldham, Burnley and Bradford and clashed with the police. Each town had its own reasons for the riots, but the underlying factors were known to be social division, rivalries between criminal gangs, poverty and racial tension between the Asian and white communities. On 7 July 2001, there was widespread destruction in Bradford's Manningham area when young men clashed with the police; over a hundred officers were reported to have been injured. The MCB sent a team of senior volunteers a few days later to hear the views of Muslim residents and observers, as well as those who played a role in seeking to contain the situation. We convened a national conference of Muslim organizations on 4 August in Oldham, to enable Muslim youth leaders, community workers, imams and other experts to share views and identify courses of action to restore confidence in community relations. There were widespread grievances under the radar, but violence was totally unacceptable and the MCB decided to invest more in our youth.

A number of investigations were commissioned, including the official central government inquiry into these events by Professor Ted Cantle. He came up with a disturbing critique of civic leadership and central government policy. According to his observation, people of diverse backgrounds were living 'parallel' or 'polarised' lives and the country needed 'community cohesion' to solve the deeper problems in our society. Professor Cantle made dozens of recommendations on housing, youth, regeneration, politics and education. He recommended that central government do more to promote a sense of the rights and responsibilities of citizenship. Perpetrators were punished through the criminal justice system, but the Asian community in Bradford, that had fully cooperated with the police, came up with complaints that the sentences were unfair compared with others facing similar public disorder charges. Michael Mansfield QC commented that the sentences were 'manifestly excessive', and the Institute of Race Relations also expressed concerns over excessive sentencing of Bradford rioters. These riots, however, were a wake-up call for the British political establishment. It also posed a new challenge to the nascent Muslim leadership.

However, the year 2001 will mostly remain stamped on the collective memory because of the September 11 terror attacks on New York (known as 9/11). Nearly 3,000 died and the damage ranged into the billions of dollars as the twin towers of the World Trade Center were brought down by two airliners deliberately ramming them, the Pentagon falling under attack from a third airliner, and a fourth crashing into a field. It was late afternoon in London and I was with my colleagues in a training session at the Tower Hamlets' Professional Development Centre (PDC) when the news broke. The ferocity of the events, seen by some PDC staff on the TV, spread an unknown fear among teachers. Managers decided to call it a day and we all headed home early.

The 9/11 attack was an unthinkable evil act on mainland America and the trauma was more than just death and destruction. A horrified world offered its full sympathy and support to America. However, it was also a global game changer. America was fuming, and under the spell of its neoconservative elite it took steps that changed the course of world history and would lead to the infamous 'War on Terror'. All fingers pointed to the terror group al-Qaeda (AQ), which had been given sanctuary by the Taliban regime in Afghanistan, as the organization behind the attacks. On 20 September, US President George W. Bush, while delivering an ultimatum to the Taliban government to hand over AQ leader, Osama bin Laden, used the term 'War on Terror' for the first time. The Taliban's demand for evidence was rejected and America (with the support of coalition forces) invaded Afghanistan in October 2001.

America did not stop there. President Bush was planning to invade Iraq for its illusory stock of weapons of mass destruction (WMDs), but world opinion was against him this time. However, British Prime Minister, Tony Blair, made up his mind and gave his unyielding support to Bush; 'I will be with you, whatever', he said in a 2002 memo to Bush on Iraq. The MCB Secretary-General, Iqbal Sacranie, met Blair towards the end of 2002 and informed him that the Muslim community, while totally against the brutal Saddam regime, was also against an illegal invasion that would bring unknown and catastrophic consequences. On 15 February 2003, there was a coordinated day of protests across the world in which people in more 600 cities in 60 countries expressed their anger and opposition against war on Iraq. Over a million people converged in central London to protest against the impending conflict. According to the BBC, the Police said it was the UK's biggest ever demonstration with at least 750,000 taking part; organisers, however, claimed the figure was close to two million. Attending with family and friends, I witnessed a sea of people in London's Hyde Park all united against launching a new war in the Middle East, though our passionate protests fell on deaf ears in Westminster. Blair claimed in Parliament that invasion was a necessity, even suggesting that Saddam Hussein could unleash an attack on British soil 'within 45 minutes' using his alleged WMDs.

The Iraq invasion commenced on 20 March 2003 with an aerial bombardment on Saddam Hussein's Presidential Palace in Baghdad. I can still vividly recall watching the night-vision news reports as luminous green explosions rocked the city while the announcers gave a running commentary on the invasion. Over 100,000 coalition troops from the United States, the United Kingdom, Australia and Poland poured into Iraq, under the protection of a ferocious bombing campaign that destroyed the country and threw the defending army into chaos. On 1 May, President Bush gave his infamous 'a job well done' speech in front of a banner that read, 'Mission Accomplished', from the deck of the aircraft carrier USS Abraham Lincoln. But the aftermath was a tragedy from day one, not only for Iraq and the Middle East but for the whole world. The destruction of Iraq's infrastructure and disbanding of the army and police forces brought the historic land to its knees (after already suffering many years of devastating sanctions). Over the years since, the loss of around a million Iraqis and the callous sectarian violence that erupted has left the country effectively lawless. To the people of Iraq, this was America's worst crime.

While the Sunni-Shia divide has been present in the Muslim world for fourteen centuries, in the aftermath of the invasion of Iraq the occupying powers and short-sighted local politicians deliberately stoked sectarian conflict. Edward Luttwak, a military strategist and adviser to a number of world leaders, pinned the blame on President Bush: 'I failed to appreciate at the time that he was a strategic genius far beyond Bismarck. He ignited a religious war between [Shia] and Sunnis that will occupy the region for the next 1,000 years.'[11] Combined with the short-sightedness of President Bush, the total lack of any post-invasion recovery plan left Iraq a dysfunctional country.

---

11. Thomas Meaney, 'The Machiavelli of Maryland' (*The Guardian*, 9 December 2015).

With American torture chambers in places like Abu Ghraib and collapsing law and order, the Iraq experiment threw the entire Middle East onto the precipice of anarchy and helped export a further rise of deadly terrorism. Many in the East and the West pointed their fingers at America's Iraq adventure as one of the main causes behind the emergence of Daesh (known as ISIS or ISIL, or so-called Islamic State) in 2014.

Tony Blair's Britain also paid a heavy price for participating in the Iraq war in terms of blood, treasure and trust in the political class, With thousands of British military personnel wounded and 179 soldiers dead, billions of pounds were lost and there were unprecedented large-scale Stop the War marches. The Prime Minister himself never recovered from the effect of going into war under false pretences and trust in Blair's government was shattered. A public inquiry under the chairmanship of Sir john Chilcot was convened by Blair's successor, Gordon Brown, in 2009, and the Chilcot Report, as it became known, concluded that Tony Blair's policy in support of George W. Bush's invasion was founded on 'flawed intelligence' and the legality for the decision to go to war was 'far from satisfactory'. Since the invasion, and following his resignation on 27 June 2007, Tony Blair has continually faced calls to be prosecuted for war crimes in The Hague for his participation in the war.

* * *

London basked with pride on 6 July 2005 after it beat Paris and won the 2012 Olympic bid. But this pride was violently shattered the next day after multiple suicide bombings across its transport network. Fifty-six people, including the four bombers, were killed in the attacks and around 700 were injured, and for the next few weeks Londoners went through a trauma of fear and uncertainty after what came to be known as '7/7'.

London Mayor Ken Livingstone was in Singapore on the day of the bombing. He gave a powerful message to Londoners via video link:

> That (terrorism) isn't an ideology, it isn't even a perverted faith – it is just an indiscriminate attempt at mass murder and we know what the objective is. They seek to divide Londoners. They seek to turn Londoners against each other. I said yesterday to the International Olympic Committee, that the city of London is the greatest in the world, because everybody lives side by side in harmony.[12]

After returning home, the Mayor organized a vigil in Trafalgar Square on 14 July to remember the bombing victims, thank emergency crews for their efforts and praise Londoners for their 'calmness and courage'. It was a sombre gathering that touched me personally and the thousands who attended from all walks of life.

Prime Minister Tony Blair, the Home Secretary, Charles Clarke, and the Metropolitan Police Commissioner, Sir Ian Blair, separately organized meetings with Muslim leaders and other senior public figures, to inform about and seek ideas on the threat of terrorism. In spite of my full time job, I managed to attend the important ones, and in the meeting with the PM the MCB Secretary-General was the first who raised the issue of the need for a Public Inquiry into the events of 7 July; the PM ignored the call.

In the post-7/7 reality, the right-wing media lost no opportunity in coming up with sensational and often outrageous headlines disproportionately attacking mainstream Muslim groups and individual public figures as somehow complicit

---

12. 'Mayor condemns "cowardly" act' (*BBC London*, 8 July 2005).

with this terrorism. This was exacerbated by skewed research by some think-tanks and far-right groups. Neoconservative political blogs like 'Harry's Place', that had previously supported the 2003 Iraq invasion, commenced trawling the statements of some Muslim scholars and then quoting them out of context and with a spin so as to make them out as a threat to British values. It appeared that Muslims were guilty before being proven innocent. Some of this 'news' was also given a voice in the mainstream media by columnists and from certain sections of the tabloid media. There were twisted news claims, such as Muslims wanting to ban Christmas, for example – a frequent but complete hoax – and an anti-Muslim climate started to grow. Ten years later this is still continuing, with right-wing television stations like Fox News that continually misrepresent and blame Muslims, and Breitbart, the 'news' website that has the ear of the US President, Donald Trump. In 2016, hoax leaflets were circulated in Manchester that Muslims wanted to ban keeping dogs as pets. This was widely reported in the right-wing press, even though their contents had been thoroughly debunked. The UK's public service broadcaster, the BBC, aired a *Panorama* programme, 'A Question of Leadership', on 21 August 2005 raising some of these many issues. It was pessimistic and took aim at several MCB affiliates. Made by veteran journalist John Ware, it was seen by the MCB as 'a deeply unfair programme using deliberately garbled quotes in an attempt to malign the Muslim Council of Britain'.[13]

A number of influential right-wing commentators blamed successive British governments for 'tolerating radical Islamists for so long'. Journalist Melanie Phillips wrote a book in 2006, *Londonistan: How Britain is Creating a Terror State Within*, about the 'spread of Islamism' in the UK over the previous

---

13. 'John Ware's Panorama programme: A witch-hunt against British Muslims' (*Muslim Council of Britain*, 20 August 2005).

two decades. The Conservative neo-con politician Michael Gove attempted to address the 'roots of Islamic terrorism' in his book, *Celsius 7/7*, in the same year: it was heavily criticized by historian William Dalrymple as a 'confused epic of simplistic incomprehension'. Some of these assertions fell in line with conspiracy theories such as Eurabia, the idea that the total Islamisation of Europe was underway. They might have sounded like fantasists, but similar theories in the past provoked anger against other minority peoples such as the Jews and Gypsies, victimizing them and providing justification for violence against them. Conspiracy theories, although baseless, are imaginative and can be portrayed as 'real' by the unscrupulous as they are regurgitated in political and media discourse.

Muslims are facing this at a time when they are still mostly a diasporic community, with high levels of socio-economic deprivation and underachievement in many areas of life, including in education. They also have little influence and political power in Europe, so are they really a threat to established democracies with powerful institutions and dominant cultures? This runs against all common sense. However, 7/7 posed a different socio-political challenge for Muslims and they were still not well-prepared to effectively handle it. Muslim organizations and Islamic leaders issued immediate statements condemning the attacks, but were not able to coherently address the issue of violent extremism before the Blair government set its agenda and narrative. Counteracting the right-wing media was also not easy. With constraints on human resources, expertise and finance, the volunteer leaderships of British Muslim organizations were struggling to cope. Blairites in the Labour government were obviously very unhappy with the MCB's role of criticising the 2003 Iraq invasion and were looking for an opportunity to marginalize it in the public domain. Counterpoised against this was a small section of Muslim youth very angry with both the government for its foreign policy and also the mainstream Muslim community leadership for its ineffectiveness. For national groups like the MCB, the situation was not easy. On the one hand, the Blair government was unhappy with the MCB for not endorsing its foreign policy and domestic security measures; on the other, sections of Muslim youth perceived the MCB's willingness to engage with government as a sign of weakness.

On 5 August 2005, Blair announced in his 'the rules of the game are changing' speech[14] a series of measures to counter the threat of terrorism, including specific points that suggested a ban on Hizb ut-Tahrir (HT) and a proposal for new legal powers to close places of worship alleged to be used 'as a centre for fomenting extremism'. Muslim groups were alarmed and despite huge differences with the HT on issues such as democracy, the MCB challenged the government to bring proof that HT had broken any law of the land. On the closure of places of worship, we consulted the police and Church establishment and asked the government to bring evidence if any mosque was ever 'used as a centre for fomenting extremism'. The government did not respond to either of these two challenges. In fact, most of the recommendations from the seven Working Groups formed by the Home Office in August 2005 on 'Preventing Extremism Together' and submitted to the Home Secretary on 22 September did not see any follow up by the government.

In December 2005, Blair finally announced he would not establish an independent judicial inquiry into the 7/7 attacks, reasoning it would divert police and security service resources, and 'We do essentially know what happened'. Instead, a senior civil servant would produce a 'narrative' on the attacks in London, using evidence compiled by the

14. Tony Blair, 'PM's Press Conference' (The National Archives, 5 August 2005).

police and two House of Commons select committees. This narrative, compiled by Sir John Gieve and delivered to Home Secretary, Charles Clarke, in December 2005, reinforced the government's position not to hold a public inquiry, much to the disappointment of Muslim groups, survivors of the attacks and relatives of the victims.

* * *

British life post-7/7 was never the same, particularly for the Muslim community. The atmosphere was thick with suspicion and the undercurrent of misinformation and Islamophobia was constant. But I was also heartened to see many in Britain's faith groups and civil society bodies lending their invaluable support to our community in its time of need. In the aftermath of the 7/7 bombings, the citizens organizing group, London Citizens, stood firmly behind its Muslim affiliates. The Trades Union Congress (TUC) also felt it necessary to come to our support. In August 2005, the TUC published a report, *Poverty, Exclusion and British people of Pakistani and Bangladeshi Origin*, that found many people from considerable parts of these two communities suffered disproportionate disadvantages: 69 per cent were classified as poor, compared with the national average of 22 per cent, and they were three times more likely to be unemployed than the majority white population.

In early autumn 2005, the TUC's General Secretary, Brendan Barber (now Sir), sent the head of the TUC's Southern and Eastern Region (SERTUC) to meet me at the East London Mosque. This paved the way for Brendan to personally visit the ELM later in the year to 'show solidarity' with us, and through that visit a personal friendship developed between us. Before leaving, he turned to me and suggested: 'Would you be willing to host our General Council at the London Muslim Centre?' I looked at him with enthusiasm and asked: 'When and how many are you in the Council?'

'It's on 22 February 2006 and there are fifty-five members in the Council,' he said.

I quickly looked at my colleagues and replied: 'It'll be a privilege to host the event. Go ahead, Brendan.' He thanked me and said his office would contact me soon.

We dedicated the whole of the LMC's first floor to the event. On the day, we warmly received the union leaders and the Teaching Union leaders were delighted to learn I was involved with the Association of Teachers and Lecturers (ATL). I gave a ten-minute welcome address, thanking them for coming and addressing the need to work together for social justice and the common good, then left the room so they could continue their business. The TUC issued a press release before the event that stated:

> Britain's top trade unionists are to meet one of London's most senior Muslim leaders for discussions on how the unions and the Muslim community can work more closely together in tackling deprivation in some of the poorest areas of the capital ... Other issues the General Council will be discussing include how to make sure that Muslim communities get to share in the benefits that the Olympics will bring to London in 2012.[15]

The LMC event led to an historic occasion when as MCB Secretary-General I spoke at the 138th TUC Congress in Brighton the following September. During my speech I brought up the difficulties faced by Muslims in the workplace: discrimination, 'misunderstandings, prejudice

---

15. 'TUC General Council to visit London Muslim Centre' (Trades Union Congress, 22 February 2006).

and the stereotyping of whole communities',[16] and how 'the essential message in the Quran is the unity of humankind and its potential as a positive force for harmony and cooperation.' In conclusion, I reaffirmed 'our determination to work in partnership with the TUC to bring greater awareness of the problems faced by Muslim workers in the workplace as well as in being members of British society', and the MCB and TUC issued a joint statement pledging 'to work together to encourage more Muslims to join trade unions, encourage better community relations and combat Islamophobia, both within workplaces and in society at large.'[17] The MCB and TUC also pledged to work together on issues of common concern, such as equality and opposition to prejudice.

As the MCB leadership's two-year term was coming to an end in June, preparations started in earnest for the next election on Sunday 4 June 2006 to elect a new team of leaders for the following two years. Sir Iqbal and I would be finishing our second two-year term as SG and DSG, respectively, and we could not, according the constitution, stand again for the same post. Iqbal had led the MCB brilliantly through the crisis of 7/7 and its aftermath, and the next leader would have a gigantic task ahead to lead it through uncharted social and political terrain. There was a natural expectation that I would stand for SG. But in spite of my added commitment towards the MCB post-7/7, I had no intention to step in, especially considering the needs of my existing teaching job. I informed Iqbal of my unwillingness to take on the position and my reasons for not doing so.

However, the MCB needed a safe and strong pair of hands in these choppy waters and towards the beginning of April

---

16. Muhammad Abdul Bari, 'Speech to Trade Union Congress', (Trades Union Congress, 11 September 2006).
17. 'TUC General Council statement jointly with the Muslim Council of Britain' (Muslim Council of Britain, 11 September 2006).

I received several phone calls from senior MCB colleagues and community elders about my intentions. I explained to each why I had made my decision, but every time I talked to them I was asked to think again. Time was passing, and one of the elders made an appointment to meet me personally to discuss the issue. He understood my reservations, saying: 'I am not in a position to arm-twist you on this, but please do not withdraw your name if you are nominated for the job. You may not be elected after the nomination.' Many things were going through my head, but as I respected him I kept quiet. Before leaving, he solicitously added, 'Dr Abdul Bari, if people in the MCB choose you, then have *tawakkul* (reliance on Allah) and please do not refuse. You are not seeking this, so God will help you.' I had lost the appetite to argue and in a quiet voice replied: 'Let me think and consult my family.'

Later that same day, I spoke with Iqbal to discover whether he also felt the same; he said he fully agreed with the idea. I thought long and hard and consulted Sayeda and our older children that night. The implications, if I became the first post-7/7 SG of the MCB, were understandably a huge challenge, both for myself as an individual as well as to my family. Our daughter Rima remained vehemently opposed to the idea, she thought I would be too busy with the MCB to attend to the family and would also be a target of the right-wing media (she was certainly right about the latter). We mulled it over and Sayeda reluctantly gave me the go ahead. I informed my senior colleagues that I would not refuse to take up the position if I were indeed chosen.

For the next few weeks, the MCB tried to streamline its work internally and in the community. The leadership and its major affiliates were aware that the Blair government, by rejecting a call for a judicial public inquiry into 7/7, was probably going to be tougher on Muslims. Sure enough, the government brought in the new Terrorism Act (2006), and some of its terms proved to be highly controversial. 'The notion that the Muslim community somehow harbours a threat to the country, and to society as a whole, is wrong and offensive',[18] the MCB commented on 13 April 2006, in response to the Act coming into force: 'The fact that a handful carried out the terrorist attacks on the 7th of July should not render the entire 2 million strong Muslim community liable to suspicion, censorship and persecution under these laws.' A month later, the MCB published its report, *Voices from the Minaret*, in Manchester, after a wide-ranging consultation and research into mosques and imams. It was conducted by an independent research consultancy on behalf of the Mosque and Community Affairs committee. The report dealt with the issues facing mosques and imams in the UK, ideas on better governance and capacity building to deliver a better service to local communities.

* * *

The MCB's 2006 Annual General Meeting (AGM) attracted significant interest from affiliates and beyond, as it was the first change of MCB leadership after 7/7 and affiliates felt it necessary to rally around their umbrella body to face the new challenges together. The Blair government and mainstream media also appeared to be keeping their eye on the MCB. It was a new phase of the British Muslim journey, and it was a different political landscape we were entering. Nobody knew how the global situation would pan out or how the government would (re)act.

On the morning of Sunday 4 June, delegates started pouring in to the LMC in east London. The weather was sparkling, but the mood was sombre because of a very high-profile police raid that happened nearby a couple of days earlier. In the early

18. 'Muslim Community Opposes New Anti-Terror Legislation and Urges Government to Exercise Maximum Restraint and Caution' (Muslim Council of Britain, 13 April 2006).

morning of Friday 2 June, a massive police operation (involving 250 officers) raided two houses in London's Forest Gate, purportedly looking for a suspected chemical bomb factory, which made national and international headlines. Under the Terrorism Act, the police arrested two British-Bangladeshi brothers, Mohammed Abdul Kahar and Abul Koyair, during the raid, and in the course of the arrest Kahar was shot in the shoulder. The police did not find any explosive devices, nor was there any evidence of terrorist activity. Details were still patchy on Sunday and delegates at the AGM were looking for further information.

Iqbal was stepping down as SG, after four years at the helm, and the hall was packed with registered delegates in the cordoned area in the middle, surrounded by a similar number of registered observers. The AGM started with Sir Iqbal's final report as Secretary-General, and questions from the floor about accountability to all the office bearers, including me as Deputy Secretary-General. Once the reporting session was over, the chief election commissioner, Judge Khurshid Drabu, took over the proceedings and with his usual mixture of humour and seriousness explained the process. Delegates were given a short but sufficient amount of time to put the names of no more than twenty-five people from the delegate list as national CWC members. The trained volunteers, led by Dr Jamil Sherif, maintained discipline during this time and collected the ballot boxes for counting. The first twenty-five people elected with majority votes were declared. In the same way, twelve regional CWC members were elected from the affiliates of twelve geographically divided regions. Once the thirty-seven names were announced, the election commissioner sought nominations for CWC membership from each of the national and regional affiliates, making the total number to over sixty. All the CWC members were then ushered to the big hall upstairs for the second phase: electing the SG, DSG and the Treasurer.

My mind was racing, I had agreed not to withdraw my name if I was nominated but I could still visualize Rima's loving but worried face. Two nominations were made for the SG – and one was indeed for me. Judge Drabu asked each of us if we agreed to stand or withdraw nomination. I finally made up my mind to stand and said so. The vote was taken and I was declared the winner. There were instant congratulations; I tried to remain calm and thank everyone, but what we as a family had been talking about had actually happened. The DSG and the Treasurer were elected in the same way, and Dr Daud Abdullah and Mrs Unaiza Malik, the new Deputy Secretary-General and Treasurer, respectively, accepted their positions. Inayat Bunglawala, the MCB's media secretary, quickly came over to me and whispered a request to prepare a brief acceptance speech for the AGM attendees who were waiting downstairs. He also asked me to talk with some reporters from the print and electronic media, including someone from the BBC. I jotted down some points in my small notebook and we all came down to the packed main hall.

Judge Drabu announced our names and invited myself and the newly-elected Treasurer and DSG to the stage. Standing alongside Dr Abdullah and Mrs Malik, I delivered my acceptance speech, which was warmly received, and the meeting came to an end. As people started to leave I stayed around for a while, mingling with some of the delegates and observers. I sat with a few senior colleagues and discussed how the MCB could handle the police operation in Forest Gate the previous Friday. We agreed that as the new SG I would visit Forest Gate the following day to show solidarity with the people there and also to uncover more facts; we informed the local affiliates of this decision overnight and Inayat informed his contacts in the mainstream media.

* * *

The following morning, I arrived at the SLS office slightly earlier than usual in order to finish a few tasks, then straight away went to Liz's office to inform her of my election to SG in the MCB; she smiled and congratulated me. I took the day off from work and headed towards Forest Gate.

By the time I reached Upton Park tube station there were quite a few people from MCB affiliates and the local community ready to meet me. We went to a nearby clothing shop where we made plans for a walk through the main high street shopping centre to the house at the centre of the police operation. A BBC journalist appeared and asked if he could follow me. He added a caveat: 'You'll have to be wired and you'll be live.' It was a new experience, but I agreed. We walked along the street and I talked with people. Some people in Forest Gate already knew me and a few joined my walkabout. Around midday we arrived at the police incident centre outside the cordoned area. I talked with the officer-in-charge who explained the situation. Some journalists were camped in the vicinity, and when they discovered I was there they were eager to interview me. The main question on their lips was what I thought of the police operation. I knew the community was unhappy, indeed some very angry, in the way the raid had been carried out, but I decided to calm the situation by saying:

> The police as public servants have a duty to keep us safe, but they also should take extra care that any operation in a neighbourhood is done sensitively and with a higher degree of evidence-based information. Given the enormity of the police operation, and that the men had no previous criminal records, I am not sure if this was the case.

The slow pace of the police investigation led to frustration in the local community and there were protests from community groups against the raid. One was held outside Scotland Yard on Friday 9 June, and on 18 June about 5,000 people marched through Newham to Forest Gate Police Station. Both the brothers were later released without charge, and the Metropolitan Police apologized 'for the hurt that we have caused'.

My visit to Forest Gate soon became international news, and when I returned to the MCB office later that afternoon I received a phone call from a close friend in Bangladesh. He told me that people there who were watching me on the TV, in the presence of uniformed British police, were very worried that I might have been in trouble! I laughed and explained what had happened, then I asked him to convey a message to my extended family and friends that I was safe. Unfortunately, the police in many developing countries are still not on the people's side. My friends could not comprehend that police in the UK have always been public servants, and instead presumed I was in serious trouble.

* * *

In spite of my busy life outside the SLS, my relationship with my manager, Liz Vickerie, was based on solid professionalism. But she called me within a few days of my election to discuss how best the SLS could accommodate my public commitment. As a pragmatic leader, she realized that I could add value to the image of the borough and the SLS through my public engagements in high places. She offered me some flexibility in the job, which would be a great help in being an effective Secretary-General. I thanked her and reminded myself that I would never take advantage of this opportunity. I also had a natural advantage in Tower Hamlets: the SLS, the MCB office and the ELM were within just a mile of each other. As a public servant, I had a permit to park my car across the borough, so I could even use my lunch break to make short visits to the MCB office or ELM if needed.

The first few weeks as SG were hectic, as I had to build a team. The structure was already there, but I wanted to streamline it and give the sixteen-odd Committees or Task Groups a big push by bringing in more younger people. With the help of a few friends, I recruited about a dozen young volunteers who started giving me unmatched support. The Youth Committee was particularly energetic and initiated several projects. One of them, the 'Young Muslims Beacon Award', hunted talent from across the country and highlighted their achievements. Summer holidays were also approaching. As a teacher I always relished the break from the grinding work in schools, but I decided to spend the 2006 break visiting various towns and cities across Britain to help connect the MCB with its affiliates and communities. I consulted my colleagues and office staff; one senior staff member offered to organize my trip from the office and a national youth leader, Hasan Patel, decided to accompany me to most places. Hasan's presence proved to be of great benefit in connecting with many youth groups across the country. The MCB affiliates were asked to inform us of proposed events; then we started preparing a rota. We sought volunteers to accompany me to various places and quite a few, including some senior leaders, enlisted themselves. The main purpose for the national tour was to introduce the MCB and what it stood for; to listen to people and learn from their grass-root work; and, of course, to share good practices. We wanted to strengthen the Muslim community and spread the message of realistic optimism amid all the challenges we were facing.

The initial plan was to visit a maximum of sixteen cities, but the number quickly increased. We advised the local organizers to include not only the MCB affiliates in their events but also others from the community and wider society.

We visited Birmingham, Leicester and Manchester more than once to attend large summer events. Places like Cardiff organized multi-faith receptions for myself and my team. It was a whirlwind trip across England, Wales and Scotland that really energized the MCB, but it also taught me and brought me closer to my colleagues within the MCB and helped build relationships with many people. Throughout the national tour that summer I found many in the Muslim community who were not aware of what the MCB stood for. Some had the negative idea that we were probably a government lackey, and indeed I was often asked about our relationship with the government. There was still great unhappiness with Tony Blair's decision to take our country to war, and my visit was an opportunity to spell out our full commitment to the community and clarify our stance against the invasion of Iraq in 2003.

Towards the end of the tour I realized that I had only five days left before re-joining my teaching job in early September, and I had hardly seen my family over the summer. I took a short break and arranged a three-day family trip to Grenada in southern Spain. It was mainly to spend quality time with the children, but also to gain some flavour of understanding of the Muslim contribution in creating an intellectually vibrant and pluralist society in Europe several hundred years ago.

* * *

Around mid-July 2006, we came to learn from a few sources that the Blair government was working behind the scenes to create Muslim bodies that would give it the support it needed. We were not surprised, Blair had been unhappy with the MCB since the Iraq invasion. One such group, the Sufi Muslim Council (SMC), appeared in the news on 19 July 2006 apparently from nowhere. Launched in Westminster in the presence of politicians, and endorsed by Cabinet Minister,

Ruth Kelly MP of the newly-formed CLG (Communities and Local Government), the SMC claimed to 'represent the silent majority' of Sufi Muslims and with a vow to tackle extremism. Politically-conscious Muslims were amazed; our media officer, Inayat Bunglawala, dismissed the SMC as 'unrepresentative and divisive' and indeed it disappeared within a few years.

While I had been travelling across the country, Pakistan's High Commissioner to the UK, Dr Maleeha Lodhi, a renowned political scientist, invited me to an event at the High Commission on 5 September as one of the two main guest speakers. The other was Ruth Kelly who, I was informed, had accepted the invitation. But as the date neared, Dr Lodhi's office informed me that Ruth Kelly had given her apology and would not be attending – I was not surprised. Dr Lodhi went ahead with the event and on the day the High Commission was packed with dignitaries from diverse backgrounds. In my twenty-minute talk I spoke briefly about my experience of the country-wide tour on the MCB's behalf and the need to reach out to all sections of the Muslim community – as well as to wider civil society – in order to heal the fractures that had been created by the London bombings over a year before. I also spoke about the need to engage and involve Muslim youth. I then said:

> Post-7/7 Britain, however, has seen a deterioration of its tolerant pluralism and community harmony. Phrases used by some public figures and right-wing media, such as Islamic terrorism, Islamo-fascism and Islamo-Nazism are simply fuelling prejudice for Muslims. Unsurprisingly it is not only affecting far-right groups but ordinary people too. We must all work to build bridges among people in these difficult times.

While our relationship with public bodies and Muslim engagement with wider society were priorities, our primary task was to work and strengthen disadvantaged Muslim communities. In order to strengthen the capacity and improve governance in our mosques, we started a '100 Mosques Capacity Building Initiative' during my first year, once we had secured some funding to employ a highly dedicated programme manager.

The MCB had already been working with the London Mayor's office and the Greater London Assembly (GLA) to improve the conditions of Muslim Londoners, and in October 2006, two important events took place as hallmarks of our collaborative work with Mayor Livingstone. First, the *Muslims in London* report was published by the Mayor's office that drew 'on a range of data to illustrate the diversity of London's Muslim communities and barriers faced by Muslims in everyday life'[19] and addressed a number of issues to improve the conditions of Muslim Londoners; secondly, the first ever public celebration of Eid al-Fitr (the celebrations at the end of Ramadan) which attracted thousands of Londoners to Trafalgar Square.

On 27 June 2007, Tony Blair finally stepped down and Gordon Brown occupied the Prime Minister's role at 10 Downing Street. On 30 June, a jeep loaded with propane bottles was driven into the glass doors of Glasgow International Airport terminal and set ablaze. It was a terrorist attack that could have easily caused great carnage and destruction, though fortunately security bollards prevented the jeep from entering the terminal and the assailants were quickly apprehended. The MCB convened a press conference on 3 July at its offices and I spoke about the need to 'collectively work to undermine and defeat the

---

19. 'Muslims in London Report Published' (*Mayorwatch*, 24 October 2006).

terrorists who seek to divide the country'. In response to a question, I said: 'When your house is in fire, your first task is to extinguish it first and then find the causes.' It was a timely press conference that brought major media correspondents in to the small MCB office; we learned later that Whitehall departments had been following the proceedings closely.

On 29 November 2007, in collaboration with three other groups (the Muslim Association of Britain, British Muslim Forum and Al-Khoei Foundation) we launched the Mosques and Imams National Advisory Board (MINAB) to standardize the governance and capacity of hundreds of mosques. It was a community-led, but government-supported, project with great ambitions (sadly, after the Tory-led coalition government came to power in May 2010, it did not see fit to support the project).

At the 2008 AGM, I was re-elected as Secretary-General of the MCB for my second and final two-year term. I continued to consolidate the work begun during my first term in a relatively positive political climate under the Brown government who, we found, took care in the terminology they used on terrorism. For instance, when blaming terrorists Gordon Brown preferred to use the phrase 'al-Qaeda-inspired terrorism': it was small gesture, but useful. Unfortunately, our relationship with the government soured in March 2009 when news broke alleging that during an Istanbul conference (which he attended in a personal capacity) the MCB's Deputy Secretary-General, Dr Daud Abdullah, advocated attacks on those who would prevent smuggling arms to Hamas in Gaza. The Communities Secretary, Hazel Blears, contacted the MCB with a strong tone and argued that as Dr Abdullah had signed the document in Istanbul (known as the Istanbul Declaration) that advocated actions against foreign forces (that could include the Royal Navy) or Jewish people around the world, the MCB should consider his position as DSG.

It was a shock to us, we were aware Daud had made a personal visit to Istanbul on behalf of an organization he worked for, the Palestine Return Centre (PRC), and like me he was also a volunteer in the MCB. When I asked him about it he candidly answered that he had signed a document written in Arabic as an individual, along with dozens of Muslim leaders from around the world, only in support of the rights of the Gazan people. He categorically denied that the Istanbul Declaration meant attacking the Royal Navy or the Jewish people. Daud was known for his frankness and also his ability to resolve conflicts; he had been part of a delegation of British Muslim leaders to Baghdad in September 2004 to attempt to save the British hostage Kenneth Bigley (a British civil engineer who was kidnapped on 16 September 2004 by an extremist group led by Jordanian Abu Musab al-Zarqawi). We responded to Hazel Blears with this clarification, but she went public and wrote a comment piece in *The Guardian* that was also published as a letter with the same claim.[20] Daud wrote a powerful comment piece in *The Guardian* in response[21] and appeared on the BBC's flagship current affairs programme, *Newsnight*, rejecting Blears' claim.

The matter was being blown out of all proportion; we felt some quarters in the establishment probably wanted to punish the MCB because of its support for the cause of justice for Palestinians. Attempts by the Government to remove an elected senior official of the MCB constituted an act of unprecedented interference in the affairs of a faith community organization. We discussed the issue among the MCB leadership circle and with the Central Working Committee, before clarifying the issue by reiterating our resolute stand against all forms of indiscriminate violence and

---

20. Hazel Blears 'Our shunning of the MCB is not grandstanding' (*The Guardian*, 25 March 2009).
21. Daud Abdullah, 'My reply to Hazel Blears' (*The Guardian*, 26 March 2009).

opposition to all forms of prejudice including anti-Semitism and Islamophobia. The relationship with the Department for Communities and Local Government, which was already weak by then, formally ended. So did our formal relationship with the government, it seemed. However, in a bizarre turn of events Hazel Blears quit the Cabinet in early June for political reasons, and John Denham took over the Ministry. John was known to be a fair-minded politician and felt that the MCB as a national Muslim body should not be left in the cold. It took us a further six months to re-establish our relationship with the Government.

* * *

Being in the public domain gave me an opportunity to meet many wonderful people and attend important events. Over the years I often encountered situations that taught me vital lessons in life, echoing my father's views expressed to me as a child that we should keep on learning until the end of our lives.

One such situation was my libel complaint against the BBC following the broadcast of its flagship programme, *Question Time*, on 12 March 2009. During the broadcast, the panel was asked about the controversial protests against British troops, who were parading in Luton on their return from duty in Iraq. During the discussion that followed, one of the Question Time panellists suggested that 'despite having been asked many times to condemn the kidnapping and killing of British soldiers, the leadership of the MCB had failed to do so'.[22] The panellist further suggested that 'the MCB leadership believed the kidnapping and killing of British soldiers to be a good and Islamic thing.' This was a shocking allegation and totally

---

22. Staff and agencies, 'BBC in £45,000 libel payout to Muslim Council of Britain leader' (*The Guardian*, 16 July 2009).

false, the MCB had a history of publicly speaking against such crimes, so I took legal action against the BBC over the issue. After prolonged negotiation, in July 2009 the BBC apologized to me in the High Court and agreed to pay libel damages, together with the legal costs; I donated all of the money to a charity.

Towards the end of my second term, I was busier than ever with the MCB. My term as SG would come to an end in mid-2010 and I felt there was still much to do. The sense of responsibility that drove me to become a community activist and brought me into the MCB's hot-seat after 7/7 was something that I never took lightly. Over the years, I met and worked with people from all walks of life – from ordinary Muslims and people from the wider society to high-flying individuals in the upper echelons of the British establishment – from the realms of politics, media, the Armed Forces, Civil Service, faith groups and even royalty. My LOCOG role also gave me an additional opportunity to meet and exchange ideas with globally-renowned individuals. Every November I represented the Muslim community in the Remembrance Day commemoration at the Cenotaph; standing with other dignitaries and armed forces personnel on this memorial day always reminded me of the great sacrifice of those who died and suffered in the Great War and in the wars that have followed.

In late November 2009, the MCB came up with the unique idea of organizing an annual Muslim dinner (we called it the Muslim Leadership Dinner, or MLD) as a means to network with leaders, opinion formers and people of excellence from all walks of life and celebrate the contribution of Muslims to British society. We agreed to have the first event in London on 22 February 2010. Preparation time was short, so volunteers and staff worked flat out to make a plan, book a venue in central London, find sponsors and invite people – Muslims and non-Muslims – from across the country. We invited a few senior leaders from the three main political parties. By the end of December we had also patched up our relationship with the Government. The evening itself, at the London Marriott, Grosvenor Square, was buzzing with energy and confidence; two Cabinet ministers (Jack Straw MP and John Denham MP) and Liberal Democrat leader, Nick Clegg MP, spoke of their optimism in the MCB's continuous work with wider society. Sadly, no senior Tory leader could attend. Professor Tariq Ramadan, as the keynote speaker, gave an excellent speech on Muslim identity and all in all it was a highly upbeat event. Since then the MLD has become a regular feature in the MCB's yearly calendar.

* * *

The MCB Annual General Meeting on 20 June 2010 was a few days away when we learned about a secret sixty-three page document that the Quilliam Foundation (QF), a think-tank formed by former Muslim extremists, had sent to senior Government ministers and their special advisers in mid-June. The strategic briefing paper, *Preventing Terrorism: where next for Britain?* was, we surmised, meant to advise the UK's new Coalition government, formed between the Conservatives and the Liberal Democrats, about the 'Prevent' programme, a government initiative launched in 2008 that aimed to 'stop people becoming terrorists or supporting violent extremists.'[23] The document did not remain secret for long, and many in the community who came across the report were shocked to know it categorized major Muslim groups as political (or entry-level) Islamists and thus 'non-violent extremists'. We expected that the Coalition government would rather listen to the recommendations made by the CLG Committee's March 2010 report on the Prevent agenda, *Preventing Violent*

---

23. HM Government, *The Prevent Strategy: A Guide for Local Partners in England* (The Stationery Office, 2008).

Extremism, but that did not happen and later in the year we learned that the government conducted its own review on Prevent that, to our knowledge, ignored opinions from the Muslim community and experts in the field on both sides of the Atlantic. It adopted a so-called 'conveyor belt theory', discussed in more detail in Chapter 7. Many believed that the government apparently preferred to take its cue from the QF's assertion on extremism. It was a missed opportunity, and naturally the new Prevent did not have the buy-in from the majority in the Muslim community and remained, and continues to remain, a divisive issue.

Chapter 5

2010: The Coming Storm

AS 24 DECEMBER 2009 moved into the early hours of Christmas Day we experienced a rare white Christmas; the 'big freeze' had settled on London. My children's eyes lit up, though they were now well into their late teens and twenties, and the house suddenly filled with laughter. I was flooded with memories of them as toddlers, myself still new to London, and their sounds of delight at the smallest of things. It was a happy flashback in an otherwise turbulent time.

As we were gazing at the snow in south London, a young man called Umar Farouk Abdulmutallab, freshly arrived from Ghana, was joining 280 fellow passengers on Northwest Airlines Flight 253, boarding at Amsterdam's Schiphol airport and bound for Detroit. The youngest son of a wealthy Nigerian banker (and one of the richest men in Africa), 23-year-old Abdulmutallab had been head of University College London's (UCL) Islamic society for a year while studying for an engineering degree between 2005 and 2008. He was gifted and well-travelled; he was also carrying a bomb.

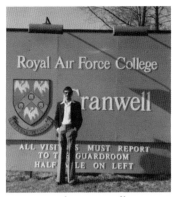

Armament Engg. Course – Group
picture with Base Commander, 1979.

Arrival at RAF College,
Cranwell, 1978.

Flying Officer BAF, 1981.

British Army Course, Kent, 1981.

HRH Prince Charles visit in 2001.

With Yousuf Islam, 2001.

MBE presented by the Queen, 2003.

Religious Tolerance in Britain Conference, 2004.

HRH Prince Charles visit to London East Academy, 2004.

HRH Prince Charles visit to London East Academy, 2004.

Cardiff Lord Mayor visit, 2006.

GLA Conference, 2007.

Visiting Royal Navy Base, Portsmouth, 2007.

TUC General Secretary Brendon Barber (now Sir), 2007.

Malaysian PM A. Badawi's visit to ELM, 2007.

TUC Conference, Brighton, 2007.

Minister Mike O'Brien, 2008.

Lord Chief Justice Lord Philips visiting ELM Archives, 2008.

With the Sultan of Sokoto at MCB office, 2008.

Citizens UK Peace Vigil on Paris, 2015.

Prof. Malcolm Grant and ELM Chair Habibur Rahman, 2016.

Prof. Sir Michael Barber and other ELM leaders, 2016.

HRH Princess Anne and ELM Archive Team, 2017.

HRH Princess Anne and ELM Chair Habibur Rahman, 2017.

The Nigerian entered the plane posing as a Sudanese refugee. About twenty minutes before the plane was due to land in Detroit he hid himself in the toilet, finally emerging covered with a blanket. Those nearby heard popping noises, then smelled a foul odour as Abdulmutallab's trouser leg and then the wall of the plane quickly caught fire. There was confusion, panic and screams. A quick-thinking passenger, Dutch film director Jasper Schuringa, jumped on the Nigerian as flight attendants rushed forwards with fire extinguishers. Spraying him down, the would-be bomber was restrained and frogmarched towards the front of the airplane, his trousers gone and clutching at agonizing burns over his legs and crotch.

For the previous three weeks, Abdulmutallab had been 'wearing in' a new type of bomb, obtained in Yemen. It was concealed in his underpants, earning him the soubriquet 'the underpants bomber', and was to be set off by mixing two explosive substances with liquid acid, similar to the bomb that British 'shoe bomber' Richard Reid had attempted to ignite aboard a transatlantic flight in December 2001. The very fact that Abdulmutallab had worn the bomb for so long (in an attempt to get used to its feel) was likely to have affected its efficacy. On touchdown in the US he was immediately arrested. Al-Qaeda in Yemen claimed responsibility for the attack, describing it as revenge for the United States' role in a Yemeni military offensive against the network.

The young Nigerian had been on the radar of several intelligence agencies, but flaws in data sharing meant his US visa was never revoked. His own father had passed on warnings that Abdulmutallab had 'extreme religious views'. Investigations pointed to an association in Yemen with one Anwar al-Awlaki, deemed by the US authorities as a 'spiritual guide' of al-Qaeda.

The episode unfortunately led to unfounded suspicions that the East London Mosque provided a platform to 'extremist preachers'. This was because in 2003, al-Awlaki, then residing in the US and an Islamic scholar of international repute, was invited by some volunteers at the ELM to give talks on early Islamic history (as did some other British mosques at the time). The alarm bells did not sound for us because al-Awlaki was then in the authorities' good books. It is reported that he was even a guest at the Pentagon after the 9/11 attacks. But that was to change and by 2009 al-Awlaki had become associated with al-Qaeda activities in Yemen, and was under surveillance. The ELM management, unaware of the extent of his radicalisation, did not object when an external organizer, who had hired one of the many rooms at the London Muslim Centre adjacent to the Mosque, invited him to speak via a video link. I was abroad on holiday in Bangladesh at the time the mosque management allowed this to go ahead. Abdulmutallab's association with an al-Qaeda leader, and then this person's association with East London Mosque – however tenuous – affected the institution's reputation for years to come. As chair of the East London Mosque Trust at the time, I was ultimately responsible – we had erred in our judgement, which I publicly acknowledged, and the ELM reviewed the situation and reaffirmed that the 'mosque will not tolerate its facilities being used for extremist groups or speakers'.[24] However, this did not stop right-wing groups or correspondents from falsely linking the ELM with Islamic extremism.

* * *

Davos is a beautiful, calm place surrounded by hills, and in January 2010 the Swiss resort was smothered in snow. I had been invited to the prestigious World Economic Forum (WEF) to join a panel discussion on 'Does Religion's Claim to Truth

---

24. 'ELM Trust Statement on Anwar Al-Awlaki' (East London Mosque and London Muslim Centre, 6 November 2010).

Lead to Violence?' and a couple of other events. It was my first such gathering and I was rather overawed to be among such heavy hitters from the global political, economic and charity scene. The environment was business-like but somewhat relaxed, and the programmes were highly professionally run. I met a number of important figures from Britain and other parts of the world and had a relaxed chat with some of them.

There were four other members on the panel with impressive backgrounds in their own fields: Muhammad Ashafa (an imam working for interfaith mediation in northern Nigeria), Edna Brocke (head of the Old Synagogue Memorial in Essen, Germany), Marcia Pally (Professor of Multilingual Multicultural Studies at New York University) and Thomas Wipf (President of the Council, Federation of Swiss Protestant Churches, Switzerland). The panel was moderated by Urs Leuthard, from Swiss radio and television (SRF). It was an insightful discussion on the causes of violence and the use or misuse of religions behind it. All contributed from their experiences, but Muhammad Ashafa stole the show. He had been a highly-bigoted religious figure in the past, but had turned from his former ways (sadly a conflict between violent religious extremists and the corrupt government practices in northern Nigeria, with widespread abuses on both sides) and had been working to bridge gaps between communities. On the return journey, at the airport I met Barbara Stocking, Chief Executive of Oxfam GB, and while travelling together we had the opportunity to discuss how our rich charity sector could help address growing social inequalities in Britain.

On my return I discovered an inquiry had begun at UCL to investigate the 'underpants bomber' affair. I was approached by the UCL Provost to join an independent inquiry panel comprising four members from outside the university (including the Chair of the panel, Dame Fiona Caldicott, who was Principal of Somerville College, Oxford as well as being the Pro Vice-Chancellor at the University of Oxford), a representative of the lay members of the UCL Council, plus two UCL staff. After much thought and consultation with my MCB colleagues, I agreed to join.

We knew the eyes of the world, and the media, would be upon us and took our task extremely seriously. For weeks we deliberated, questioned witnesses and combed through the evidence provided from a variety of sources. After several in-depth discussion sessions, we concluded in October 2010 that there was no evidence Abdulmutallab had been radicalized while a student at the university, or that conditions there were conducive to his radicalization.[25] We did say, however, that the university's approach to freedom of expression and hosting visiting speakers left students open to risks in the future. Our report called for a number of improvements, including a better vetting system for guest speakers and more communication between staff and students. The inquiry suggested a review of the university's code of conduct on freedom of speech to 'reduce the future risk of students being radicalised'. However, we conceded that these measures alone would 'not eliminate the risk of radicalisation of UCL students'. The report's findings were not popular with several neoconservative commentators, who held fast to their belief that the university must have been in some way complicit with Abdulmutallab's descent. Perhaps these critics wanted us to 'prove' that the world-renowned British academic institution was culpable. But we reported our findings accurately, objectivity and to the best of our professional ability. Our remit was limited to Abdulmutallab's life at UCL, not to find where and how else he became radicalized.

* * *

---

25. 'Umar Farouk Abdulmutallab: Report to UCL Council of inde-pendent inquiry panel' (UCL, September 2010).

Soon after my arrival in England I learned a British saying: 'It never rains but it pours', and I should have seen the political storm clouds gathering on the horizon. After our panel began looking into the Abdulmutallab affair, another controversy erupted.

As the end of January 2010 approached, arguments raged inside the MCB about attending Holocaust Memorial Day (HMD), the annual commemoration of the world's worst genocide. We had only attended once before – in January 2008 – since its inauguration in 2001. Our 'boycott' was national news and had brought us negative press: something not all of my colleagues, or some of the activists in the Muslim community, fully understood. But the Israeli invasion of Gaza (Operation Cast Lead) and the resulting massacres of Palestinians created such anti-Israeli sentiment among the MCB's 500-strong affiliates that colleagues decided not to attend in 2009. Why was this a big issue? Surely sending someone to a national memorial such as this was a no-brainer? The answer was not as simple as 'anti-Semitism', at least not in our eyes. Instead it lay in the recent history of how this day had come about.

During the late 1990s, Britain's Jewish community was lobbying hard for an official Remembrance Day to commemorate the horrendous crimes against humanity committed during the Holocaust. On 10 June 1999, Labour MP (later Greater London Assembly member) Andrew Dismore asked Prime Minister Tony Blair about the creation of such a memorial day. Blair replied: 'I am determined to ensure that the horrendous crimes against humanity committed during the Holocaust are never forgotten. The ethnic cleansing and killing that has taken place in Europe in recent weeks are a stark example of the need for vigilance.'[26] A consultation

---

26. *Hansard*, HC Deb., 11 June 1999, col. 408.

followed suit towards the end of that year to which the MCB responded in December, saying:

> The [MCB] notes that the consultation document acknowledges that the troubling repetition of human tragedies in the world today restates the continuing need for vigilance ... We also note that one of the aims and objectives of the Holocaust Remembrance Day is to 'reflect on recent atrocities that raise similar issues.' However the Muslim Council of Britain urges the Government not to miss this excellent opportunity to articulate its vision of a multi-cultural Britain by naming the Remembrance Day as European Union Genocide Remembrance Day rather than Holocaust Remembrance Day. The title conveys a powerful message. It needs to be more inclusive to be really effective and cohesive.[27]

At any rate, the government of the day didn't listen to the MCB's suggestions and went ahead with the new Holocaust Memorial Day. Meanwhile, my MCB leadership colleagues continued to call for a more inclusive day commemorating the deaths in places like Rwanda and Bosnia, along with the Holocaust. The MCB did not send official representatives to the ceremony, which was widely presented as a 'boycott' by sections of the media, and the issue became the subject of frequent (and fiery) internal debate within the organization.

At every meeting before HMD, arguments would arise about attending. Every year, the majority would vote not to go and colleagues would try to explain (without great success, unfortunately) that non-attendance was on the basis

27. Reported in, Muhammad Abdul Bari, 'Draft speech: Trade unions and the Muslim Community' (Trades Union Congress, 12th April 2007).

of principle and did not constitute a boycott. For example, in January 2003 Iqbal Sacranie, the then Secretary-General, wrote to the Chair of the HMD National Event Planning Group, based in Edinburgh, saying:

> The Muslim Council of Britain have conveyed their reservations in the previous years that the Holocaust Memorial Day National Event should be an inclusive event. I have been advised by the MCB Central Working Committee to reiterate the British Muslim community's unequivocal denunciation and condemnation of the Nazi holocaust against the Jewish and some other non-German communities before and during the Second World War. We are one with fellow members of the British Jewish community in their pains and anguish over this savage and shameful event in recent history. There is great concern in the community that our government needs to do more to make clear its moral outrage or has it exercised its considerable economic and political influence in order to bring about an end to both the Israeli occupation and unceasing brutalisation of the Palestinian people and the deadly violation of their human rights. More recently, hundreds of children and civilians have been killed … I hardly need to say that our reservations concern only the ceremony and not the Nazi holocaust per se … Genocide is the most abhorrent and outrageous crime against humanity and we should all stand together in opposing it, whenever and wherever it happens. However, given its present construct and the deep anguish felt in the community about the happenings in the Occupied Territories, we believe in the foregoing it may not be appropriate

for us to take part in the ceremony. But please convey our deep sense of agony over the Nazi Holocaust.[28]

Two years later, *The Guardian* published an article, 'Holocaust Memorial day is too exclusive', quoting Sir Iqbal saying: 'Every year since the HMD was inaugurated in 2001, the MCB has been subjected to intimidating smears of anti-Semitism in the press. We have been accused of wanting to "scrap" the HMD out of "hatred" of the Jewish people. This is hysterical nonsense.'[29]

In my second year as Secretary-General, we finally voted to attend the 2008 memorial. However, the ghastly Israeli aggression in Gaza during the 2008–2009 Cast Lead operation put paid to attendance the following year. Some might allege that this was a sign of the MCB's latent anti-Semitism, but hand on heart, I have never entertained such notions and I can say that like me many other Muslims have never held any ill-feelings or animosity towards the Jewish people and their unique place in history (and suffering); in fact, myself and many others within the MCB had worked alongside Jewish colleagues and counted figures from the Jewish community among friends. However, what rankled was the way HMD was used to become a litmus test of the MCB's adherence to 'British values'. For example, Blair's CLG Minister, Ruth Kelly, declared in October 2006:

> There are also some people who don't feel it right to join in the commemorations of Holocaust Memorial Day even though it has helped raise

---

28. For further details see, 'Holocaust Day: MCB regrets exclusion of Palestinian genocide' (Muslim Council of Britain, 27 January 2003).
29. Iqbal Sacranie, 'Holocaust Memorial day is too exclusive' (*The Guardian*, 20 September 2005).

awareness not just of the Jewish holocaust, but also more contemporary atrocities like the Rwanda genocide. That's also their right.

But I can't help wondering why those in leadership positions who say they want to achieve religious tolerance and a cohesive society would choose to boycott an event which marks, above all, our common humanity and respect for each other.

When society's core values are transgressed, it can, as a minimum, lead to resentment. But at worst if we fail to assert and act to implement our shared values this makes us weaker in the fight against extremism and allows it to flourish.[30]

The MCB regarded its autonomy and democratic ethos as sacrosanct, and such attempts to push it towards a certain course of action could only backfire. For me, they should not be linked but this was not an easy issue and was one that others, better than myself, had also tussled with.

In my fourth and final year as Secretary-General, a huge row began brewing within the organization about the next HMD, which would take place on 27 January 2010. I had spoken with a few senior leaders in our decision-making body, the Central Working Committee (CWC), and tried to reverse the decision of non-attendance once and for all. By this time, quite a few CWC members were ready to reverse the decision, but there was still formidable opposition and by a majority decision at a meeting in November 2009 we decided, once again, that we would not attend in 2010. I came up with a plan to convince the CWC members to reverse their stance. The next meeting, on 17 January, began with a tense atmosphere. The Chair of

---

30. Ruth Kelly, 'Britain: our values, our responsibilities' (The National Archives, 11 October 2006).

the meeting fought hard to keep the calm and I put my case as powerfully as I could; HMD was in ten days' time.

Heavyweights entered the debate on both sides and the arguments and counter-arguments flew back and forth. Those in favour to attend held up the principle that it was morally right to participate while also being firmly and vocally opposed to Israel's illegal and oppressive policies in occupied Palestine; those opposed pointed out that HMD could not be sanitized from the political context, it had not been renamed 'Genocide Memorial Day', and it should not be construed as anti-Semitism. They highlighted that prominent Jewish intellectuals like Antony Lerman and Norman Finkelstein also critiqued such an exclusive commemoration.

At the end of the meeting, to my relief, a majority decision was carried and we agreed that the MCB would attend Holocaust Memorial Day in 2010. This put an end to an episode that had divided the MCB for nearly a decade and caused us a great deal of reputational damage. As I was in Davos on the day itself, the organization sent a senior leader, Dr Shuja Shafi, a recently retired NHS consultant microbiologist, long-standing interfaith activist and head of our Health and Chaplaincy committee (later the MCB's Secretary-General, 2014–2016), on our behalf. The event passed with all the solemnity and decorum you would expect and the MCB was lauded for its decision. Individual and group learning is not often straightforward.

* * *

February broke and with it a coldness that lingered long into the morning air. While nature provided a physical chill, a different type of chill was received when we became aware of the preparation of a Channel 4 documentary centred around Tower Hamlets, where the East London Mosque was situated.

Rumours spread that journalist Andrew Gilligan, who had resigned from the BBC's flagship *Today* programme in 2004 following a controversial report into the government's alleged 'sexing up' of an Iraq weapons dossier and the subsequent death of Gilligan's government source, the scientist David Kelly, was working with Channel 4's current affairs programme, *Dispatches*, to produce an exposé of a group close to the mosque. We suspected this was the Islamic Forum of Europe (IFE), which I had helped form in 1988 with diasporic Bangladeshis to support the professional development of the new community. The IFE was now run by a network of friends and activists with strong connections to the ELM. In the heated and febrile atmosphere of Tower Hamlets' tribal politics, which traced its way back to Bangladesh's pained independence in 1971 (with a broadly 'secularist' camp on the one side, and a more religious one on the other), the IFE had started out quite well, attracting mainly first generation Bangladeshi professionals. By the time I had moved on in the mid-1990s, and became more involved with Citizens UK's early chapter in the East End (The East London Community Organizations, TELCO) and in the formation of the Muslim Council of Britain, the Islamic Forum Europe gradually turned into a community body. In recent years it has been painted by one side of the tribal divide as an 'Islamist' organization.

Gilligan was something of an obsessive when it came to east London. As *The Daily Telegraph*'s London editor, he had been writing in his columns and blogs about the election of members of the anti-war Respect movement to Tower Hamlets council in 2005–2006. Many of Respect's members were local Bengali activists and Iraq anti-war protestors, and in their individual capacity some of them were local IFE activists. Things had been much polarized in Tower Hamlets since the local Labour Party was placed in special measures, over a decade earlier. The intervention of anti-war orator (and Scottish ex-Labour MP), George Galloway, who had helped found Respect out of the massive 2003 'Stop The War' movement and who was elected as the Member of Parliament for Bethnal Green and Bow in 2005, changed the political dynamics in Tower Hamlets. Some saw this as 'entryism' of radical groups into local institutions and organs of influence and power.

However, the interest in what became known as 'Islamism' – or politically-inspired Islam – in the East End of London began with some former members of the radical pan-Islamic political group, Hizb ut-Tahrir (HT), which became very active during the 1990s. At one stage, Tony Blair wanted to ban it but this didn't materialize, though HT remains banned in Germany and several Middle Eastern and Asian countries. Author, and later Quilliam Foundation founder, Ed Husain was one of HT's east London members; a local lad and son of Bangladeshi parents. By his own admission he was caught up in an identity vacuum, belonging neither to his father's culture (suffused with its subcontinent flavours, where English was most definitely a second language) or the western culture of his non-Muslim contemporaries at school. The HT boys were angry: at the poverty and racism around them; the lack of acceptance into wider society; and at the abuse, as they saw it, heaped onto the *ummah*, or the worldwide family of Muslims, in places such as Bosnia and Palestine. They were also youths looking to rebel – not into gangs, or drugs or music, but through a romanticized revival of faith. Burning with zeal, Husain joined the Young Muslim Organization (YMO – one of the oldest Muslim youth groups in Britain, later on affiliated with IFE), but finding that too limiting was then drawn into HT; the 'conveyor belt' to extremism.

During the 1990s, the young members of HT would come hectoring and barracking our congregation and imams, claiming we were taking part in haram (forbidden) activities such as democracy and voting. They accused us of being 'sell outs' and tried to make our life difficult. Later HT gave birth to an even more extreme group called al-Muhajiroun (AM), which was led by self-styled 'Sheikh' Omar Bakri Mohammed (some in the media called him 'the Tottenham Ayatollah') who later fled to Lebanon. Al-Muhajiroun is currently a banned organization in Britain, run by one of Bakri's followers, the lawyer Anjem Choudary, and has alleged links to both the 2013 Woolwich killers of off-duty soldier Lee Rigby and scores of fighters in Syria, Somalia, Pakistan and other conflicts. It was only when a fellow HT activist murdered a Christian student at his college did Ed Husain claim he had finally seen the error of his ways. A few like him have experienced this journey from one extreme to another, with a common outcome – they have all been a thorn in the side of the mainstream Muslim community, both before and after their change. As they shifted to the other end of the spectrum, without any sense of irony on their part, they now see the Muslims they had previously smeared as 'sell outs' when they were themselves extreme in their views as 'religious extremists'.

In his book, *The Islamist*, Husain chronicled how groups such as the IFE were, in his view, part of a conspiracy to overthrow democracy and install an Islamic caliphate. But to suggest there were cadres of highly-trained sleeper agents, waiting to take over modern pluralist and stable democracies, was far from reality. The issue of political Islam and Islamism rapidly gained currency, especially after the 9/11 and 7/7 atrocities. For most practising Muslims, Islam is a comprehensive way of life. It teaches and inspires individuals to be socially active for the good of people and society. While politics and religion are now mostly separate in the West, for reasons of history this has not always been the case in the Muslim world. Even today there is no reason to expect that all non-Western societies will arrive at Western conclusions regarding secularism and liberalism. The West arrived at secularism after horrendous religious wars due to Christian Europe's historical inability to peacefully live with religious diversity. Historically, Islam never quite had that problem, and so Muslims never felt that religion and politics needed separating.

Political parties in the Muslim world, and even Muslim organizations in the West, that uphold the idea that 'Islam should guide personal as well as social and political life' are now lumped into this misunderstood box of 'political Islam', and the more controversial neologism of 'Islamism'. To many people today, the word 'Islamist' means an extremist or even a 'terrorist' – yet there are peaceful Islamic political parties (for example, the Ennahda party in Tunisia) that have shared power with secular groups – even given up the reins of government – in the interests of people and democratic stability. The general dearth of religious literacy, as well as the lack of a proper understanding of the social reality facing minority religious communities in Europe, added to the suspicion. In the post-9/11 world, the continuous supply of 'expert opinions' on Muslims from sections of the media exacerbated the negative narrative on Islam and Muslims. Perhaps one could argue that Muslims were also too insular, too absorbed in their own world. And perhaps some in Tower Hamlets, a microcosm of the chaotic politics of Bangladesh, were too absorbed in the jungle of local politics.

Extremism on either end is probably the easiest option for some people – one can go from one extreme to another like a pendulum. But staying consistently on the middle-path with principle, as Islam teaches its followers, is not that easy. People in the middle of the road are criticized from both extremes and in the process they have to endure harsher criticism than most; they need to be very thick-skinned. Sticking to principles and moderation has its own penalty: Muslim groups and individuals in recent British public life, in spite of their limitations and weaknesses, have been treated unfairly by the political class because of their disagreement with some policies. But by keeping faith in the centre-ground of life and working close with robust elements of civil society, such as those that are fighting for social justice and remaining steadfast, they can weather this.

* * *

It is impossible for an outsider to understand this without knowing something of the context and complexity of Tower Hamlets' Bangladeshi identity. Most of the local Bangladeshis who made up the East London Mosque's congregation hailed from greater Sylhet, in north-eastern Bangladesh and abutting the Indian province of Assam. In fact, probably over three-quarters of British Bangladeshis come from that region. Many had arrived with families, rural folk who struggled to adapt to urban life in cosmopolitan cities. Many of them were interlinked in some way with one another in Tower Hamlets. People lived, breathed, ate, worked, gossiped, even fought and generally shared their lives together within a few square miles of the crumbling Victorian estates. The close patchwork of estates and families had not stopped the rise of overcrowding and deprivation as traditional industries disappeared.

The history of Bengali men arriving in Britain dates back to the seventeenth century, mostly lascar seamen working on ships for the Empire. Before the First World War, there were 51,616 South Asian lascars living in Britain, the majority of whom were of Bengali descent. In 1971, following the emergence of Bangladesh as an independent country, many Bangladeshis, particularly from the Sylhet region, migrated to Britain as a result of changes to Britain's immigration laws. The ever-changing Tower Hamlets became their home, as it had once been to Huguenots, Jewish, Irish and (more recently) those fleeing the wars of Somalia. As the Bangladeshis moved in, the now-affluent Jewish community – who had fled to Britain in their thousands from pogroms in Russia and Eastern Europe in the late nineteenth and early twentieth centuries

– moved out, or had already left. The Bangladeshi men who comprised the majority at this point worked in the garment and textile, or restaurant trades, often in buildings that were still owned by Jewish landlords. Racial tensions in the area began simmering between the Bangladeshis and bigoted local thugs.

Where once Oswald Mosley's Blackshirts had marched against the Jewish communities in 1936 – leading to the famous Battle of Cable Street – there was a large rise in the number of physical attacks on Bangladeshi immigrants by white skinhead gangs, particularly around the Brick Lane area. Residents began to fight back by creating committees and youth groups, with anti-fascists joining them. From the Bangladeshi community this was led mainly by first-generation youth. On 4 May 1978, a 25-year-old Bangladeshi garment worker, Altab Ali, was murdered in a racist attack as he walked home from work. This led to over 7,000 people, mostly Bangladeshis, marching in a demonstration against racist violence and walking behind his coffin to 10 Downing Street. His murder was the trigger for the first significant political organization against racism by local Bangladeshi activists.

As most people hailed from rural religious, naturally conservative backgrounds, mosques and prayer places sprang up to serve them across the East End of London. One was the historic Brick Lane Mosque, which started life in 1743 as a Protestant chapel for London's French Huguenot community, then became the Spitalfields Great Synagogue for Jewish refugees in the late nineteenth century – where in 1904 Jewish anarchists pelted ultra-orthodox religious Jews with bacon and fought pitched battles on the Day of Atonement. It finally reopened in 1976 as Brick Lane Jamme (Great) Mosque. The other was the East London Mosque, London's oldest mosque, which moved to its present site in 1975. When the ELM Management Committee undertook construction of a major multi-purpose community complex (later known as the London Muslim Centre) towards the end of the 1990s, local Muslims responded with extraordinary zeal and financial sacrifice. The LMC has been attracting politicians, ambassadors, lawyers and journalists from all backgrounds ever since. The Queen even spoke of it in her 2004 Christmas message.

With varied traditions these two institutions – the East London Mosque and Brick Lane Mosque – were laying the foundations of Bangladeshi Muslims' religious identity in London in the 1970s and 1980s. Today the *adhan* (call to prayer) emanating from its minaret is as much a part of the character of East End life as was the sound of Yiddish on the streets 100 years earlier.

* * *

I became Chair of the ELM's Board of Trustees in 2002. During the period of my leadership of the Muslim Council of Britain (2006–2010), I had made a few attempts to resign from the post at the ELM because I was overworked. But I was persuaded by my fellow trustees to 'stay for just another year, Dr Bari bhai'. And so I did. I had a strong team of dedicated volunteers and I did not have too much day-to-day involvement in the affairs of the mosque. I was working for the local education authority, so I could just about fit it in with my other responsibilities.

Following the 7/7 bombings, when volunteers from the mosque rushed to help the wounded, the ELM began to come under a greater public spotlight. The activities of younger volunteers were more likely to be noticed and the 'old ways' of doing things were starting to show strain. We had speakers coming from overseas and sometimes their 'unreconstructed' (read: conservative, orthodox or literal) views jarred with the sensibilities of a modern, secular society. Hostile articles on blogs and elsewhere started attacking us with excerpts of unpalatable speeches – typically about gays, Jews, women, or quotes from religious texts mostly taken out of context – often organized by third parties renting meeting rooms in the LMC.

As a community institution, we took our reputation seriously: we had to, as we were a registered charity. But our procedures and management weren't always up to the task, we have already seen what happened with Anwar al-Awlaki. Today we take great pains in vetting all speakers and organizations using our facility, to such an extent that some Muslims in our community now think we are too 'politically correct'. Given the nature of what were usually openly Islamophobic blogs, we often tried cross-referencing the information they leaked or alleged (about our speakers) with more authentic sources, rather than resorting to knee-jerk reactions. Of course, this took time and often we were working reactively with occasional mistakes. In trying to spend time finding out about speakers, we encountered another difficulty: most of the hostile blogs were seemingly deliberately targeting some of the Muslim community's more popular theological figures. We had to be careful not to disallow someone on the basis of a possibly dubious story and thus risk alienating an entire congregation; it was not easy to strike a balance. On individuals we were not sure about we contacted the local police for their advice.

The visibility generated by the mosque bred envy and criticism within some quarters of our own community, too. The political divisions back in Bangladesh had entered local political and religious circles, leading to accusations from one side or another about their complicity in various events. These two tribes would often polarize Tower Hamlets and still do, sadly feeding into the hostile narratives about the ELM and IFE that a few right-wing commentators and journalists have loved to repeat ever since. This they have been doing often without counter-checking the facts or informing their readers or viewers that their sources of information often came from one side or another in this internecine struggle. The reality is that most people know one another in our community. There were intermarriages, yet cousin fought cousin in gang wars, drugs tore families apart and the divisions of 'back home' had been imported into secular politics – even into the mosques.

With local politics divisive, and religious leaders sometimes sucked into communal and political matters, it was only a matter of time before the ELM was in someone's sights; someone in the mainstream media. That was when we came to learn about the *Dispatches* programme.

* * *

Channel 4 broadcast 'Britain's Islamic Republic' on 1 March 2010. The production company had written to us on 17 February, giving us just over one week to respond to several of their allegations. Sadly, our robust responses were hardly used or were presented in a cynical fashion. In addition to some choice quotes and undercover footage of a few IFE activists claiming to have 'their people' inserted into positions of power, there were curiously dark readings of common Islamic phrases, such as *da'wah* (meaning introducing Islam or 'to invite' someone to learn about Islam, commonly translated as to 'proselytize') to creepily insinuate an Islamic takeover was being planned. In essence, the programme alleged four things: that the mosque professed tolerance and moderation but in reality condoned and supported violent extremism; that it had obtained £10million of public funding and had diverted some funds intended to combat violent extremism to an 'extremist' group, the IFE; that it knowingly permitted extremist speakers to speak at its premises; and finally, that it was deceiving worshippers about the true nature of activities and was complicit in 'abusing the House of Allah'. These were serious allegations!

An ordinary citizen who had not entered the mosque would have been appalled and confused by these allegations. Because of this type of twisted narrative surrounding established Muslim bodies since 7/7 and then through to the murder of Lee Rigby in Woolwich in 2013 and beyond, the community has felt it is 'in the dock' and subject to murky journalism. The film showed the IFE as some sinister, all-powerful body infiltrating the local council as part of a greater master plan to turn Tower Hamlets into an 'Islamic state'. Loud-mouthed nobodies and activists with tenuous connections to the mosque were painted as some kind of fearsome cadres. Those of us who knew the IFE, and disagreed with it at times after it turned into a community body, knew it was being painted into some grand role it simply did not and could not fulfil. It simply didn't have the kind of structure or personnel, let alone finances, to achieve these alleged goals.

Accusations of 'entryism' against the IFE, and by default the mosque, were also lined up from one of our local MPs, Labour's Jim Fitzpatrick. He had walked out of a Muslim wedding ceremony at the mosque complex the year before after complaining about segregated seating, despite having accepted the invitation in advance knowing full well about the segregated seating arrangement, which was mostly in line with traditional Bangladeshi custom. It was a private wedding event, so he was publicly criticized by the local people for his outburst. Another antagonism came from Tower Hamlets' local 'secular' Bengali faction, unhappy with the area's 'religious' faction (both, in fact, could be blinkered by their tribalism). Local political bust-ups were given a national stage. In a comment piece in *The Guardian*, the MCB's former spokesperson, Inayat Bunglawala, suggested that many of the people interviewed on the programme actually had hidden agendas of their own and were using Gilligan and the programme to voice their own grievances that they could no longer 'take the votes of local Muslims for granted'.[31] Surprisingly, not a single existing or former senior or even middle-ranking IFE leader was brought in to 'prove' the theory of a takeover. As for the mosque, it had its share of weaknesses, but the lazy journalism, combined with the complicity of ideologues with hidden agendas, and political factions with axes to grind, was mindboggling.

How much of these allegations were actually believable? Was there really something going on that I did not know about? I was pretty knowledgeable about the borough, as I had been working as a teacher for its Education Authority since 1997. While there was a strong presence of Bangladeshi-origin councillors in its Council chamber, including some with conservative religious practices, at that time there were hardly any Bangladeshis in the Tower Hamlets senior management team (except for a short period in the future when one Mr Lutfur Ali was deputy Chief Executive) and certainly none from the IFE. There was only a small handful of Bangladeshis in middle management. Yes, many Bangladeshis worked in administrative or reception positions in the Council's various premises, as well as in schools across the borough, of which some may have had links with the IFE. But how could such ragtag junior staff possibly plan for an effective 'takeover' of the borough? To most people I spoke with, the theory was meant to undermine whatever little progress the community had been making. But for many outside the borough and unfamiliar with Tower Hamlets they must have felt there was no smoke without fire, and herein lay the danger. The drip feed of suspicion about a Muslim organization would not be limited to one group, but would feed into the narratives of the far-right and so-called 'counter-jihadist' movements that have always scare-mongered about London becoming 'Londonistan' and Europe turning into 'Eurabia'.

---

31. Inayat Bunglawala, 'Watch out: democratic Muslims about' (*The Guardian*, 3 March 2010).

Neither the IFE nor the ELM were approached much in advance to give an account of the other side of the story – the production company simply dropped a list of accusations to us in a letter a few days before broadcast and asked for a response. Yet by nature, mosques are public places and it is easy to walk into the East London Mosque. Journalists go there almost daily, as do members of other faiths, the police, local officials, schoolchildren and dozens of other outside representatives. Most of those who would later on begin pillorying the mosque on social media, where conspiracy theories ran wild, would never actually bother to visit it or see for themselves the boring reality. Mainstream TV channels, like Channel 4 and others, needed to internally review their own procedures to determine whether they, through slapdash journalism, are contributing to community tensions and the rise of Islamophobia.

Of course there are issues within traditional Muslim organizations. There can be an element of loose talk and thoughtless conspiracy theories in some which I find frustrating; 'high in rhetoric and low in output' as they say. There can also be cultural gaps in understanding; the lack of religious literacy in our society is astounding, perhaps partly as a result of the decline of organized religion (perhaps people don't have regular contact with a faith via a church, temple, synagogue, etc.). This affected British Muslims too. I have been across the country and found many Islamic centres, mosques and community organizations that are poorly-run with limited resources and not-so-satisfactory internal and external communications. In the midst of post-7/7 challenges, the Muslim community needed (and still needs) to invest in these areas.

The Dispatches film wanted to prove that Muslims were self-ghettoizing. This theory gained traction not just on the right but in mainstream media and political discourse as well. Muslims were being seen as different from other Britons, perhaps because many of them did indeed 'look' different. Again and again, politicians would look at our community with suspicion and terror, even when polls came out showing that an overwhelming proportion of British Muslims felt loyalty to this country, a higher figure than the 'native' white population. Many Muslims in the past had fought for the Empire; most were and are proud of being British and Muslim. Only a tiny fraction has been involved in any form of violent extremism.

The idea of 'entryism' was even more pernicious than that of self-ghettoization. It presented Muslims as being engaging, but only in organized attempts to infiltrate, subvert and take over. Some articles, especially after the *Dispatches* programme, repeated the highly-charged innuendo that Muslim groups were privately 'committed to replacing democracy with a theocracy based on Islamic law.'[32] This not only made any Muslim organization suspect, it also made the very idea of Muslims organizing suspect. Under this intense scrutiny, it was difficult for Muslims to carry out the kind of meaningful democratic engagement that we were so often pilloried for not joining. Thousands of pressure groups and lobbying bodies from secular and faith communities, dealing with single or multiple issues, exist in this country. Without them, the interests of the many different people that make up modern Britain would be ignored or trampled by the powerful majority. Muslims needed to make themselves heard in this process.

* * *

On the wider charges of extremism, I believe that *Dispatches* really missed the mark. In an attempt to give the programme

---

32. Telegraph View, 'This secretive agenda must be taken seriously' (*The Telegraph*, 28 February 2010).

a gravitas it sorely lacked, it had tried to link Muslims in the East End to a web of international extremism, making much of the links between Muslim organizations here and their supposed connections with foreign Islamic groups. This alarming portrayal can only be justified by those who are determined to believe that British Muslims are innately dreadful. Alternatively, they are ignorant of the fact that Muslims have been living as minorities in many places over millennia. Or, they assume that decades of living in Britain's particular social and political climate have left things completely unaltered; Muslims who have lived here for decades, or people who were born and bred here, are still too 'backward' to be unchanged by the experience of living in a pluralist society. Perhaps we are seen as intrinsically alien to British society and culture. In those scenarios, the mind is already set.

Most Muslims, like any other people, are getting on with their lives and contributing to their local communities or other areas of our national life. They have been positively integrating with wider society, irrespective of the constraints and the challenges they have faced over the past decades and especially in the aftermath of the 7/7 atrocities. The truth is that despite the disproportionate media scrutiny, uniquely complementary British and Muslim identities are merging and emerging in the UK. There are definitely teething problems, but the situation is far better than in many other European countries. This emergence requires diverse socio-cultural expressions in a confident and stable society to grow into and mesh with those of mainstream society. Britain has always been enriched by the diversity of the people who came to its shores and Muslims, like Christians, are as diverse as global humanity and historically they have flourished in a pluralist environment. The British model of dealing with pluralism has already set an example of better social cohesion compared to many other developed nations. Yes, there are hiccups, but top-heavy condemnation of a relatively new and disadvantaged community may exacerbate alienation and disenfranchisement of younger Muslims to the detriment of social cohesion.

Perhaps the saddest aspect of the approach taken by the *Dispatches* film makers was that it seemed to give Muslim communities less reason to see themselves as British. The single most potent allure of British society has, for hundreds of years, been liberty – the liberty to adopt and maintain different philosophies, lifestyles and beliefs – that has been hard-fought for in civil and sectarian wars, revolution and counter-revolution for a thousand years. Those great struggles, physical and philosophical, were more often than not centred on religious freedom as Protestants, Calvinists, Methodists, Catholics and others all vied for the space to be who they were and practise as they wished. By setting preconditions for Muslims who want to be part of that, we do not allow them this most fundamental of advantages to the British way of life. We do not offer them liberty, and without that the notion of Britishness is a hollow one.

No doubt there is a tiny minority of Muslims who are willing to resort to violence to get their way. Sadly a few hundred have already ended up in faraway lands, such as Syria, to engage in terrorism in the name of Islam and die in a proxy war unleashed by regional and global powers in the aftermath of the (illegal) Iraq war; some are returning but they must be challenged at every turn as a matter of our civic and Islamic obligation. There are also some Muslims who hold views that are contrary to the mainstream. But the challenge of living in and maintaining a liberal democracy is to work with this fact, not to push people further away or underground. After all, the mainstream view itself on issues as varied as women's rights, or gay rights, was deemed unsavoury only a few decades ago! Our views are evolving, too. Human identities are multiple and as such complementary. If people from diverse backgrounds across the UK self-identify as Muslims, that is their right. If they set up organizations that defend their interests, that is their right. If Muslim organizations wish to contribute to Britain's cultural and political life, that is not only their right but their patriotic duty. In an age when so many people feel politics is pointless and political leaders are out of touch with people, anyone who wants to take part in public life is an asset to the nation as a whole.

Those behind *Dispatches* might have felt they had to teach Britain's, or Tower Hamlets', Muslims a lesson about democracy. But they would do well to remember that democracy is often messy and difficult, and means having to deal with people with whom you disagree. If the programme makers were incapable of doing this, then they were the ones who needed a lesson in what it meant to be British. I continued to ask myself: if this had all been a grand Islamist plot, and indeed a group was in control of both mosque and borough, was there any evidence that the 'Islamists' had succeeded? Tower Hamlets overall remains as diverse, tolerant and anti-fascist as it had been a century ago. To categorize a highly-diverse but socially deprived borough as 'taken over' or as 'Taliban-like' as some US websites now do is fanciful in the extreme and also dangerous. This type of narrative has fed into the agenda of violent anti-Muslim groups, who have been popping up and 'invading' British mosques, as witnessed by the rise of the English Defence League and Britain First. And it has led to the sort of views which perhaps then influenced Donald Trump with his infamous 'travel ban' for Muslims.

* * *

As I was readying myself to step down from my position as head of the MCB, and my daughter was preparing to get married, another man was in the centre of the media crosshairs: the former leader of the Labour council in Tower Hamlets, who was later deselected over a trumped-up dossier alleging his links to, you guessed it, the IFE.

Politics in Tower Hamlets' was dirty and Lutfur Rahman, a former lawyer who was snapping up people's votes, was at the centre of a negative campaign from disgruntled members of his own Labour Party. Originally Rahman had been selected as the Labour Party candidate, but after allegations that he was closely linked to the 'fundamentalist' IFE and had signed up fake members to win the selection, he was removed from consideration. Whatever the rights and wrongs of Rahman's cause he was no radical religionist, and like most other local politicians he had courted many for their votes. So he stood as an Independent and would soon become the first directly-elected Mayor of Tower Hamlets. As soon as he was elected the first executive mayor, on 21 October 2010, a familiar pattern emerged. The IFE and Lutfur Rahman were interchangeably attacked, with the ELM also being occasionally muddied as an 'IFE-controlled mosque'. It was all black and white, without any nuance at all. And the whirlwind had only just begun.

Media attacks were hurled at the ELM for much of 2010, which was an unwelcome distraction for the management team and myself from the normal duties of serving the community. The ELM was viewed with considerable pride by our community in the East End, and highly rated by Londoners; Muslims and non-Muslims alike. This unrelenting media sniping needed to be stopped, so I decided to confront this directly on the BBC's straight-hitting programme, *HARDtalk*. Questions were tough, but in an exclusive thirty-minute interview with Stephen Sackur on 13 December I frankly explained what was going on in the ELM, including that there had been some honest but undesirable mistakes made by the management. The truth was that a 100-year-old British Muslim institution was delivering an enviable service not only to the local community and Muslims but also to wider community and society. The interview removed some of the toxic clouds surrounding the mosque and Tower Hamlets' Muslim community and the level and ferocity of attacks gradually decreased to more manageable levels. Since then, we have further strengthened our policies and procedures and restructured the media and public relations department. The ELM is still in a learning curve, but many things have or are improving.

* * *

Politics was moving fast in Tower Hamlets. In March 2014, just weeks before the mayoral and council elections, the BBC broadcast a *Panorama* documentary presented by John Ware, 'The Mayor and Our Money', which made serious allegations about Mayor Lutfur Rahman's suitability as an executive mayor. On 4 April, Eric Pickles, then Communities Secretary, appointed auditors from PWC 'to carry out an inspection of the council'. On 16 April, the Metropolitan Police said there was 'no credible evidence of criminality'[33] to substantiate allegations made against Rahman and it was not investigating him. Lutfur Rahman stood for the Mayoral job again and was re-elected on 22 May 2014.

Later, Rahman was challenged by four Tower Hamlets residents in an election petition under the Representation of the People Act (1983), and on 23 April 2015, at a special High Court hearing, Election Commissioner Richard Mawrey drew a curtain over Lutfur Rahman's political career by declaring the previous May's election null and void, saying the Mayor had 'driven a coach and horses through election law and didn't care'. Rahman was removed from office with immediate effect and the former Mayor was personally debarred from standing for elected office until 2021. Rahman's supporters

---

33. Caroline Davies, 'Police find no evidence of criminality by Tower Hamlets mayor Lutfur Rahman' (*The Guardian*, 16 April 2014).

were horrified, while his opponents were ecstatic. In a fresh and well-fought election on 11 June 2015, Labour's John Biggs won against Ms Rabina Khan, an independent (but Rahman supporter) writer-turned-politician. Whether this will end Tower Hamlets' divisive politics is a matter for the future.

During this political turmoil in the borough, the ELM remained totally non-partisan and was busy with building another multi-million pound project: the female-focused, nine-storey Maryam Centre on its Fieldgate Street side. This again received extraordinary public support from the East End's Muslim community and the building was completed in summer 2013. After eleven years as Chairman I decided to step down, but remained part of the Trust. With nearly three dozen projects and about two million footfalls every year, the ELM was now recognized as Britain's premier Muslim community complex. The new leadership decided to consolidate and maximize its effectiveness.

When the new management of the adjacent synagogue decided in the summer of 2015 to sell the building, finding it difficult to run because of the dwindling Jewish population in the East End, the ELM (its nearest neighbour) felt it necessary to buy the property. The forty years of excellent neighbourly and brotherly relationship (the mosque provided funding for the synagogue's roof repairs a few years prior to the sale and enjoyed excellent relations with its congregation) was a big factor in the ELM's decision. Fortunately, it was the blessed month of Ramadan and the leadership proposed to the Friday congregations to raise the money needed to buy it. The response was overwhelmingly positive and inspirational. In an exceptional month-long fundraising campaign, the money – consisting of donations and loans – was raised. With the acquisition of the synagogue building, the ELM diversified further.

With its fascinating background, the ELM also felt that it had a responsibility to keep its history alive and to pass on that history to the new generation of Muslims. As a result, the ELM Archives Project was launched, consisting of a professional group of archivists and historians from diverse backgrounds, including mainstream archiving experts, to preserve the mosque's history. The archive team, chaired by historian and author (and my MCB colleague) Dr Jamil Sherif, was tasked with the collation of ideas as to how the ELM could accommodate another Abrahamic institution – the old synagogue building – to bring communities together. It is now given to the National Zakat Foundation as a lease, but the idea of a heritage or interfaith project is always in mind and an appropriate decision will be taken by the Trust when the time is ready.

On 30 September 2015, BBC Two featured a documentary film on the ELM, 'Welcome to the Mosque', by award-winning filmmaker Robb Leech. Leech was given exclusive access to the mosque over several months and the resultant film gave a personal account of his experience of the life in a mosque. With a very different approach to the *Dispatches* programme, Leech revealed the day-to-day lives of Muslims as they prayed, studied, reflected and socialized and showed, in fact, what it was like to be an everyday Muslim living in Britain. Devoid of political or ideological bias, the film was highly-rated. 'The reason I made the film, and the reason why I'm a filmmaker', Leech said, 'is to provide insight rather than to make a [specific] point. It's about allowing people to see something they normally wouldn't be able to see, in a palatable way that they can engage with and then talk about.'[34]

Nowadays, the East End is changing fast. With the expanding financial sector in Canary Wharf (it remains to be seen how it is affected by the uncertainty surrounding Brexit) and with Shoreditch establishing itself as 'Tech City', Tower Hamlets

34. Alun Evans, 'Robb Leech Takes You Inside Britain's Largest Mosque in His New Documentary' (*Vice.com*, 29 September 2015).

is a savvier and more expensive place than when I arrived all those years ago. Money is moving in, while many of those who settled there in the 1970s and 1980s are being priced out. These are the inevitable realities that the community at large and people around the ELM have to grapple with.

Chapter 6

Summer 2012: Britain at its Best

FTER THE CHANNEL 4 *Dispatches* programme in March 2010, I gradually became used to the extra media pressure on the ELM. Thankfully, a brighter summer beckoned, and with it, hopefully, a breeze of respite. As the weather improved, so my mood lifted. London basked in high temperatures during the second half of my summer school term and I was feeling more peaceful: my fourth and final year as Secretary-General of the MCB would come to an end at the organization's Annual General Meeting on Sunday 20 June. The feeling was liberating and I began counting the days until I stepped down from the toughest voluntary job in my life and unburden myself from the pressure of the MCB's multi-dimensional work.

The two-year-term elected term of the MCB's Secretary-General (an honorary post) is probably one of the most demanding voluntary jobs in the British Muslim community. It requires 24/7 commitment, and what makes it more arduous are the ever increasing belittlements from the right-wing British media and unhelpful attitudes from the political establishment. The MCB had severely constrained financial resources and was unable to employ even a small number of senior staff to run an office and support the elected officials – a fact often astounding to many, both within and outside the community. However it was the sad reality.

I was limited to serving two consecutive terms, and constitutionally barred from contesting the top post right away in the 2010 MCB election. The feeling that I would not be the 'Chief Fire Officer' (an endearing term given to me by a former manager in my teaching job) of the MCB anymore, and to some extent the British Muslim community, was itself comforting. At last I would have some really free days during my school holiday periods. How wrong I was!

British Muslims are known to be among the most charitable people (at least in terms of humanitarian donations and building mosques or community centres), but as a relatively new community with multiple demands we have not yet prioritized our support for organizations or umbrella bodies that have the potential to enhance the community's capacity for advocacy, public relations and engagement with mainstream society. In its absence, there has been unremitting negative media, often exacerbated by a few cynical neoconservative think-tanks and digital media outlets that amplify anything negative about Muslims. The difficulties faced by the MCB in becoming financially secure have probably cost British Muslims dear, as their representative body could not always rise to meet the needs of the hour.

With the emergence of a bright young selection of Muslim professionals, things may be improving. However, the challenges have also multiplied and diversified and the race appears to be unwinnable, at least in the short term. I am sure this will change, but it is going to take time.

* * *

The summer holidays had started and with the election of a new Secretary-General the MCB's immediate headache was no longer mine. The construction of the nine-storey complex at the East London Mosque, to better facilitate and expand women's activities, was continuing full swing. The ELM was already a large institution, with thousands of people visiting the complex every day for prayer and other social or educational purposes. The female-focused multi-purpose extension, named the Maryam Centre, also received overwhelming support from the community. I was a bit hesitant at first and thought it was too ambitious a project for us to start, especially when the world economy was in slowdown, but seeing the enthusiasm in the management and volunteers, I relented. Women, including young girls, from among the volunteers and in the local community came up with their own innovative ideas to raise funds. This was exactly what happened a decade earlier when we were building the London Muslim Centre, and the moral support from the wider community was very encouraging. So, while I was free from MCB's burdensome tasks I remained busy in my summer holiday, watching the Maryam Centre come into shape – and making sure we did not suddenly run out of cash.

At the same time, something special was happening in my family during that summer; our beloved daughter, Rima, was getting married that October! Our first child and only daughter, who had completed her Masters in Pharmacy from Kings College London and was working for the Royal London Hospital, had grown under our eyes. Most credit was due to my beloved wife, Sayeda, who took the burden of raising our children onto her broad shoulders. I was fully aware of my role in the family and to our children as a father – a uniquely complementary role that Islam has demanded – but sadly, since the 7/7 attacks in 2005 I was in effect a semi-absent father. Work with the MCB was often all-consuming and I would come home late at night almost every day; but I never forgot to keep Sayeda informed of my whereabouts. When I kept on failing to arrive home at my appointed time, it became amusing to my children; the only thing I could do was to put on a brave face and apologize. I learned a few things about life from my wise father: 'never ignore your health and under no circumstances ignore family responsibility', he would say. Yes, I was often away from my family during that period when the children were growing and they needed me, but I always compensated by making time for special occasions. They knew it was not deliberate and home and family keeps on giving me an anchor to hold onto, solace and joy of life.

We were clear about our role as parents, and towards the end of Rima's university life we started talking with her about marriage. According to our religious tradition, the choice of spouse ultimately lies with the girl and boy; parents and other adults are there to advise, assist or facilitate. In some communities, not based on Islamic principles, cultural practice leads parents or family members to coerce or even force their youth, mainly girls, to get married (often at an early age). On the other extreme, some parents have little clue about their children's life in adolescence or early adulthood. In spite of clear Islamic rulings against the practice of forced marriage, some keep on doing this for so-called 'family honour' reasons or probably for vested economic interests. The forced marriage that we hear about in some cultures, including in some Muslim communities, has nothing to do with Islam. Our Prophet nullified forced marriages if they came to his notice. This selfish or ignorant practice destroys many young people's lives.

Finding a suitable match for beloved children has always been a parental worry and dilemma. Towards the end of 2009, we came across a young Bangladeshi-American man through one of my nephews who had been living in Queens, New York. Once we were introduced with him and exchanged our family details, he came to London and met Rima. Our eldest son,

Raiyan, accompanied her as a chaperone when they talked while visiting a few places of London. Once he returned to New York they talked further over the phone. Within a few months we understood they would hopefully be a good match. Sayeda and I visited New York with Rima and visited their house to meet him and his family. Rima gave her consent and a wedding date in October 2010 was agreed. The main ceremony would be in London, and we tasked Raiyan with managing the event.

October arrived. The formal marriage (*nikah*) ceremony was solemnized in East London Mosque a day before the wedding dinner. The dinner went smoothly with scores of guests from all backgrounds, including quite a few of my friends from wider society. One was LOCOG's (London Organising Committee of the Olympic and Paralympic Games, the committee that organized London 2012) CEO Paul Deighton (later Baron Deighton, KBE who served as Commercial Secretary to HM Treasury from January 2013–May 2015). In fact, he came exactly on the time written in the card, but by that time only a handful of guests had arrived; I felt very embarrassed and apologized for not telling him about our 'Asian timing' of starting events late! He was very patient, and with a smile said: 'Don't worry, Muhammad, I can use the time for some much needed relaxation in a coffee shop nearby.' Some communities are poor at not valuing time properly, but I was blessed to somehow develop a habit of keeping good time during my secondary school days, mainly because of reprimands from a few close teachers. I still remember the proverb, 'time and tide wait for none'; time is more than money, in reality time is life. A small but powerful chapter of the Qur'an (*al-'Asr*, chapter 103) contains the priceless teaching of Islam on the meaning and importance of time.

The wedding was jovial, though for myself it was mixed with sobriety, too. I struggled to hide my feelings that Rima would from then on spend most of her time away from us;

she was not only a daughter, but 'motherly' too. In a child's marriage there is this natural mixed feeling in parents and I could also sense what Sayeda was going through emotionally, especially over the past few weeks; without Rima around, hers would be the biggest emptiness in life. After the dinner, and when most of the guests had departed, close family members from both sides came together to pray for the happy future of Rima and her husband. We came home late, exhausted and empty but feeling grateful to God. Sayeda and I had a long sleepless night.

* * *

In January 2011, there was an announcement about job-cuts in the Tower Hamlets Education Department, where my unit was based. The Department was faced with significant budget cuts, and although I was assured that I would not be affected in the short term, there was no certainty in the long run. Liz Vickery, the long-serving SLS director and our overall manager, was experienced in handling these challenges, but she was worried and worked tirelessly for a 'soft landing' in the SLS. With her negotiating skills, she convinced the borough to minimize the negative impact job losses would have on the SLS and made sure the service was not terminally affected. She was constantly keeping us informed of the situation. Shortly after we learned that over half-a-dozen out of around sixty of my close colleagues, some nearing retirement age, would be leaving voluntarily with a reasonable monetary package. One colleague was known to be going on a world trip: how I wished I could do that! My formal retirement was still some time away and so I kept quiet. I was still paying off an Islamic finance mortgage and Sayeda was working as a part-time nursery nurse near our house.

Time was passing and the decision to take voluntary redundancy was just a week away. There was some fear that our well-resourced SLS might gradually become impoverished because of the sudden departure of these teachers, some renowned in the education world. One morning, I was working in the IT room when my line manager silently came over to me and softly gestured for me to have a quick chat with her. We went to a small room nearby and with a neutral face she said: 'Sorry to take you from your work, Muhammad. You'll by now be aware that the option of taking a voluntary redundancy is closing in a week's time. To my knowledge, the Authority has given a good package to those who want to leave. You don't have to, but have you ever thought of taking this offer?' For a split second I was taken aback, was she indirectly suggesting that I leave the job? She had probably read my mind because with a smile she immediately said: 'Muhammad, we know what you do outside your work in the community; this brings great benefit to many of us. I just felt I should talk to you on this. To be honest, the education cuts are going to affect our support service heavily in the long run. Protecting frontline services in schools is a priority for the borough. I'm not sure whether SLS will remain as a premier service in future as it is now.'

I quickly organized my thoughts and asked her how much she reckoned I would get if I took the redundancy. She asked about the length of my pensionable service and calculated a rough estimate. It sounded good to me, but I needed to think properly and consult with my family and close friends. I thanked her for approaching me on this and told her that I would get back to her the following day.

I could not concentrate on my work properly for the rest of the day, a difficult decision lay ahead of me. That night I sat with Sayeda and Raiyan, our eldest son, who at the time worked for an investment bank. We discussed all the factors surrounding our family, the package on offer, earnings from my pension and most importantly what I would do once I took early retirement. It was a long, deeply practical discussion. I was happy to see Raiyan talking with maturity and offering his opinion like a true professional. Sayeda was indecisive, but Raiyan was able to demonstrate the benefits early retirement would bring. We came to the conclusion that I should not lose the chance and according to Islamic spirit, we sought guidance from God and slept on the issue.

The next morning I felt convinced that I would be leaving my job. Life was already looking different as I drove to work, and the first thing I did was to enter Liz's office and inform her of my decision. She smiled and said: 'You've taken a brave but probably a wise decision'. We sat down to calculate the exact amount of my pension and severance pay, and I came out of her office feeling relaxed. The information that I had also joined the list of leavers spread quickly among my colleagues. They were indeed very surprised; some asked me what I would be doing. I smiled and said: 'I'm not really sure yet, but one thing is certain: I'm not going on a world tour'. I also had a philosophical answer: 'You know, there is no retirement in life'. They knew I would probably be busier than ever with charity or community work.

All the formalities were followed up by the office with great efficiency. During the rest of the week I informed the relevant teachers and the students in my allocated schools of my decision. They were similarly surprised, and I must admit I felt a sense of loss. Over the next few days I completed all my reports and cleared my desk. As a number of other teachers were also leaving the SLS, the atmosphere was sombre, to say the least. I was also going through a mental change of becoming a free man, but I also knew it would probably lead me to a busier life. As the spring term came to a close, one late afternoon colleagues organized a farewell event for the leavers. It felt like a momentous occasion, a chapter closing, with heartening words spoken about us. When speaking about me, Liz coined her unforgettable phrase: 'As the head of the MCB since 2006, Muhammad was probably the chief fire officer of the Muslim community'. It wasn't something I'd ever intended to be, but it was apt in a way.

On the first day of April 2011, I woke up with a weird feeling. I no longer had to follow the maddening routine of rushing to work. I tried to spend some extra time in bed, attempting to go back to sleep, but it was not easy. A sudden thought crept into my mind: 'Did I make the right decision?' I allowed my mind to wander around lazily for a while and then woke up, determined that I had to use my time more effectively from then on. In hindsight, I now feel it was the proper and most wonderful decision.

* * *

Following my early retirement, I decided not to take another paid job, at least not for a year. Close friends suggested I needed some rest, and I also thought it was time for me to slow down, but I soon found myself rushing around again. I had decided to divert my attention to LOCOG and the approaching Olympic and Paralympic Games, prioritizing my work with young people as well as pursuing more writing on parenting, youth and identity issues (as well as socio-political issues). I updated the contents of my 'Building Families' parenting course and made it a social enterprise: 'No retirement from voluntary work', as the saying goes!

Since 2006, when I joined the LOCOG board, I had been attending regular quarterly meetings of the Board, meeting relevant senior officers on issues of school involvement, helping in the areas of equality and diversity and attending meetings with the IOC (International Olympic Committee) and IPC (International Paralympic Committee) officials when they visited London. I informed the LOCOG Board Chair, Lord Sebastian Coe, and CEO Paul Deighton (later Baron Deighton) of my increased availability. I also expressed an interest in the post-Olympic and Paralympic legacy in the

East End. They were eager that my experience in education and links with communities could be further utilized; I was already part of LOCOG's Nations and Region's Committee, and once I started giving more time I was gradually pulled into more commitment.

The London Organising Committee of the Olympic and Paralympic Games developed itself as an inclusive body since its formation in 2005 after London was chosen as the host for the 2012 Olympic Games by the IOC. In February 2010, Archbishop Desmond Tutu visited the London 2012 Olympic Park, which he described as: 'It is exciting. It is wonderful, isn't it?'[35] and later addressed LOCOG's staff, myself included. I found the Archbishop full of energy and optimism as he spoke and inspired the team at our office in Canary Wharf. He asked LOCOG to sign a leadership pledge so that it would fulfil its obligation of incorporating Diversity and Inclusion (D&I) considerations in every key business decision it made. This was consistently and enthusiastically followed up; the majority of contracts were awarded to small businesses, allowing smaller firms to gain a slice of the 2012 pie. Larger firms were also obliged to undertake specific actions that fell within D&I requirements, and the process of creating employment opportunities within LOCOG was made smoother.

There was progress at the Stratford Olympic venue too. In spite of global financial challenges, LOCOG's efforts in finding private sponsors was impressive. There was no room for complacency, but LOCOG found itself ahead in most areas of IOC and IPC requirements compared to other Games in similar timeframes in the past.

* * *

---

35. Staff and agencies, 'London 2012: Desmond Tutu visits "wonderful" Olympic site' (*The Telegraph*, 4 February 2010).

As 2011 began there was guarded optimism in the Middle East. A chain of events was set in motion on 17 December 2010 after a young Tunisian street vendor, Mohamed Bouazizi, set himself on fire following a long period of abuse and corruption from local officials in the capital, Tunis. This initiated the 'Arab Spring', capturing the mood of a people dying for change. Human beings often need inspiration or a spark to act, and the self-sacrifice of Mohamed Bouazizi was spectacular in creating a social avalanche in the Arab world.

The Tunisian autocrat, Zine El Abidine Ben Ali, resigned under pressure and left the country as the Middle East was rapidly infected with a desire and passion for freedom – and change. The Arab world's most populous country, Egypt, paved the way when its strongman president, Hosni Mubarak, resigned in February 2011. Cairo's Tahrir Square became a symbol of hope across the Arab world as it filled with thousands upon thousands of protesters, all defying the regime. Spontaneous protests spread to Yemen and Syria as a region that had been frozen in time for decades, if not centuries, suddenly appeared to be waking up. But the 'Arab Spring' proved short-lived and within a few years, the protests were stifled and in some countries, like Syria, civil war was to follow. Apart from Tunisia, which is still holding its nerve due to a pragmatic approach to politics, this has led to the worst refugee crisis for Europe since the Second World War.

In summer 2011, two events closer to home unnerved us all. The first was the dreadful massacre of seventy-seven young people on 22 July – first from a car bomb in Oslo that killed eight people and injured 209, and then the calculated murder of sixty-nine young people and the injury of 110 in a summer camp on the island of Utøya – sent shock waves across the continent. These acts of terrorism were carried out by a 32-year-old Norwegian far-right extremist, Anders Behring Breivik, who on the day of the massacre electronically distributed texts of his manifesto, entitled *2083: A European Declaration of Independence*, describing his ideology of hate for Islam and feminism. He advocated the deportation of Muslims from Europe. He was arrested and later sentenced to twenty-one years of preventive detention in prison. To modern Europe's nightmare, far-right groups have been on the rise for some time, often with increasing electoral support.

The other event was an unexpected series of violent riots across London and some English cities, between 6–11 August, which started in response to the fatal shooting of a north London man by a police officer. This led to widespread disorder, looting and arson in several London boroughs and in some English cities and towns. The rioters' behaviour generated serious debate on issues like race and economic inequality, on the one hand, and the breakdown of social morality, gang culture and criminality on the other. The wanton destruction caused by sections of youth and fuelled by social media platforms such as Blackberry messenger and Twitter showed a new phase in modern social malaise.

However, there were also some inspirational examples during the week that shone some light on human goodness. Tariq Jahan lost his 19-year-old son, along with two other young Asian men, to a speeding car in Birmingham as they were protecting local businesses. Their deaths sparked fury, but Mr Jahan helped avert revenge attacks by urging the crowds to 'calm down and go home, please.' Turkish shopkeepers in north London demonstrated exemplary community spirit in protecting their stores, and ordinary mosque goers in east London chased off rioters from the streets of Whitechapel. Faith indeed played an important role in helping Muslims behave positively; it was the month of fasting (Ramadan) and for Muslims Ramadan has always been a season of spiritual harvest and effective restraint from evil and criminal acts. A question that came up frequently in the following weeks and months was what caused such sheer criminality and nihilism to manifest in these ugly riots? Was it widening social and economic inequality, the decline of trust in established authority (such as politicians), the gradual waning of a moral compass with a 'me-first' philosophy of life and the weakening of family structure giving rise to a lack of basic discipline at home, in schools and our streets? There was no simple answer to this complex and deep issue, but given that London 2012 was just a year away, the riots were seen by many as a bad omen. All sections of our society, from police to politicians to ordinary citizens, expressed revulsion at the mindless criminality of a few. The country prepared itself for any eventuality during London 2012.

* * *

As 2011 gave way to a new phase of my life, I reminisced over my involvement in LOCOG. Towards the end of the 1990s, my commitment to a few voluntary bodies grew significantly, and since its inception in 1997 the MCB had taken on a policy of proactively engaging with wider society as part of its 'working for the common good' agenda. This included engaging with the political establishment at both national and London level. After the London mayoral election in 2000, the MCB created a London Affairs Committee to work with the Mayor and City Hall. As Deputy Secretary-General since 2002, I took a special interest in engaging with the Mayor's office on areas such as education and employment: areas that disproportionately affected the diverse Muslim communities in greater London. Most Muslims were living in the inner city areas and many were struggling to raise their children's education and economic prospects. For all these, I occasionally visited City Hall and met some senior officials.

As the idea of a London bid for the 2012 summer Olympics was taking shape, the MCB was keen to play its part. To be successful, London's offer needed political consensus and public support. The bid team, headed by former Olympic champion Lord Sebastian Coe, was preparing to prove that London would showcase itself as a world city and Britain as a country that was at peace with itself. Two prominent figures in the MCB, Sir Iqbal Sacranie, our Secretary-General, and Tanzim Wasti, Chair of the MCB's London Affairs Committee, fulfilled the role of 'bid ambassadors'. Their work included lobbying various Muslim ambassadors for their countries to back the London bid. The merits of London's multiculturalism was much discussed in the run up to the Olympic bid and finally in putting the case in Singapore. In the presence of high-profile individuals from the British establishment, the bid team was able to prove London's superiority over its rivals: Paris, Madrid, New York City and Moscow.

After the bid was won, two Olympic bodies were formed: the Olympic Delivery Authority (ODA), to build the venues and infrastructure, and the London Organising Committee of the Olympic Games and Paralympic Games (LOCOG) for staging the Games. The plan was to use a mix of newly-built and existing venues as well as temporary facilities. Some, such as the Excel Arena and Earls Court Exhibition Centre, were well known locations in London, while others were to be held in different parts of the country. Towards the end of 2005, I was made aware by City Hall that my name was being discussed in regards to a non-executive position on the LOCOG board. I was invited by the late Redmond O'Neill, the Mayor's senior policy director, for a chat in his office. Without any introduction, he asked me: 'Muhammad, would you consider joining London 2012's LOCOG Board?' Without a pause, he continued: 'But bear in mind, the DCMS (Department for Culture, Media & Sport) and the LOCOG board have to agree with your appointment. Plus, there will be an intense scrutiny on your suitability. Your past in Bangladesh as well as present here in the UK could be looked into by our intelligence branch.'

I was completely taken aback, to say the least. Although I had never participated in any competitive sports in my life, as a sports-loving person (I was always a part of sports teams, including athletics during my stay in the Bangladesh Air Force) this offer was music to my ears. Redmond could sense my feeling, saying that he would pass on my name, if I agreed. I was over the moon.

Sometime in December I received an invitation to meet Lord Sebastian Coe, Chair of the LOCOG Board, in his office on the twenty-third floor of the Barclays Bank building in Canary Wharf. As I arrived, Lord Coe greeted me with a broad smile and natural warmth. It appeared he had already gathered information about me and we had a good long conversation about his vision for London 2012. His enthusiasm was infectious, and he clearly had a passion to make these the best Games ever and leave a lasting effect on the city. At some point he proudly mentioned his Indian connection, as his maternal grandfather was Indian Punjabi. It was a very good meeting, but before introducing me to a few senior staff, he informed me that he had already sounded out my name with the DCMS and hoped everything would be fine in a few months for me to join them at the next Board meeting! I was tremendously excited.

Lord Coe (or 'Seb', as he asked to be called) then took me to meet Paul Deighton, the CEO of the organizing committee, in his office on the other side of the hall. Another warm personality, Paul was a former investment banker who had been the Chief Operating Officer for Goldman Sachs in Europe. But he was also a sports enthusiast and personally very amiable. I found in Paul a determined 'doer'. It was the early days of LOCOG, with only a handful of employees, but both Seb and Paul had a clear vision and determination of what needed to be achieved in 2012. I met a few more staff before leaving. I had already made up my mind to give my best to LOCOG if I were to be formally accepted as a non-executive director. I joined the March 2006 board meeting once the process was complete and my seven-year journey towards the most exciting world event had begun.

Although I was very busy with the MCB after my election as Secretary-General in June 2006, I put aside designated quality time for LOCOG and routinely contributed to its steady expansion month by month. It was a huge experience and I was enjoying it until one problem arose during the renewal of my LOCOG membership in 2009. It should have been a formality, but it was not. One day in late May, after three years on the body, I received a phone call from Lord Coe. He informed me that there was a 'small hiccup' with my renewal, but he assured me: 'don't worry, I'll sort this out and come back to you'. I was surprised and asked him if he was aware of the reason, but Seb only hinted that it was from the top and would not divulge. He sounded determined and advised me to miss the next board meeting, which was on Thursday 28 May. I had full confidence in Seb, so I did not press him, but I kept on wondering what the 'hiccup' could possibly be? I could guess only one reason: politics. Maybe, after Boris Johnson had replaced Ken Livingstone to become London Mayor the year before, the Tory establishment would want to go for my replacement. I did not want to think about it too much and left it like that. I missed the board meeting on Thursday, but to my relief Seb called me on Friday and affirmed that I would remain a board member.

A very personal memory for Sayeda and myself was one of our few visits to Buckingham Palace. One evening, I was with Sayeda at the Palace for an event. Towards the end, as people were leaving, we were relaxing and thinking about leaving ourselves, but then we realized we were not far away from Her Majesty The Queen, Prince Charles and Princess Anne. I felt they were also not in a hurry to disappear and I knew Princess Anne well through my duties with LOCOG; I had also met Prince Charles quite a few times. I thought, 'why not spend a few informal moments with them?' So we drew closer and greeted them properly as and when approaching all royals. Our short hello became a few minutes of relaxed conversation on various issues, such as community relations, pressures on the Muslim community and the challenges of modern life. Sayeda and I parted from them with a fond recollection.

* * *

The regeneration of Stratford in east London, with the new Olympic Park, and of the neighbouring Lower Lea Valley, was a driving factor behind the bid. Soon after the bid was won, tens of thousands of people started work to transform a disused area, much of it contaminated wasteland, into a state-of-the-art Olympic park with major facilities including a new stadium, aquatics centre and velodrome. Effective reuse of some of the new facilities and a post-game reduction in the size of others were all part of the plan.

The Olympic Delivery Authority (ODA), under the chairmanship of Sir John Armitt, worked hard to complete the massive venue (about 500 acres or 2 square kilometres) in the Olympic Park on time. The Olympic Village and Westfield shopping centre also added to long-term regeneration of the area. The enhanced transport network in Stratford, with improved overland rail and London underground services, was incredible. The venue construction and preparations by the ODA, in full consultation with LOCOG, needed a high level of dedication, coordination and professionalism.

The challenges of holding a world-class event in a democratic country are immense. People participation is vital, and a government cannot simply bulldoze its will on them. London's high traffic congestion was a particular worry, and with millions of extra people arriving during the summer Games in 2012 the situation could easily become chaotic. Given the summer riots in 2011, and a high level terrorism threat, security was another major issue for the organizers and police. The government, LOCOG and the London Mayor's office were fully aware of the risks and challenges, and necessary preventative measures were taken well in advance. It was absolutely vital that London's traffic was kept moving during the events. It was also crucial that London and the rest of Britain be kept safe, so that the Games could go ahead smoothly. The huge investment in transport, security and communication made sure there was no gap in the tactical and strategic planning. The synergy between people, government, media and other stakeholders was proving concrete in the run up to the Games; everyone wanted to be a winner. From the moment I joined the Board in early 2006, I had seen LOCOG grow from infancy to near adulthood in late 2011. Construction of most of the venues in the Park was going at full swing, and I had visited the site quite a few times already. By the end of 2011, the Olympic Park was ready to be handed over to LOCOG for carrying out successful test events to prepare for the real Games.

* * *

There were some challenges with ticket sales in the beginning. LOCOG's plan was to keep tickets affordable to most and to ensure that seats did not remain empty, as had happened in many previous Games. The six-week application period the previous year to pre-register for tickets was met by a huge demand that massively exceeded supply, especially in some popular events. The demand for the Opening Ceremony attracted more than two million requests, and for Athletics there were more than a million requests for the Men's 100m final, alone. There was so much demand for Track Cycling, Swimming and Artistic Gymnastics that tickets were put to ballot.

As 2012 got underway, there was a sense of great anticipation in the United Kingdom. Everyone's eyes were fixed on two global events: the Diamond Jubilee of Queen Elizabeth II ... and the London 2012 Games. The British economy was still struggling, but the whole nation was in full Olympic and Paralympic mode. The Queen's Diamond Jubilee marked the sixtieth anniversary of her accession to the throne. The Queen Elizabeth Diamond Jubilee Trust, chaired by former British Prime Minister, Sir John Major, was officially launched on 6 February 2012 to 'support charitable projects and organizations across the Commonwealth, and ... place great emphasis on enriching the lives of individuals, by focussing on areas such as the tackling of curable diseases and the promotion of all forms of education and culture.'[36] In a statement from Buckingham Palace, the Queen gave a special message of thanks, saying: 'In this special year, as I dedicate myself anew to your service, I hope we will all be reminded of the power of togetherness and the convening strength of family, friendship, and good neighbourliness.'[37]

The aim of London 2012 was to bring the world to the capital city to ignite a spirit of peace and harmony. The whole of Britain was reeling with a feeling of positivity and optimism, and excitement grew as the month of the Games approached. The LOCOG was in a unique position to showcase the best of Britain in the presence of athletes, spectators and visitors, and with London's large number of disabled people, the Paralympics had a chance of receiving wide support across the country and beyond. London's attractiveness was multiplying as time passed. More than 300 languages were spoken in this great city, with at least fifty non-indigenous communities of 10,000 or more. It could proudly claim that virtually every race, nation, culture and religion would be in its midst. It was necessary that London 2012 shared the burden and economic

---

36. Written evidence, 'The role and future of the commonwealth' (Foreign and Commonwealth Office, 6 February 2012).
37. HM Queen Elizabeth, 'The Queen's Diamond Jubilee Message' (Buckingham Palace, 6 February 2012).

benefit of the Games with all, and the CEO of LOCOG, Paul Deighton, personally chaired the Diversity Board to oversee diversity and inclusion and to ensure that the Olympic and Paralympic values of excellence, friendship, respect, courage, inspiration and equality prevailed throughout the Games.

Diversity and inclusion extended to global Muslims, including British Muslims, as the Olympic events would be falling in the month of Ramadan. There was some worry in the sporting world that because of their fasting commitment some practising Muslim athletes would either be disadvantaged in the competition or even avoid taking part in the Games altogether. Medical research was carried out in some countries on fasting and individual performance. It was found that fasting itself would not be a much of negative factor, but deprivation of sleep would most probably be, because of the pre-dawn wakeup and meal intake. In any case, from the organizer's side we had been planning for some years how best to accommodate the fasting Muslims – athletes, volunteers known as Games Makers, guests and others involved – in providing prayer facilities and the halal food needed for pre-dawn and sunset meals.

As a result of the proactive steps taken by LOCOG, the necessary arrangements were planned well ahead for the Olympic Park, including the Olympic village, and across other venues. London's Muslim centres and mosques particularly were invited to offer generosity to visitors during the fasting month, opening their doors and welcoming athletes, spectators and visitors from around the world. Similar relevant arrangements were made for other faith communities. Citizens UK, the premier citizens organizing body, organized an *iftar* (fast breaking) event for athletes in Tower Hamlets' York Hall. As a result of this gesture to faith, London 2012 became the most faith-friendly global event in the world.

* * *

Being the only non-white board member, I had some advantages as well as occasional disadvantages compared to other members of LOCOG's board. As someone with a strong community connection myself, I could see the importance of the strong community focus of the Games. This was indeed LOCOG's strength, and as part of its 'Nations and Regions' team, led by Sir Charles Allen, I tried to reach out to more of London's communities. My presence at various events did probably raise some curiosity among IOC and IPC members, who often visited us from all corners of the world as part of their monitoring, assessment and evaluation of the progress in the run up to the Games. My attendance at these visit-related events increased significantly after April 2011 in various places of the British political establishment, such as the 'Westminster village'.

A Finnish university (University of Tampere) organized a seminar at the British embassy in Helsinki and invited me to hear my perspectives on the Games. There were many expatriate Brits at the event, and this was soon after the 2011 England riots so they were obviously worried about London's security and transport during the Games. I was aware of the close work between LOCOG and the Metropolitan Police on security and I knew the progress on enhanced transport facilities in London. In response to a question on the topic I said:

> As a Londoner I am conscious of the security threat during the Games, but as a LOCOG member I am also aware of the measures that are being taken by the police and the security services. I believe, when an overwhelming majority of the British public are fully in tune with the government and LOCOG in seeing the best of Britain during London 2012 I am confident we can deliver the most successful and peaceful Games next year.

Through such meetings and events I encountered many politicians and other senior dignitaries in the political establishment. From its inception, LOCOG was being developed as an uncompromisingly professional body and engagements were always business-like. My LOCOG colleagues were a wonderful group of enlightened people, including celebrities and renowned professionals as well a member of the royal family (in spite of her busy schedule, the Princess Royal hardly missed any board meeting). Although I clarified to Lord Coe and others that I could not or would not claim to represent any community, as it would be arrogant to do so, they valued my presence and contribution and on any community-related issues they would seek my opinion. I was probably seen as a symbol of diversity in modern Britain and inadvertently was an ambassador for Britain's communities.

Over this long period of LOCOG membership, I encountered only a handful of humorous moments with senior establishment figures regarding my visibility at those events. I could sense that some found it difficult to reconcile my presence among all the high-profile people at such gatherings. If I translated this into words it would read like this: 'How could this Asian guy with a beard be here as part of the LOCOG board?' If I felt a slightly odd glance or uneasy body language from someone I just looked the other way: I pretended I didn't notice anything. Some guests, of course, innocently asked about my 'journey' into LOCOG and how I was contributing to the organization. My response was usually frank information about myself and what I was up to. Due to my public role in the MCB, especially after 7/7, I was quite well known to a few of the senior politicians in the Labour government. With the change of government in 2010, they were replaced by Tory and several Liberal Democrat politicians.

One incident in the House of Lords was a little amusing. At one high-profile event, as I entered the hall I could see a

well-known minister and my LOCOG colleague Lord Colin
Moynihan (then-Chair of British Olympic Association). As I
walked straight ahead I first met the minister. I did not really
notice, but I felt that the minister, whose knowledge of the
security services was quite deep, was somewhat shocked to
see me there. As I passed and approached Colin, he warmly
grabbed my hand and gently pulled me into a corner and
started laughing. I knew Colin could laugh his heart out,
but I was a bit puzzled and kept looking at him. He asked:
'Muhammad, did you notice that the minister seemed shaken
to see you here, she cringed! What's the matter? What did you
do to her?'

I started laughing as well and repeated the question: 'Did
you notice it?'

'Yeah, I noticed it all and it was hilarious!' he said.

I briefly told Colin that I had encountered her a few times
in the past in my role as the MCB head, and had disagreed
on some government policies that she advocated: 'Maybe
because of that,' I ended.

Colin said with a smile: 'Forget politics, Muhammad. But
this is going to be etched in my memory; I can never forget
how she cringed.' He laughed again. Since then, whenever I
met Colin he used to start with a laugh and before going into
any discussion would remind me of the saga.

* * *

Summer 2012 started with unusually regular sunshine and
London was already in a great mood. The transport system
was also behaving extraordinarily well; there was no sign of
road works on any of London's main roads. However, trouble
was brewing. Although security firm G4S had been made
the official 'security services provider' the previous year,
and included training and management for a 10,000-strong
security workforce, it admitted on 11 July 2012, barely two

weeks before the Games were due to start, that it 'would not be able to deliver the numbers of security personnel that they had promised'.[38] It could have been a major glitch, but the Government had a contingency plan. The Defence Secretary announced that up to 3,500 extra troops would provide security duties during the Games, and the Home Secretary told MPs there was 'no question of Olympic security being compromised'.[39]

The overall security issue, because of overseas terrorism from groups such as al-Qaeda or attacks from 'lone wolves', had always been a matter of concern. The UK had been on high alert since the 7/7 atrocities, and the government assured the public of its maximum preparation to thwart any terrorist attack. I was not privy to the deeper level of our security measures, but I was confident that Britain – with its resources and expertise as well as support from other countries – would be fully prepared for any eventuality. It was only made public in May 2016 via *The Guardian* newspaper that the British government had covertly funded a film, *My 2012 Dream*, featuring Muslim athletes competing in the London Olympics that was 'shown on 15 TV channels [including Al Jazeera and the British-based Islam Channel] and watched by 30 million Muslims worldwide.'[40]

Tens of thousands of volunteer Games Makers were all recruited on time and trained in a range of skills. With full public support, the Games Makers, police and the military were positioned in the Olympic Park and other London and out-of-London Olympic venues. It was an extraordinary

38. Szu Ping Chan, and agencies, 'Timeline: how G4S's bungled Olympics security contract unfolded' (*The Telegraph*, 21 May 2013).
39. 'Home Secretary Theresa May's statement to the House of Commons this morning' (Home Office, 12 July 2013).
40. Ian Cobain, A. Ross, R. Evans and M. Mahmood, 'Government hid fact it paid for 2012 Olympics film aimed at Muslims' (*The Guardian*, 3 May 2016).

show of unity and synergy that produced exceptional human warmth, humour and togetherness during the Olympic and Paralympic Games.

The Opening ceremony on 27 July, directed by award-winning film maker Danny Boyle, was absolutely stunning. It involved 10,768 athletes from 204 countries. The ceremony, featuring our rich British life, received widespread acclaim from the British public as well as throughout the world. The Royal involvement, with an acting debut from the Queen, had been kept such a closely-guarded secret that even key members of the Royal Family did not know. It was disclosed later that the idea was originally floated by Danny Boyle. Another attraction was Muhammad Ali, the boxing legend and BBC's 'Sports Personality of the Century' as well as a renowned civil rights campaigner, who made a special appearance at the beginning. *The New York Times* headlined its review: 'A Five-Ring Opening Circus, Weirdly and Unabashedly British', calling the ceremony a 'noisy, busy, witty, dizzying production'.[41]

The nation was glued to the television and people were pouring into the Olympic Park. Team GB surpassed all expectations and raked in twenty-nine Gold Medals. The home team took third position in the medal table, after the US and China. 'The London 2012 Olympic Games delivered the biggest national television event since current measuring systems began, with 51.9m (90% of the UK population) watching at least 15 minutes of coverage', reported the BBC.[42] The 2012 Summer Olympics also proved to be a wild success in Olympic history. When I was asked to contribute a short piece on the Games for the LOCOG website I wrote: 'It started with passion, and ended with inspiration. London 2012 has delivered a stunningly successful Olympic Games

41. Sarah Lyall, 'A Five-Ring Opening Circus, Weirdly and Unabashedly British' (*The New York Times*, 27 July 2012).
42. 'London 2012 Olympics deliver record viewing figures for BBC' (BBC Media Centre, 13 August 2012).

and is now preparing for the Paralympic Games. The theme "Inspire a generation" has captured the mood of the nation with high spirit and euphoria. From organisers to volunteers to athletes: people from all sections of life have made this success possible.'

The nation basked in the glow of success. Particular praise was heaped on the tens of thousands of Games Makers, as well as the police and the armed forces. On behalf of the whole nation, Lord Coe praised the Games Makers, saying: 'Our volunteers have been sensational. They've had boundless enthusiasm, goodwill, humour – they've done it with grace. And they have in large part been the face of these Games.'[43] Britain was now a 'world superpower in the field of sports', and a Muslim community that had felt beleaguered since 7/7 once again felt it was a stakeholder in Britain's achievements. Mo Farah sparked the nation's spirit and imagination as a long-distance runner, and after his victory he prostrated himself on the ground in line with the traditional Islamic practice of humility at the height of one's success. Britain had given him the best opportunity to succeed: a 'proof of great multicultural Britain', according to comedian Eddie Izzard.[44]

The weather, transport and security – the three uncertainties of London that many were worried about – were spectacularly favourable. The Olympic Park in Stratford and other venues were buzzing with Britons and international visitors. I was able to invite my children to the opening and closing events. After the night events, the streams of people from all corners of London would return home in the early hours – walking or using public transport – without fear or tension. It was London at its best, and I wished that it could have remained so all the time.

---

43. 'London Olympics: Coe praises UK "spirit of generosity"' (BBC News, 13 August 2012).
44. Eddie Izzard 'Mo Farah is proof of great multicultural Britain' (CNN, 13 August 2012).

The billions of pounds of public money used to transform a derelict industrial dumping ground into a modern urban park, with huge sporting venues connected by modern transport infrastructure and one of the largest shopping centres in Europe, was indeed a worthwhile investment. The deprived East Enders in the six host boroughs (Newham, Tower Hamlets, Hackney, Waltham Forest, Greenwich, Barking and Dagenham) housed significant numbers of people from the BME (black and minority ethnic) communities, highlighting modern London's distinctive diversity and creativity. London 2012 provided Londoners with a thrilling regeneration that will continue for decades to come.

* * *

Paralympian Baroness 'Tanni' Grey-Thompson, in a presentation at St Paul's Cathedral prior to the start of the Paralympic Games, paraphrased Nelson Mandela: 'Mandela once said that sport has the power to change the world, but I believe it goes beyond this. Paralympic sport has the power to change the world. The Paralympic Games will show the world what extraordinary athletes can do, who happen to have a disability. These Games will inspire a generation to think differently.'[45] With the world's most successful Olympic Games over, LOCOG prepared itself to welcome the Paralympics. The ceremonial cauldron was lit in London's Trafalgar Square by Claire Lomas, who was paralysed in a horse riding accident. From 29 August–9 September, the nation was once again gripped with another spectacular sports event. London Paralympics 2012 was about raising the profile of Paralympic sports and to demonstrate exceptional performances to the widest possible audience.

---

45. Kevin McCallum, 'Madiba's magic lives on in Rio' (IOL, 12 September 2016).

The primary legacy of the Paralympic Games was about changing perceptions of disability in the world. By nature it has been an embodiment of the human spirit to conquer hurdles. Seeing human beings with disabilities overcome and break barriers of physical or psychological limitations is truly an inspiration. With over 4,000 Paralympians from 166 countries this became the second biggest show on Earth. It was really heartening to see the British rushing early for Paralympic tickets, with most of the quarter million tickets sold; on a par with the enthusiasm shown for the Olympics. It was a tribute to the way Paralympic sports had moved forward. Holding the Paralympic Games in London felt like the Games were truly coming home. The origins of the Paralympics date back to when Ludwig Guttmann, who fled the Nazis before the outbreak of the Second World War, established the first spinal injury centre at Stoke Mandeville hospital in Buckinghamshire in the late 1940s. He introduced sports into the treatment and rehabilitation programme for those with spinal injuries and other disabled people. An annual event at first, by 1952 more than 130 international competitors were taking part in the 'Stoke Mandeville Games'. The first unofficial Paralympic games took place in 1960, running alongside the Summer Olympics in Rome, as the Paralympic movement grew. Separate organizations were formed to serve athletes with other disabilities e.g. for amputees, the visually impaired or those with cerebral palsy, and in 1982 the International Coordinating Committee of World Sports Organizations for the Disabled (ICC) was established to govern the Paralympics and to represent the Games in dialogue with the International Olympic Committee (IOC) and other global organizations.

A new governing body, the International Paralympic Committee (IPC), with a clear vision 'to enable Paralympic athletes to achieve sporting excellence and inspire and excite the world' replaced the ICC in 1992. The IPC included more than 100 member nations as well as the international federations that represent different disability groups. The Paralympic motto, introduced in 2004 at the Paralympic Games in Athens, was 'Spirit in Motion', with the Paralympic values 'Determination, Courage, Inspiration and Equality'. The motto and the values truly represent the human spirit of resilience.

Sadly, there are still parts of the world which have yet to create the minimum facilities required for disabled people in real life. As an SEN teacher, I was lucky to see the bright faces of many disabled British children, some of whom – owing to the facilities they received in schools – were able to outshine other children. The Paralympics would help overcome inhibitions arising from a disability in real life.

Britain came second in the medals table in Beijing and with Paralympics GB's 300-strong team of athletes we expected to remain second in the medal list in 2012. Comparing the number of medals, Paralympics GB did come second behind China with 120 medals, but in the official medals table we were 'pipped at the post' as Russia won just two more golds than the British team. But the 2012 Paralympics exceeded all expectations, raised more money than ever before and were seen around the world by more people than ever before. During the Paralympic Games LOCOG members, including myself, were involved in awarding medals to the winning Paralympians. It was a privilege, and I proudly did this for half a dozen Paralympians in various sports.

* * *

London 2012 was one of Britain's greatest peacetime achievements, a 'yes, we can' attitude filled with confidence and ambition – not only in sports, but also in creating social harmony and defeating the political fractures in our society. London 2012 created a sense of belonging and an ethos of inclusiveness amongst all Britons. The political class and media establishments voluntarily put themselves under a culture of self-regulation for the common good, and it worked. Was it worth spending all that public money for this one-off global event? Well, the transport and other tangible infrastructure, as well as intangible goodwill and positive image of Britain, were phenomenal. Legacy was at the core of holding the London 2012 Olympics and Paralympics, and the London 2012 legacy document stated that: 'After the Games the Olympic Park will be transformed into one of the largest urban parks created in Europe for more than 150 years'.[46] So although British taxpayers paid a much higher bill, of £9.3billion, most British people felt it was money well spent. Globally, however, there is a need for genuine discussions as to whether these highly expensive international games have essentially become elitist. For poorer nations with weaker economic infrastructure they have indeed become a luxury, and this is an issue the Olympic and Paralympic Movements need to address.

Sport is colour-blind and it unites people of all backgrounds. Whether for fitness or competition, sport is excellent for national health and social togetherness. Given the modern challenges of obesity and mental health amongst many children in our society, it is common wisdom to invest in sports facilities across the country. This will not only address some of the challenges our children face but will also enhance feelings of fellowship and team spirit amongst people.

It was also a heartening period for the nation's Muslim citizens, as the near absence of post-7/7 prejudice and suspicion helped them to give their best to contribute towards the success of London 2012. Given how negatively sections of our media and political class treated Muslims in the aftermath of the cold murder of Lee Rigby in 2013, and the rise of Daesh (or ISIS) in 2014, the social harmony and inclusivity they enjoyed in 2012 was exceptional and enviable.

---

46. Muhammad Abdul Bari, 'London 2012: A Global Prospect for Harmony Amid Challenges' (*Huffington Post*, 09 January 2012).

Chapter 7

Radicalization and Terror

A FTER THE 7/7 bombings hit London in 2005, we prayed that the bombers were not from the Muslim community. We could sense the consequences if they were – 9/11 had already heaped incalculable problems upon Muslims – it would be portrayed as Britain's 9/11. The Metropolitan Police confirmed there were four blasts with more than fifty casualties, twenty-two people were in serious condition in hospitals, and over 700 were wounded. The Queen visited the Royal London Hospital, near the East London Mosque, in Whitechapel, and the media was full of speculation.

The following days, everyone looked sombre and worried at work. Britain was on full security alert and it was difficult to concentrate on the tasks at hand. When the announcement of the identity of the four bombers was released a few days later, it was our worst nightmare come true. We were horrified to learn they were, indeed, Muslims: the ringleader was Mohammad Sidique Khan (30), and the others were Shehzad Tanweer (22), Hasib Hussain (18) and Germaine Lindsay (19). The first three were of Pakistani descent from Leeds; the fourth was Jamaican-born from Aylesbury in Buckinghamshire. Two of the bombers left videotapes describing their reasons for becoming what they called 'soldiers'. About two months later, Al Jazeera broadcast a videotape of Khan that said 'we are at war and I am a soldier'.

The feeling was excruciating; how could these ordinary young people kill dozens of innocent commuters in our own city? Why did they put such an unbearable burden on their own families and the communities they originated from? My immediate thoughts were about handling the initial crisis and wondering how we as Muslims would live with this bleak future reality. In Friday sermons, British imams spoke of their horror and about Islam's robust teachings about the preciousness of human life and the need to work for the common good. After the prayer in the ELM, we brought together a few dozen community leaders and interfaith friends in Tower Hamlets and organized a vigil near Aldgate tube station. It was still closed and cordoned off by police and the mood was solemn, but determined.

Two weeks after 7/7, on another Thursday, four attempted bomb attacks disrupted part of London's public transport system at around midday; a fifth bomber dumped his device without setting it off. Police were already under a huge strain and on 22 July they shot and killed a Brazilian man, Jean Charles de Menezes, at South London's Stockwell tube station, believing him to be one of the men wanted for the attacks of the previous day. It was a tragic mistake and the police expressed their regret. On the same day, the ELM was surrounded by armed police officers and the mosque evacuated and searched after a bomb scare. By 29 July, all four suspects from the 21 July attempted bombings had been arrested and the tense situation calmed somewhat.

* * *

Although 9/11 was an historic disaster in the Muslim world, for Britain it was the 2005 London bombings that transformed the socio-political landscape vis-à-vis its Muslim citizens. Despite quickly becoming the new 'suspect community', we were fortunate to receive the support and solidarity of many of Britain's faith groups, trades unions and many civil society bodies that were working for social justice and equality.

In August 2005, the Home Office set up seven working groups comprising academics, community organization representatives, Parliamentarians and civil servants, under the broad name 'Working together to prevent extremism'. These groups covered: education, engaging with women, imams and the role of mosques, regional and local initiatives, security and policing, tackling extremism and radicalization. The purpose was to find the causes of terrorism and its cure. Some from the wider MCB circle took part in the working groups and made valuable contributions. The findings of each group were collated and with dozens of recommendations submitted to the Home Secretary, Charles Clarke, in late September and compiled and published as a report in November. Most working groups were critical of British foreign policy and the report contained sixty-four recommendations to tackle extremism and radicalization. The government, we feared, wanted a profound shift in our mind-set and culture. Although British foreign policy came as one 'key contributory factor' to the terrorist threat, the government was not ready to hear this criticism.

The Blair government made attempts to portray mosques as 'incubators' of violent extremism in order to bring in measures to close them. But the reality was quite different. On 6 October 2005, the government launched a Consultation Paper, *Preventing Extremism Together: Places of Worship*, 'to explore ways in which communities can be supported to address the problems of radicalisation and extremism in their midst' with a closing date for responses of 11 November. It was the month of fasting, when imams and mosque committees were particularly occupied with Ramadan. The MCB was given an extra week for submission of its response; it carried out a nationwide consultation with the community and convened a special conference at the LMC in London's Whitechapel on 12 November. More than 150 leading scholars and community leaders, belonging to various schools of thought from across the country, took part a day-long discussion on the issues of radicalization, extremism, terrorism and places of worship. It prepared a robust response rejecting the government's attempts to criminalize mosques.

The Right Reverend Tom Butler, the Bishop of Southwark, came out strongly against the proposed powers outlined in the Consultation Paper, saying: 'Of course I support the principle of dealing with extremist activity, but targeting places of worship under blanket provisions is excessive and disproportionate'[47] He mentioned that there was only one place of worship, Finsbury Park mosque, where any potential link between a place of worship and terrorist activity could be found. That issue had been resolved by the management committee itself, within the present law. The British Sikh Consultative Forum came to a similar conclusion about the government's Paper.

After the terrorist attack on Glasgow airport on 30 June 2007, we organized another conference of scholars and community leaders at the Islamic Cultural Centre (Regent's Park Mosque) on 7 July 2007, the second anniversary of 7/7. In my keynote speech, I explained what the MCB did after the attack and what it had been doing to empower the community through a number of strategic initiatives such as the Footsteps Project (inspiring school children by introducing Muslim role models), its Leadership Development Programme – helping to

---

47. 'Home Office Proposals for legislation on places of worship' (Church of England, 13 October 2005).

empower young Muslim leadership – and the 'Mosque 100' project to improve the capacity and professionalism of at least 100 mosques. I said: 'British Muslims are unreservedly united in rejecting acts of terror. The safety and security of our society is NON-NEGOTIABLE.' The meeting ended with a Joint Declaration: 'Together We Will Defeat Terrorism'.

* * *

The government's counter-terrorism strategy, CONTEST (with four strands: Prevent, Pursue, Protect and Prepare) was launched in 2003 against the threat from international terrorism, and was later revised in March 2009. As a strand of CONTEST, Prevent was launched in 2006 with the objective of stopping people becoming terrorists or supporting violent extremism. The Department of Communities and Local Government (CLG) provided financial support at the local level through the 'Preventing Violent Extremism' (PVE) programme to build resilient communities. The CLG has distributed over £18 million since 2007 to regional government offices and another £45 million for the period 2008–2011 through its Area Based Grant for PVE.

Although successive governments have expressed their commitment to protecting freedom of speech, many in the Muslim community have become nervous because of Prevent's disproportionate focus upon Muslims. Prevent was seen to be conflating security with the ideals of 'community cohesion'. There were also worries that the Prevent policy was creating internal friction within the Muslim community and drew envy from other faith groups, thus leading to polarization. Some local councils and Muslim groups received Prevent money but spent it on good causes other than purposes intended for the programme. Others were even unwilling to take the money. One organization, the An-Nisa Society, used the money for a project on self-development work with Muslim boys in the

London Borough of Brent. It concluded that 'the government needs to [realize] that it is not possible to deliver "security led" initiatives through Muslim community groups ... Security needs to be addressed separately by experts in this field.'[48]

In early 2009, the government came up with CONTEST 2, which went further than challenging violent extremism; it widened the definition of extremism to include those who would hold views that clashed with 'shared British values' such as democracy. The MCB organized a consultation meeting in Birmingham Central Mosque on 21 March to discuss a response. We agreed that shared values such as personal integrity, good neighbourliness, industriousness and justice were in fact universal and needed to be promoted and practised. Shared values could not be prescribed or imposed on citizens and people should not be criminalized for having opinions on these issues. At the end of March 2009, I was invited to give a seminar at the Las Casas Institute, in Oxford University's Blackfriars Hall on the topic of 'In Defence of Shared Values: The Muslim Council of Britain's Perspectives'. I said: 'There must be a basic acceptance, on all sides, among individuals and among groups that Britain has a set of organic values which are arrived at through consensus and accommodation, not through diktat and bluster. It allows us all to be able to say, with one voice that we reject hateful speech.' My speech was later published as a Las Casas Institute booklet towards 'emerging work on institutions, inter-religious dialogue and the nature of secularism in the European arena'.

Because of the ongoing criticism of its overall ineffectiveness, a review of Prevent was initiated by the CLG under a parliamentary committee led by Dr Phyllis Starkey MP towards the end of the Labour government under Gordon Brown. After hearings and written submissions, including

48. Salaam, 'Preventing Violent Extremism (PVE) & PREVENT – a response from the Muslim community' (Salaam, 24 September 2009).

from mainstream Muslim groups such as the Muslim Council of Britain, the committee published a report on 30 March 2010, *Preventing Violent Extremism*, saying Prevent was stigmatizing and alienating a whole community. There were suggestions that it should be scaled back considerably towards more evidence-based targeted intervention, and resourced to address the social and economic difficulties of Muslim communities. The review also made recommendations to separate the 'Channel' programme (a multi-agency approach to protect vulnerable people by identifying individuals at risk of terrorism) from the CONTEST strategy and place it within the context of other crime prevention initiatives.

* * *

However, following the May 2010 election the new Tory-led coalition government bypassed the CLG report. Instead, it initiated its own review in November 2010 and this time no mainstream Muslim group was seen to be consulted. A new Prevent initiative was launched that put 'extremist ideology' at the heart of the threat. The government decided upon a bizarre, but not publicly declared, 'no platform' policy towards many bona fide Muslim groups that were not considered sufficiently 'moderate', or were improbably deemed 'nonviolent extremists' in an academically-weak 'conveyor belt' theory of the path to violent extremism.

The conveyor belt theory held that individuals started off as being angry or disaffected and through a linear progression turned to more religious and/or politicized 'non-violent extremism', and finally to violent extremism or terrorism. It was a temptingly simple idea, and one which has taken root among some political commentators and journalists as well as being parodied by some Muslims. However, despite its media and political popularity, the theory remains academically discredited and lacks evidence to back it up. In reality, some extremists have been in gangs, most lack religious knowledge, some have rarely attended mosques and a few are converts. Most encounter radical groups and preachers via other means such as the internet, not in mosques as some detractors desperately suggest. In practice, radicals have more often than not been ejected from mosques. Socio-economic and political factors, social exclusion and mental health also play an important role. Some extremists have been highly secular: they go to nightclubs, pick up girls, drink wine and use drugs. Some go through the criminal justice system and have come into contact with the police. Some get radicalized in prison. The generation gap with parents or imams, lack of empathy from adults, and persistent negative depiction in the media also make young people vulnerable. Some may suddenly turn to impulsive religiosity ('born-again' Muslims) without a basic knowledge of Islam and its teachings: with little religious knowledge they see Islam as a radical ideology.

The conveyor belt theory had already been disproved by an MI5 Briefing Note, *Understanding Radicalisation and Violent Extremism in the UK*, published in 2008. Based on hundreds of case studies, the report concluded: 'there is no single pathway to violent extremism'. Also in 2008, in his book, *Leaderless Jihad: Terror Networks in the Twenty-First Century*, the highly experienced forensic psychiatrist and former CIA case officer, Marc Sageman, rejected 'the views that place responsibility for terrorism on society or a flawed, predisposed individual.' As the coalition government's civic conversation with majority Muslims had been put on hold since their election in 2010, it had to find fringe groups or think-tanks with Muslim connections to show it was somehow consulting with the community. But what the government failed to realise was that the community didn't trust its small coterie of approved groups or individuals. The new Prevent was losing its 'buy in' from those who mattered most for its success.

Nobody would disagree with the need for an effective counter-extremism measure to safeguard vulnerable individuals, especially impressionable children, at risk of radicalization and extremism. Like sexual grooming, radicalization that leads to extremism has affected some within the Muslim community. But the Prevent strategy was seen by many as stifling Muslim children's natural expression in the school environment, and damaging relationships between families and teachers and police. It was having a negative effect on open debate, free speech and political dissent, helping to sow a mistrust of Muslims. The student community was convinced Prevent had a negative impact on free debate and relationships among students, particularly in higher education institutions. The National Union of Students (NUS) expressly opposed Prevent. In an open letter to the government, the NUS president, Megan Dunn, reaffirmed that the NUS was 'committed to ensuring legitimate, proportionate and effective measures are in place to prevent students becoming engaged with or sympathetic to violent terrorism.'[49] However, she went on to say:

> The Act and the associated regulations introduce numerous practical issues which we worry risk being potentially counter-productive to the stated aims of the programme. These concerns include issues pertaining to academic freedoms, and so the quality of education and research that we deliver; the implication of students being monitored on the basis of their race, religion or mental health conditions; the role of academic and non-academic staff in universities and colleges and their relationship to students on

---

49. Megan Dunn, 'Our open letter to Jo Johnson on the Counter-Terrorism & Security Act' (NUS Connect, 21 September 2015).

campus; the regulatory status of students' unions
as charities and not public bodies; and the ability
of students and staff on campus to campaign on
political issues.

The government's Counter-Terrorism and Security Act
(CTSA) 2015 put Prevent on a statutory footing and placed a
legal obligation on teachers and other public sector workers
to have 'due regard to the need to prevent people from being
drawn into terrorism'. In reality, it put extra pressure on
people to keep an eye on colleagues in the workplace. In the
education sector, this led to a surge in referrals from schools,
and some young Muslim children were subjected to confused
referrals arising from Prevent. Safeguarding of children is vital,
but incidents of schoolchildren questioned by Prevent staff for
making spelling mistakes – such as 'terrorist house' instead of
'terraced house' and 'cooker bomb' instead of 'cucumber' – did
not help allay community misgivings against Prevent.

On 10 July 2015, in an open letter, 280 academics, lawyers
and public figures made an unprecedented intervention
claiming that the controversial law would 'make Britain less
safe as it will force radical political discussion underground'.[50]
There had also been increased calls for a reform of the Prevent
strategy. Prominent individuals like David Anderson QC (the
former independent reviewer of terrorism legislation) and
human rights group Rights Watch UK expressed concerns
about the discriminatory nature and effectiveness of Prevent.
The Labour party consulted Muslim groups such as the MCB
to develop positive alternatives to Prevent. In April 2016, the
UN special rapporteur, Maina Kiai, similarly commented on
the negative effect of Prevent on British schoolchildren, and
the following month Nils Muiznieks, the Council of Europe's

---

50. Robert Verkeik, 'Government deradicalisation plan will
    brand Muslims with beards as terrorists, say academics' (*The
    Independent*, 10 July 2015).

Commissioner for Human Rights, said Britain's Prevent 'risks isolating the very communities whose cooperation is most needed to fight violent extremism.'[51] On 29 September 2016, more than 140 writers and experts, including Karen Armstrong, Marc Sageman and Noam Chomsky, expressed concern 'with the implementation of "radicalisation" policies within the UK Prevent strategy'.[52] But successive governments paid no heed.

In my capacity as an advisor to Citizens UK's Commission on Islam, Participation and Public Life, I visited major cities across the country and learned about community misgivings with Prevent in most places I went. However, we also heard support for the programme in a few cities. After further inquiry, we learned that the delivery of Prevent was being made in the name of 'Safeguarding Children'; this makes good sense, as no parent will object to safeguarding of their children, but it failed to address the underlying concerns about the strategy.

Since Prevent's inception, the threat of far-right extremism in Europe has also grown and that reality cannot be ignored any further. In the aftermath of the brutal killing of Birmingham grandfather Mohammed Saleem by a Ukrainian neo-Nazi in April 2013, Prevent took far-right extremists more seriously, and after the vicious murder of Jo Cox MP by a white supremacist in June 2016, Prevent has been dealing with a significant number of far-right referrals. The mowing down of a Muslim worshipper outside a north London mosque by a far-right extremist in June 2017 further highlighted the threat from far-right terrorism, along with the Daesh-inspired terror attacks by radicalized Muslims that had caused havoc in Manchester and London prior to that. There is no room for

---

51. 'Commissioner on UK "Prevent" strategy and education' (Council of Europe, 17 May 2016).
52. Marc Sageman, Noam Chomsky, Humayun Ansari, et al., 'Anti-radicalisation strategy lacks evidence base in science' (*The Guardian*, 29 September 2016).

complacency or finger-pointing; we all need to work together to eradicate the menace from our midst.

Today's suicide terrorists are internet-savvy; they are often radicalized with the aid of social media, such as Twitter, WhatsApp and Facebook (and other, more secretive networks) outside of any institutionalized religious structure. Some parents are unaware of the world of social media or wider youth culture; as they lack the confidence in communicating with their own children, young people lose their anchor from their own tradition and culture. British Muslims themselves, being the worst victims of violent extremism, have consistently and robustly opposed terrorism. Successive British governments eventually took a level-headed approach towards IRA terrorism, and where historically the Catholic community as a whole was blamed for the criminality of a few, no-one seriously believed that the Catholic Church was responsible for the actions of armed groups. It is unfortunate that the same principle has not yet been extended to Muslims. Unlike others, they are disproportionately affected by the constant diminution of their reputation in the name of counter-terrorism. Some Islamophobes have even accused the religion of Islam itself for any criminal act by an individual of Muslim faith – no matter how far the individual is from his or her religion. This has proved to be a recipe for alienating Muslims and polarizing society.

The community is often accused of 'not doing enough' to defeat terrorism, but the unfortunate reality is that voices of sanity within the community are not (often enough) amplified in the media; even major outlets such as the BBC have sometimes appeared more interested in featuring extremists such as Anjem Choudhary (who was finally jailed in 2016 for his vocal support of ISIS) than hosting mainstream Muslim commentators. There is also another reality: in the midst of continuous scrutiny and often negative media, the community has been struggling to articulate its voice.

The political class and media establishment should rise above short-term rhetoric and see Muslims as part of the solution, not the problem. Genuine involvement of communities is needed to instil a sense of confidence and keep it – not continually talking them down. In order to defeat the menace of violent extremism, some of it coming from abroad, it is essential we all work together. It is simply common sense that in a mature democracy like ours, government works in collaboration and partnership with all citizens, irrespective of policy differences. On this I think Parliamentary select committees appear to better understand the social and community dynamics than government and politicians as a whole.

* * *

When three bright teenage girls: Shamima Begum (15), Kadiza Sultana (16) and Amira Abase (15) disappeared from east London's Bethnal Green Academy on 17 February 2015, it was a terrible shock. There was concern they were heading to Syria to join the so-called Islamic State, or Daesh, and Prime Minister David Cameron said it was 'deeply concerning'. The families were devastated and the Archbishop of Canterbury, Justin Welby, felt it was a 'nightmare situation' for them. I appeared on BBC Breakfast television and said: 'the girls were talented and dynamic but impressionable and that they could end up "with the vilest and most dangerous group on earth" was heart-breaking for the parents.' The families were struggling to cope and they expected moral support from the East London Mosque, the ELM's media officer went that extra mile to empathetically handle the situation from the beginning (this was featured in Robb Leech's 'Welcome to the Mosque' on BBC Two in September 2015). The fear that the girls were heading to Syria to join the world's most notorious terrorist group proved to be correct within days. As CCTV footage of the three girls passing through the doors at Gatwick Airport was released to the media, it was known by then that they were heading for Turkey. Ultimately, they ended up in the terrorist-held territory in Syria.

The mystery was how could these 'straight-A students' dodge their families, school and police so cleverly? It was a soul-searching question, and through this one thing became clear: As David Cameron said, 'the fight against [extremism] is not just one that we can wage by the police and border control. It needs every school, every university, every college, every community to recognise they have a role to play'.[53] The allure of extremism, or the glamour of 'fake jihad' in faraway lands is dreadful. Since 2014, thousands of young people from across Muslim majority and minority countries have made their journey to Daesh-held territories. An estimated 850 British men and women, including some young and talented schoolchildren, joined the group over the last few years – before Daesh was ousted from Mosul and other places in Iraq and Syria. Nearly half are reported to have returned and 15 per cent killed. One of the three girls, Kadiza Sultana, was reported to have made attempts to come back but died during an aerial bombardment in summer 2016; the other two have also most probably been killed. Their deaths should have laid bare the poisonous lies of the group and prevented other vulnerable young people from joining them. However, the nihilistic cult has also inspired 'lone wolves', hidden in society, to commit callous acts of mass murder – so we must remain vigilant.

Ever since the spectacular rise of this vicious group in Syria and Iraq, there has been speculation about its emergence. One thing that gradually became clear was that many of Daesh's military commanders were former henchmen of Iraqi dictator Saddam Hussein. As the post-invasion US administration in

---

53. '"Syria-bound" London girls: PM "deeply concerned"' (BBC News, 21 February 2015).

Iraq callously decided to disband the army and Iraq's basic infrastructure without any forward plan, these ruthless people were suddenly unemployed. It was at that point that some of them found a haven in terrorist groups and were joined by other people of a similarly evil nature. Together, they resorted to slick online propaganda to attract impressionable young people from across the world to their wicked cause.

This is of course one side of the story. But why and how do people, especially teenagers like the Bethnal Green girls, living in comfort in a stable and diverse democracy such as Britain, become brainwashed such that they leave everything behind and join a death cult? Radicalization that leads to violence is indeed a serious problem for many countries, and Daesh-linked innovative terrorism and far-right extremism is on the rise across Europe. Defeating such terrorism needs an open mind to find the root causes involved. Being fixated on one community (such as Muslims) or one reason (such as religion or ideology) has in many cases led to the wrong conclusions and damaging consequences for community relations. One thing is certain: those who sign up to nihilistic violence do not follow logic. Most of them are too exposed to dangers of skewed ideology, utopian ideas, hateful politics, hatred or grievances. Individual anger or frustration, family disorder, lack of positive role models, and socio-political strain (or a blend of such) could all be a catalyst for their actions. It is now very clear that there is no single pathway for extremist violence; no 'silver bullet' or 'one size fits all' cause.

At a base level, we cannot ignore socio-economic deprivation and political unfairness. We cannot ignore young people's teenage vulnerability either, their (sometimes) lack of self-worth and sense of ownership in life. An easy access to the online world is empowering to many, but destructive to those young people who are not properly supervised. In fact, many parents do not have a basic knowledge of the harm online attractions such as pornography and radicalization can bring to their children. Some online predators prey on young people's vulnerability through the 'dark web'; sometimes friend-to-friend peer-to-peer networks.

An absence of greater empowerment and civic engagement can be factors in radicalisation, too. The effect of foreign policies in the Middle East and the hurtful consequences they have brought cannot be ignored, nor successive governments' stubbornness in talking down a community and the inadvertent depiction of Muslims as moderates or extremists. All are factors that have alienated some. Giving the impression of spying and intelligence-gathering on Muslims, rather than working for greater cohesion and connecting communities through two-way positive integration, has proved unhelpful. Community 'buy-in' is fundamentally important to eradicate the menace, as it is the parents and communities that suffer primarily by the loss of their teenage children to the groomers of extremism or faceless terrorists. Their pains and needs must be heard.

* * *

Extremism is nothing new in human society. There were two occasions in Muslim history when violent extremism rattled peace and stability. One was in the early period of Islam, during the time of the fourth Caliph, when Muslims faced unusual violence from a group known as Khawarij or Kharijites ('the Seceders'). The Kharijites developed extreme doctrines beyond mainstream Islam, they espoused *takfir* (declaring other Muslims who did not agree with them as 'kafir', or infidels) and resorted to violent means, including assassinations, to eradicate their opponents. As the first three generations of Muslims were deeply rooted to Islamic values, traditions and spirituality, they were able to gradually root out the Kharijites. The other challenge was in the late eleventh century, from a branch of the Ismaili sect of Shia

Islam, whose leader was Hassan-i Sabbah; they wreaked havoc in some parts of Iran and Syria. Sabbah's group became known as the Hashshashin, or 'Assassins' in English. However, they were stamped out mainly by the Mongols.

Over the last few centuries, Muslims were subjected to several humiliating phases due to internal failings and external onslaughts, such as colonialism, but had not experienced the existence of death cults such as al-Qaeda and Daesh until relatively recently. In modern times, the Japanese kamikaze pilots of the Second World War would probably qualify as the first such example of a death cult. They would load their planes with bombs and fly them directly into the target in suicide attacks. Between October 1944 and August 1945, nearly 4,000 such attacks were said to have taken place. Later, suicide attacks were perpetrated by the Liberation Tigers of Tamil Eelam (LTTE, the 'Tamil Tigers') in the 1980s and 1990s. They targeted Sinhalese economic and military interests in Sri Lanka and used suicide attacks as a weapon to achieve their political goals, and even assassinated the former Indian Prime Minister Rajiv Ghandhi in a suicide attack in 1991. But al-Qaeda and Daesh-linked suicide terrorism in western countries today cannot be explained by any other rationale except nihilism.

Daesh claims that it wants to restore Islam's early caliphate, but any Muslim – or even non-Muslim – who knows the basic history of Islam would reject their claim as anti-historic, delusional and treacherous. Their nihilism leaves no room for any negotiation or political solution. What benefit do 'lone wolf' attacks in western cities bring other than frightening ordinary people and provoking a backlash against Muslims? The very act of inciting terror in the hearts of defenceless civilians, the wholesale destruction of buildings and properties, and the bombing and maiming of innocent men, women and children are all totally forbidden in Islam. Terrorism, including state-sponsored acts of terror, is antithetical to religious principles. As the texts of Abrahamic faiths come from the same source, their scriptures contain 'violent' passages that can be quoted out of context and used for violence. Religious texts should be understood in their proper context, mere translations into different languages and reading without understanding the historical context can be dangerously misleading.

Muslims are the worst sufferers from Daesh-linked suicide attacks in our cities, and they must invest in raising their game in the social, economic and political arena. They must initiate a deeper study into the root causes for the continuous phenomenon of disproportionately higher number of Muslim youths in the criminal justice system. Only then can they employ appropriate resources to remove the problems. It is time our communities build inner resilience, secure their home front with effective parenting, and improve engagement with their own young people who are the assets of any society. By involving more talented and professional young Muslims – boys and girls – in the affairs of the community they can strengthen an alliance with wider society and better tackle Islamophobia. Professionalizing numerous institutions that the first generation has built over decades will also improve their service to local communities. Better resilience helps us effectively address internal as well as external challenges.

Human beings are born free with freedom of thought, and our mind is a mysterious reservoir of limitless thoughts and ideas that can swing like a pendulum from one end of the spectrum to the other. Proactive and creative people can have valuable ideas in life, including radical thought, which can make an active contribution and bring positive change. They are not only acceptable but encouraged in successful countries, as long as their actions do not cause harm to others and they fall within the law of the land. Radical ideas can kick our mind into high gear and push us to make sense of them. Education opens the door for curiosity, ideas and creativity to act. 'Our brain is a parachute that only works when it is open', is a good metaphor for blue-sky thinking, but it is a parachute that needs to open at the right time! Radical thinking needs to be brought into effective action by proper debate in an open environment for the good of society. The British education system, especially at university level, has always encouraged radical thinking and unconventional ideas that have led to great good for the country over the centuries.

Muslims are supposed to be a middle-path community treading the 'middle way' (Arabic: *wassatiyya*) of life. While Islam accommodates radical ideas it detests extremism, as mentioned in the Qur'an; 'do not commit excess in your religion' (*al-Nisa'* 4: 171; *al-Ma'idah* 5: 77). The Prophet as an exemplar to Muslims advised and practised moderation in life. Needless to say, unlawful killing is clearly forbidden (haram; *al-Ma'idah* 5: 32). As for the few verses of the Qur'an (the so-called 'sword verses') that some extremists exploit for their criminal acts and some Islamophobe academics cite to demonize Islam (e.g. *al-Baqarah* 2: 191 and *al-Tawbah* 9: 5), the historical fact is they were revealed at a time when Muslims had endured more than a decade of extreme persecution. Eventually they fled to a safe land, but even that was invaded and they faced extermination by the pagans. These verses relate to physical battle. Even then the Qur'an tells believers to maintain justice and forgive the opponents, and not to linger on hostility.

* * *

Islamophobic groups such as the English Defence League (EDL, a far-right street protest movement formed in 2009 in opposition to what it considered to be a spread of Islamism and Shariah in the UK) and Britain First (a far-right nationalist political party formed in 2011 by former members of the British National Party) took advantage of anti-Muslim sentiment and became emboldened to corner the community further. The EDL orchestrated a number of violent demonstrations against mosques in major cities, and threatened a big demonstration in front of the ELM in 2010. However, local civil society groups formed an alliance, United East End, and thwarted the demo by organizing a counter-demonstration with 5,000 local people. Probably a coincidence, but in February 2011 – on the day the EDL organized a big confrontational march against Muslims in Luton – Prime Minister David Cameron gave his 'muscular liberalism' speech at the Munich Security Conference, which to many eyes seemed aimed directly at Muslims. Many thought it was ill-advised, as the tone and some of the comments put further pressure on the Muslim community.

Things improved during the brilliant Olympics year of 2012. However, on 22 May 2013, the callous murder of fusilier Lee Rigby in broad daylight by two young Muslims of Nigerian-origin in Greenwich (London) shattered the positive atmosphere. The fallout was grave: anti-Muslim incidents rose sharply and one mosque in north London was torched to the ground. A BBC survey in September 2013 showed more than a quarter of young adults (27 per cent) in Britain mistrusted Muslims. In 2014, news of 'Operation Trojan Horse' broke. This was an alleged organized attempt by school governors and teachers of Muslim background to introduce an Islamist or Salafist ethos into several schools in Birmingham; an attempt to 'Islamise' state schools with Muslim-majority pupils. This story was perpetrated on the basis of a letter regarded by many as fake, and the allegations were vehemently denied as absurd by the individuals involved. But the ensuing trial-by-media put huge pressure on the entire Muslim community. In spite of criticism from some in the education sector, a retired senior police officer and security expert (Peter Clarke) was appointed by the-then Education Secretary, Michael Gove, to investigate the allegations. In the subsequent report, *Report*

*into allegations concerning Birmingham schools arising from
the 'Trojan Horse' letter*, Clarke saw 'co-ordinated, deliberate
and sustained action ... to introduce an intolerant and
aggressive Islamic ethos' into some schools in Birmingham.
However, the House of Commons Education Committee's
official response, *Extremism in schools: the Trojan Horse
affair: Ofsted Response to the Committee's Seventh Report
of Session 2014–15*, asserted that: 'No evidence of extremism
or radicalisation, apart from a single isolated incident, was
found by any of the inquiries and there was no evidence of a
sustained plot nor of a similar situation pertaining elsewhere
in the country.' In May 2017, the case against five senior
teachers accused of professional misconduct in the 'Trojan
Horse' inquiry was dropped. Sadly, the fallout and reputational
damage to British Muslims has been massive.

According to the House of Commons Women and Equalities
Committee report, *Employment opportunities for Muslims in
the UK*, published in August 2016: 'Muslim people suffer the
greatest economic disadvantages of any group in society.' The
unemployment rates of Muslims were more than twice that
of the general population (12.8 per cent compared to 5.4 per
cent) and 41 per cent were economically inactive (compared
to 21.8 per cent of the general population). Muslim women
were three times more likely to be unemployed, because of
the 'triple penalty' impacting on their job prospects – being
women, being from an ethnic minority and being Muslim.
This recognition by MPs was a genuine reflection of the
reality being faced by many. However, the most discussed and
besmirched group of British citizens has been Muslim youth.
A jointly-funded research project[54] by the National Youth
Agency (NYA) and Muslim Youth Helpline (MYH) in 2007
found that the main concerns affecting Muslim youth were:

54. Rabia Malik, Aaliyah Shaikh and Mustafa Suleyman, *Providing
Faith and Culturally Sensitive Support Services to Young
British Muslims* (Leicester: The National Youth Agency, 2007).

relationships; mental health issues; religion; sexuality and sexual health; and, the criminal justice system. Identity and a sense of belonging; integration; lack of infrastructure to cater for their needs; unwillingness or the inability of older Muslims to relate with them; and, discontent over foreign policy were also highlighted. Added to this, racial and religious prejudice has lowered their career prospects in recent times.

While known to have a strong attachment to Britain, many young Muslims feel that they also have to frequently prove their loyalty as well. Muslim students make up a significant proportion of Britain's education sector, including further and higher education. As they hail from incredibly diverse backgrounds, young Muslims can be ambassadors for Britain abroad; the majority are raised and schooled with fellow British citizens. Some may display overt religiosity in their dress and expressions, but many are remarkably similar to any other young modern Briton in their hopes, aspirations and dreams. Many of them are serving the nation through charity work and contributions in other areas of life.

The rise of right-wing political parties using anti-Muslim rhetoric in some parts of Europe, although not yet electorally successful, is also worrying. It is an irony that a continent that suffered from the evils of bigotry in the last century appears not to be taking the rise of new bigotry seriously enough. It took the cold-blooded massacre of seventy-seven young Norwegians in July 2011 by far-right 'Christian' extremist, Anders Behring Breivik, to create some alarm within Europe's political class. It was a horrendous wake-up call to home-grown extreme nationalism and far-right violence. During his trial, Breivik made vitriolic attacks on European leaders for their 'impotence' to stand up against a Muslim 'conquest' of Europe. He was propounding the 'Eurabia' fantasy that is central to the so-called 'counter-jihadist' movement propelled by anti-Muslim ideologues. Sadly, such Islamophobia has been desensitized in recent years (it has 'passed the dinner table test', as Tory politician Sayeeda Warsi said in January 2011). Even raising the issue of anti-Muslim bigotry in modern Britain can invite accusations that Muslims are playing the 'victimhood' card. Yes, some in the community are not savvy enough to articulate their opinions well, but many think that post-7/7, the lacklustre response of successive British governments to rising Islamophobia has not helped the situation.

* * *

Young people, whatever their backgrounds, are the assets of any country. Successful nations genuinely invest in properly raising their future generation. Parents, communities, religious institutions, youth groups – in fact the whole of society including the government – should concentrate on helping vulnerable young people and protect them from any harm. The British Muslim community and its important institutions must make it a priority to empower their youth for the better future of all.

The greatest concern a parent has in our time is safeguarding a child from abuse, paedophilia and extremism. Parents should be on their guard by making their homes a loving and inspirational place to live. Education providers, youth services and religious institutions have a major role to play as well. By nature, children in the adolescence-to-adult transition, because of their physical and hormonal changes as well as ever-changing social milieu, are volatile and painfully vulnerable. Arrogance, rebellion and resentment are part of their growth and some may indulge in drugs, criminality or unworthy sexual practices. It is the job of the adult to address these issues by valuing them and accepting their mistakes. We have to build a world based on better equality and basic justice such that no other ugly menace arises in the future. Our higher education institutions have a major role to play in encouraging creative ideas to flourish, even if they are often deemed 'radical'. Muslim students today are very different from what they were even couple of decades ago – overwhelmingly British born, more confident and more assertive. It is important that our policy makers keep pace with social changes and allow education campuses to remain as the bastion of free-thinking. This will help in building a confident society and reduce bigotry.

Young people, by nature, are driven by idealism. Many joined underground communist movements in the last century, either for national liberation or social justice (or both). The Muslim youth are crying for positive changes everywhere, and in spite of the odds around them they have a huge potential in the West. In Britain, some of their potential is being employed in the voluntary sector, through social media and informal groupings they are helping themselves and the people around them with enterprise and civic engagement. Increasingly in many Muslim countries, from Indonesia to Morocco, young entrepreneurs, both men and women, are driving the economic growth by initiating thousands of start-ups in the business and new technology sectors.

* * *

Violent extremism in a small section of British Muslims cannot be seen in isolation to the malaise in other Muslim majority countries, particularly in recent times. For decades, a number of these countries have been run by corrupt, incompetent rulers and tin-pot dictators – secularist or nationalist, monarchic or military – or 'elected dictatorships' with sham democracies, where leaders win nearly 100 per cent of the vote. These despots and deep-state shadowy gangs, some with the blessing of foreign powers, preside over failed politics and dismal economies. Rule of law, freedom of expression as well as minimum accountability of governance and economy have all but vanished from these countries.

Others have weaponized sectarian or social division to increase the lease of their political life. Far removed from Islam's egalitarian model and teachings of running public affairs, they have proved themselves unfit to run their countries and their historic people. On the other hand, non-stop meddling by some western countries in the politics and economies of sovereign nations for the 'national interest', aided by direct military invasion in some cases, has created toxicity inside those countries and across the world.

With nowhere to pin their hopes, many grabbed the opportunity of the so-called 'Arab Spring' that started in Tunisia at the end of 2010 and rapidly spread to a number of Arab countries. But this was foreseen as a death knell by the despots in power and reactionary forces, encouraged by silence from the western powers, nipped the Arab awakening in the bud. The distraught Arabs felt betrayed. In the absence of effective religious and spiritual voices, as well as a dearth of alternative citizen leadership, people's frustration and anger has turned into meaningless violence and nihilism. Anarchy in the Arab world and poverty in Africa are now directly affecting Europe with an unprecedented rise in refugee numbers. Some say: 'the chickens are coming home to roost.'

The radicalization and terror that we see today emanating from some Middle Eastern countries and influencing some Muslims did not grow in a vacuum and can only be contained and defeated through 'human' solutions. Creating an environment of good governance, accountability, a safe and stable political space for all citizens and better economic infrastructure are basic to any people. As politics deals with power and power corrupts people, there must be well-established public ethics supported by a strong civil society that has the courage and ability to defend the weak from the strong and the poor from the rich. A live and robust civil society remains constantly on guard against misuse of power.

If errant politicians or ambitious military officers attempt to temporarily push the boundaries of legitimate power, civil society fights tooth and nail to redress it. In developed democracies civil society is a blessing, where people can speak through the ballot box, minimize political errors and change leadership in a peaceful manner. Civil society often needs champions: individuals, institutions, or both. Martin Luther King, in the US in the 1960s, and Archbishop Tutu in South Africa were exemplars as such individuals.

Sadly, over the last few decades only a handful of developing countries have been able to cross the threshold of political peril and improve the socio-economic conditions of their people by means of representative governance and the rule of law. The Arab world's renowned political Islamic theorist, Tunisia's Rached Ghannouchi, spoke on the causes that are known to drive some people to terrorism in his own country. According to the Ennahda leader, terrorism is in part a product of dictatorship, though poverty and unemployment are important factors in explaining the appeal of terrorism to young people. Many of those who were angry and turned to extremism had been raised in marginalized and poor areas. He believes that a misunderstanding and misinterpretation of Islam coupled with a dysfunctional upbringing and lack of education have played a role in feeding terrorism. 'Freedom alone does not change much in the lives of people if it is not supported by the rule of law and inclusive economic growth', he asserts.[55] There is no magic wand to uproot violence and terrorism from the world. As for Muslims, they must go back to the basic principles of their religion, such as justice, if they want 'religious' answers to the extremism and violence in their midst. The way out is a war on ignorance and a massive jihad (utmost effort) to improve knowledge

55. Ahmed El Amraoui, 'Tunisia's Ghannouchi: Poverty is a root cause of terror' (Al Jazeera, 14 Nov 2015).

and education in order to bring about sane politics and a sustainable economy.

* * *

Acclaimed researchers and writers like Karen Armstrong, a British scholar of comparative religion, have tried to explain a 'big picture' reality of terrorism emanating from some Muslim countries. Contrary to the opinions of many politicians and think-tanks, in a 2015 interview for Qantara.de, an internet portal aimed to promote intellectual dialogue between the Western and Islamic world, she criticized the narrative that Islam is essentially more violent than Christianity and points out that there is a 'long and inglorious tradition of distorting Islam in Europe'.[56] She observed: 'The caricature of Islam's Prophet in the West as a violent, epileptic, lecherous charlatan since the time of the Crusades has not gone away; this twisted image of Islam developed at a time when Jews also were caricatured as the evil, perverse and potent enemies of Europe.' This is more or less uncontroversial among academic experts of Orientalism, such as Zachary Lockman and many others who are well-versed in history. In a 2014 comment piece in *The Guardian*, Armstrong attempted to get to the root cause of religious violence and concluded that in fact, the barbaric violence of Daesh 'may be, at least in part, the offspring of policies guided by [western] disdain'.[57]

It is true that government agencies and departments like USAID (US Agency for International Development) and DfID (Britain's Department for International Development) and numerous international western NGOs have been giving invaluable help to developing countries, including

---

56. Claudia Mende, 'Islamist violence is "in part a product of Western disdain"' (Qantara.de, 11 February 2015).
57. Karen Armstrong, 'The myth of religious violence' (*The Guardian*, 25 September 2014).

the Muslim world. But in the absence of any long-term and serious capacity-building project to bring good governance (not 'exporting' democracy) through genuine representative and accountable governance, their efforts will remain short-term and hollow. Individual philanthropy in many western countries, such as Britain, is enviable. But if their leaders do not prioritize in building the infrastructure of developing countries, and aid is not replaced by mutually beneficial trade, things will not change. What is required in the twenty-first century is transfer of knowledge, know-how and capacity-building for political stability and sustainable economic growth in developing countries.

In spite of their historic presence in the West, there is still an unwritten culture of prejudice against Muslims; even after generations have lived as citizens they are still seen as immigrants. In the post-9/11 world they are often seen with the prism of security and, some suggest, as a 'suspect community' subjected to 'McCarthyism'. Muslim women who are increasingly asserting their presence in public life are the worst sufferers of ill-treatment, just because of the dress worn by some. Things are far better in Britain, but we need to raise the bar of our success criteria in achieving community harmony by proactive engagement with the wider society. By choosing Sadiq Khan as their Mayor with a large mandate in May 2016, Londoners showed Britain's success in celebrating diversity. Many feel this will help in enhancing Muslim engagement in civic participation for the common good.

* * *

In the period leading up to the 2015 United Kingdom general election, the Conservative Party had been losing votes and support to a nationalist Eurosceptic party called Ukip (the United Kingdom Independence Party). In a bid to prop up his leadership and restore the support of his own Eurosceptic

MPs, David Cameron, the British Prime Minister, promised a vote on 'Brexit' – whether the UK would remain in or leave the European Union. After a surprise win on 7 May 2015, with an increased majority, Cameron announced that the United Kingdom European Union membership referendum would take place on 23 June 2016. The run up to the referendum was highly-charged, and emotions ran high on both sides. On 16 June, the Labour MP for Batley and Spen, Jo Cox, who was in the Remain camp, was shot and then stabbed multiple times following a constituency meeting in Birstall, West Yorkshire. The death of a highly respected public servant and philanthropist with two young children horrified the nation. The suspect, named locally as Tommy Mair, apparently shouted 'Britain First' (perhaps in reference to the British far-right political party) as he shot and stabbed the Labour MP.

The violent death of Jo Cox was not only unbearable to her family and people close to her, but a wake-up call for the whole country. I was stunned by the cold-bloodedness of the murder. Her death touched my family as well, as both Jo and her husband Brendan were my friends and we were privileged to host them one evening at our house in Merton, south London, in 2008. I first met Brendan quite by chance, probably at a party conference either in 2006 or 2007, and since then we had kept in touch with each other. One day, when we were having a telephone conversation, he unexpectedly asked me: 'Muhammad, why don't you visit us on our boat?' I was not sure what exactly he meant by 'boat', so felt a bit surprised.

I paused for a while and asked: 'Boat?'

He laughed on the other side and said: 'Jo and I are boat dwellers. We live on a canal in west London.'

I was trying to figure this out – a successful professional couple living on a boat! I was aware of impoverished boat dwellers in Bangladesh, known as the Bedey Community, who live in their boats on the waterways in some places. I used to see them in my childhood almost every year when we were surrounded by water. In the monsoon, when boats were the only means of communication, they used to come to our village to sell merchandise like children's dolls; some of them would show magic tricks that hypnotized our young brains. So, I was curious to see the modern boat dwellers in London. I hid my surprise and said: 'Oh sure, I will come, inshallah.' We fixed a date.

I went to their boat one late afternoon. It was a mid-sized affair with the basic amenities of life amid other boats moored nearby. Jo and Brendan greeted me warmly and explained how they used to move from place to place. It was a new experience for me. They cooked a delicious vegetarian dish and Jo was very sociable; I learned she was working for Oxfam and I could feel her passion for the world of charity; giving and serving those who needed some extra help to stand on their feet. Before leaving I asked them if they would accept an invitation to come to our house. They readily agreed.

After returning home that night I narrated my experience to Sayeda and the children. She exclaimed and on her own said: 'Really, we must invite them!' Our four children also wanted to see them. We agreed on a suitable date for dinner and they came to our house. In spite of the age gap (our oldest child, Rima, was ten years younger than her), Jo became friendly with all of them. Sayeda cooked some South Asian vegetarian dishes for them and we ate together and discussed almost everything under the sun. Jo's openness and liveliness made us feel as if she was part of our extended family. We learned about her intention of becoming an MP and we wished her good luck. They spent a few hours with us and left a loving memory. After our dinner, I kept in occasional touch with both of them. I met Brendan a few times here and there, but never found an opportunity to meet Jo again. She became an MP and was always busy, so our communication became infrequent.

Her sudden death was terrible news for our family, especially for Sayeda and Rima. How could people kill someone like Jo, who was giving her best to people of all backgrounds, inside Britain and abroad? After her death, Brendan mentioned in a BBC interview: 'She just approached things with a spirit; she wasn't perfect at all you know, but she just wanted to make the world a better place, to contribute, and we love her very much.'[58] I could not agree more.

The unexpected marginal Brexit victory has left Britain more polarized than ever before, with an immediate surge in xenophobic attacks across the country. A 40-year-old Polish man was murdered in a suspected hate crime in Harlow, Essex, in August 2016. Abuse and attacks on vulnerable people and women wearing the hijab, particularly, are now a big worry. To 'continue her work and to highlight the issues she cared about so deeply', Jo Cox's family, friends and colleagues established a charity (the Jo Cox Foundation) and on 16–18 June 2017 organized country-wide neighbourhood celebrations: 'The Great Get Together'.

Jo was a remarkable woman with many qualities. As she announced in her maiden speech to parliament a mere year before she was so brutally murdered: 'We are far more united and have far more in common than that which divides us'. Her death should be a reminder to all that fear, hatred and violence are not the answer to any social or political problem in a civilized society. Jo's husband and supporters are determined to keep her legacy alive through bringing people together on issues that unite us.

---

58. 'Jo Cox "died for her views", her widower tells BBC' (BBC News, 21 June 2016).

236

Chapter 8

Family, Faith and Community Spirit

A S I WRITE THIS, my mind turns again to my childhood. I grew up in a village surrounded by unadulterated farmland and the idyllic beauty of rural Bangladesh. In winter, under an endless blue sky, the whole area was speckled with the golden glow of mustard fields. In summer, the heady aroma of plants and fruits mingled with the smell of raw or ripening crops created a hypnotic scent. We ran around and played without any fear or inhibition, even in the thundering clatter of the monsoon rain.

Showered by unlimited love from my parents, my childhood was filled with peace and tranquillity. My father and mother seemed meant for each other and they gave me unrestricted freedom. In addition to his work in the fields, my dad would help my mother with most household chores, and I honestly can't recall hearing any arguments between them. My mum was quieter, but she had such a strong personality that no one, including my father, would dare to provoke her. Mind you, nagging her was my favourite childhood pastime – I enjoyed pushing her just to see her loving angry face – but she knew I was playing and would only return her infectious, loving smile. I was always playing, flying my kite, shouting, singing, breaking things and getting up to all sorts of mischief. Yet she never once stopped me or told me off. But there were unwritten rules in our village and they were affectionately enforced by the elders so that we did not go too far.

As I grew older, during my secondary school years I developed a taste for learning and became a 'bookworm'. My mother would steal up quietly behind my chair and comb my thick hair with her soft fingers. I used to stop reading, close my eyes and enjoy her touch. Sometimes I stood up and reciprocated with a big hug. Those were blissful moments, and I think now that she would smile if she knew how much I enjoyed playfully teasing my own children, especially our first child and only daughter, Rima, who is now a mother herself.

My father was exceptionally sociable and full of life, the eldest of his generation in our big Sikder clan. He had the innate ability to create rhymes while talking to others and composed poems whenever he wanted, all without writing. His humour and poetry often attracted people into conversation with him. He was also a famed singer of what we now call 'Nasheed', meaning 'the praise of God and Prophet Muhammad (peace be upon him)', and was a hugely popular figure in the whole area. Perhaps today we might call him a 'mystic', though I struggle for the right words to encapsulate what seemed like a saintly person to my young eyes. In those early years, I was always chasing my father; he was my world. I was hyperactive and full of energy, but he showed me, his youngest son, endless patience. I grew up as a free-thinking individual, but with an urge like my father to serve people.

Fast forward, away from our families in Bangladesh, to when Sayeda and I were raising our four children in the 1980s and 1990s in cosmopolitan London. We also enjoined the spirit of freedom in them, so that they grew with a sense of responsibility. All are now professionals, individuals of their own but closely connected with family and community.

I always felt indebted to my parents for the common sense wisdom they applied to raise me. Their education did not go beyond primary school level, and they did not attend any parenting classes, but their parenting skills were innate and, as I understand, were effective in their time.

As I was becoming more and more involved with young people's lives, through my voluntary work as well as teaching career, I observed a huge gap in contextual parenting skills in our communities, particularly among first generation BME people. As a result, I could see many young people becoming disconnected from their own families and becoming demotivated or getting involved in delinquency. In 1990s east London this was a worrying phenomenon to many parents. It was in the late 1990s that an internet-based group of young professionals approached me and asked whether I would be willing to run an education-related online course for parents. I agreed and started preparing materials The process turned into the seventeen lecture parenting course that ran for several years with hundreds of parents around the world.

* * *

Children are an adornment of our life, and raising them with a good education and moral upbringing is a job that requires knowledge, patience, dedication and planning. Children have the right to life's necessities such as food, shelter, clothing, education and medical treatment if they are ill. They deserve constant and age-appropriate physical, emotional and intellectual nourishment. In all religious and cultural traditions, the mothers' position is higher than that of the father, not just because they bear the burden of pregnancy but also because as primordial leaders they provide a better lead and vision to the next generations. 'Paradise lies at the feet of the mother,' said Islam's Prophet. Mothers have to be particularly careful about their own health, food habits, diet and lifestyle

– particularly during pregnancy. Perhaps some women may be disinterested, out of their own choice, to undertake motherhood in the rush for life and the individualistic frame of mind in the consumer culture of today's world.

Raising children effectively at home prepares them to enter adulthood smoothly and also for civic engagement in life. This then becomes the vehicle for handing over the baton of responsibilities or leadership from one generation to the next, helping to cement a community and a nation in a vibrant democracy. For Muslim communities coming from diverse backgrounds and the four corners of the world, settling in a secular, multi-ethnic and cultural Britain has been (at times) difficult. But building families and raising children through effective parenting can guarantee a better future. Thus we can prepare future generations with an ethos of active citizenship and fuller engagement with society.

The best way to build a society is to build homes and families. Home is a place where children start their life. A stable family environment with warmth and care is essential for their healthy and balanced growth. Society consists of families and stands on the shoulders of house-makers: the parents and available adults. Strong families create strong moral values in children, such as love, respect, loyalty, care, patience, sacrifice, fairness, integrity, compromise and inclusivity. They also nurture an ethos that encourages consultation and daily problem solving. All this depends on planned, assertive and positive parenting from the early stage of a child's life. Society needs strong families, it cannot sustain itself with weak families that fail to produce better citizens, and a society that fails to value the importance of family and community through positive parenting will face challenges that will come back to haunt it. From faith perspectives, marriage-based family life generally leads to better stability that is needed to raise children as responsible human beings.

Like any other relationship commitment, marriage is not problem-free; but an ethos of marital union teaches couples to be more compromising, with a sense of responsibility that an alternative system may not provide. Unfortunately, the institution of marriage and family as the core of human society has been weakened by pressures of individualism, commercialisation and rampant consumerism. Increasing amounts of domestic violence, mostly by men, leads to parental separation which then negatively affects children's lives. Unrestricted consumerism and the negative intrusion of modern technological gadgets into people's lives have reduced the time for physical communication and relationship-building; many people now spend more time online than in the company of their near and dear ones. Increased loneliness and loss of childhood innocence are now affecting many children in the developed world. All this is putting additional pressure on public sectors such as education, health, law and order and social services – meaning the national economy. Recent findings have indicated that rates of depression amongst teenagers have soared in the past twenty-five years; children from rich families are far more likely to develop mental health problems than less affluent youngsters.

Parenting is an inter-generational task for the development and sustenance of a stable, peaceful and successful society. In a modern diverse society such as ours this is also cross-cultural. Through positive parenting, a family plays the central role of a nursery and a school, to produce a conscientious and humane generation that is outward looking and forward thinking. Parenting, unpaid and often unrecognized by many, is definitely a demanding task but it is by far life's most fulfilling job. It is challenging and more stressful for low-earning people, but even then it is deeply enjoyable and often adventurous. To people of faith, parenting is ever-important for this life and the life to come, with children as '*amana*', meaning both 'test' and 'trust'. Believers are not supposed to fail in this.

According to Islamic teachings, there are three seven-year stages of parenting guidance. The first seven-year phase is about providing limitless love, warmth, care and safety to a child in a positive home environment, where a child grows with productive physical activities and play. The mother, father and other adults contribute to this wonderful human growth process. Man and woman are a pair, and love between mother and father is the essence of human continuity. This love converges and finds expression in their child as a bundle of joy. A new-born child is showered with love from both parents and the adults around it and a new dynamic grows in the family. The natural demand of love for children is giving them freedom and allowing them to grow with freedom of thought. As children come to the world with sharp brains, they learn and memorize words and rhymes easily. Parents can help them with unforced, age-appropriate learning.

In the second seven-year phase, the emphasis should be on children's education and learning through unlimited love and well-thought-out plans and positive discipline. During this phase, their physical and mental skills develop sharply and they need social and life skills as well as positive self-esteem through knowledge of their own selves – their gender, faith, ethnicity and many aspects of multiple but inclusive identities. Encouraging conversation at home raises them intellectually and gives them an emotional attachment to their own family, faith, community and nation; they learn to respect others around them. Simple household chores equip them with confidence, a joy of helping and a sense of responsibility. As adolescence starts in this phase, with hormonal changes that have a physical and emotional impact, discipline could be an issue or concern for some. Parents, teachers and other professionals should be aware of this transition and equip themselves to handle this appropriately. It is important adults develop suitable behaviour strategies and consistently employ them with empathy.

There are various age-appropriate discipline techniques, such as reward and sanctions, which may also be applied during the various phases. Children need freedom, but as they grow positive and creative discipline is vital for their success. Love and care should be constant in a child's life. Discipline has a spectrum and this starts with modelling good behaviour at one end and confronting bad behaviour with sanctions at the other. Children will make mistakes, as we all do, and we should treat children as children, not young adults. It is vital that parents give consideration to a child's age, mental maturity and temperament. Before employing any discipline technique the values, beliefs, education, customs and culture should be kept in mind. Proper communication is vital; shouting and telling off undermine a child's self-worth. With increased importance given to 'positive parenting' at home and 'assertive discipline' in schools, children should be prepared to sail through this phase of life with basic family, civic and social responsibility.

The third seven-year phase is about being friendly with children and building a lasting relationship based on mutual trust and understanding. By this time, children are in the teenage phase and beyond, preparing for full adulthood and brimming with ideas and energy. They should be mentored wisely and shown respect and never undermined or ridiculed. Wise parents never forget that children have arrived in this world at a time which is different from theirs. This mental adjustment is vital for a respectful and gradually interdependent loving relationship. Family values that fit with modern life, as well as healthy eating and an ethical but balanced lifestyle with awareness of the proper use of electronic gadgets, table manners, respect for others and integrity, are the ingredients of success.

Children are by nature inquisitive and generally adventurous. They are idealist, impressionable and often vulnerable. The tendency to rebel against the status quo is in their nature, and without a rock in the family and the community they may enter the adult world with a weak moral anchor. Without a strong but rational discipline, young people may harm themselves and may engage in behaviour which could be damaging to themselves, their family and to wider society. Schools are often at the sharp end of this indiscipline and delinquency. With difficulties at home, such as mixed messages from adults or domestic violence, children may be at a loss of what to do and where to go. A 'blame-game' between parents, schools and society can make the situation worse. As a behavioural support teacher and community activist for nearly three decades, I have seen that a positive home environment and a happy family are essential to give young people a better chance to succeed in life. Young people's potential delinquency and criminality can better be tackled in our core human organization – the family – as community and society begins at home. All have a role to play in society, parents should feel empowered and other agencies including schools also have major responsibilities. Pointing fingers at one another for a child's 'problem behaviour' does not help.

In these days of consumerist culture and the intrusion of social media, young people could easily be glued to a TV or computer, or nowadays their smartphones. Uncontrolled use of these gadgets with immersive screens can insulate the mind from the real world and isolate children from people around them. In addition to making children physically inactive, potentially leading to obesity, this can make them dull and socially passive for the rest of their lives. Children need motivation to 'get going' every day. They need to be inspired with an inner desire to be involved with physical, emotional, social and cognitive forces to activate their positive behaviour. They often need visible or nearby role models as well as effectual rewards and sanctions as triggers. Parental role-modelling is known to be most effective with children, and successful parenting styles and techniques are also important for a better impact upon them. Undemanding engagement and common sense parenting with positive, rational and authoritative approaches help a lot.

Children are the natural inheritors of this Earth. Our future generations need to be equipped with positive character traits – both inner and outer – such as integrity, trustworthiness, friendliness, etc. At its core, we need a positive home and a vibrant community where no-one is left out; where children flourish uninhibited and are not harmed in the street or online by sexual predators or extremists; where elders and frail people are properly looked after; and where people in neighbourhoods not only tolerate one another but also show genuine respect.

* * *

The family is at the heart of any nation, and the most effective as well as cost effective way to build a nation is to invest in family as it prepares future generations. A positive family environment creates an ethos of care within the family, stimulates creativity and entrepreneurship, keeps children away from meaninglessly wasting their lives and reduces inequality within family members. To make the world a better place we must invest in human beings within the family structure. Most families endeavour to perform well, and whether nuclear or extended, elders in a family try to instil in the younger generation the character traits that are needed to succeed in life and raise the standard of a nation. From interdependence and mutual support in the family environment children learn the ethos of selflessness and the spirit of giving. If they are not well-prepared from an early age, problems with children normally arise when they enter into adolescence, when natural physical and emotional changes take place. It is a common wisdom that a family and society that does not invest in its children and keep them on track early in life will pay dearly later – socially, morally and economically. Spending quality time with youngsters and employing age-appropriate discipline are vital. The universal principle is: prevention is better than cure.

One of the biggest sources of stress in many families is the absence of a father, or a father figure, at home. Children born into families with delinquent fathers are naturally disadvantaged. By failing to stay around to raise their children, men can cause or exacerbate the rise of problem children in society, which can eventually lead to social breakdown. There are many reasons for social problems, for example in the UK it is known that three-quarters of young offenders come from households where fathers abdicate their parental responsibilities. Government programmes for 'righting the wrong' are vital in helping people in a broader perspective, but even a highly efficient and well-resourced government cannot cure all family failures. Constructive parental engagement and communication with their children is the first step on the ladder to a more equal and successful society, where no group is missed out or disadvantaged. Encouraging and helping parents who are struggling is obviously a better way to produce positive results. The quality of parenting received by children is a better predictor of their success in adult life. There is no perfect parenting, as human beings will always err, but continuous effort in creating a better family will minimize the risk of failure. Marriage-based stable families with an ethos of compromise and sacrifice have an overall advantage.

Creating strong and healthy families can help us create a more equal society where fewer people control power and wealth. An unequal society can bring collective failure in the end. Parents who are equipped with the necessary skills to support themselves and can prepare the future generation to effectively shoulder future responsibility help in better social mobility and reduce inequality at the very grassroots level. Just as it is socially respectable in developed countries to learn how to look after one's physique through exercise and fitness classes, so should we have parenting classes to learn better techniques to raise children. Better public awareness of the need to equip parents with effective parenting skills will take away any stigma there may be on parenting support. The basics of looking after a child are embedded in human nature. Unlike other mammals, we take a far longer period in raising children with human values, but all parents need some practical tips or 'tools of the trade'. Thus, parenting education should be seen as highly respectful and aspirational. Professionally-run parenting classes can also be linked with one's career progression.

My entry into the world of parenting towards the end of the 1990s was partly because I needed practical skills as a father to raise our four children and also due to an urge to bring positive changes among parents in Tower Hamlets and beyond. Coincidentally, when I was running the online parenting course I was invited by the Support for Learning Services (SLS) management to attend the course 'Strengthening Families, Strengthening Communities' (SFSC) that was mentioned in Chapter 2. This thirteen-week course, with a three-hour session each week, was culturally sensitive and has been running across the borough ever since. In 2004, I decided to devise my own course by blending well-established values of faith traditions and ancient wisdom with the contemporary challenges and opportunities faced in a modern society. I made sure that the content and longevity of the course worked best for busy parents, so I experimented with a five to eight week course with around two hours per week of teaching. The course was aimed at lone parents as well as couples. Over the years, this 'Building Families' course developed into a fifteen-hour programme spread over six sessions with two-and-a half hours every week. After I stepped down from the leadership positions of various Muslim organizations, I turned this parenting programme into a social enterprise under the banner 'Amana Parenting' and have been running workshops across the UK and in some global cities of Europe, Asia, Australia and North America ever since. With changing social dynamics and global inter-connectedness, I have been continuously updating its contents to address the diverse needs of parents from any background.

The programme deals with the practical day-to-day issues that parents face in a secular/liberal society such as Britain. It also deals with the long-term strategic objectives of investing in our future generation for the 'good in this world and in the Hereafter' (*al-Baqarah* 2: 201) in a non-prescriptive and non-judgmental manner. It aims to help parents to make sure that the individual worth of a child, albeit in the context of social and civic responsibility, is inculcated in them from their early life with a loving relationship, tough love, inspirational family environment and positive discipline techniques. Children are gifted with ingenuity and the job of parents is to make sure they grow with full potential to become a force for good in society. The course is based on five components: balanced growth and development; parent-child relationships; positive discipline; family and community perspective; faith, culture and spirituality.

* * *

Children raised with parental love, positive discipline and in happy family environments have the potential to be better equipped with social skills and confidence later in life. If they live with or are in direct touch with members of extended families they will have an advantage in developing more empathy and less individualistic attitudes, as well as better skills in life. An extended family consists of parents, grandparents, aunts, uncles, and cousins living in the same household or nearby. Elderly members or couples, such as grandparents, moving in with their son or daughter due to old age or frail health, is an example. I know quite a few Asian families that are still living with traditional extended families, where three or four generations live under the informal direction of a patriarch or a matriarch. The issue of elderly care and child-rearing in extended families is normally handled with care and patience. Although this may put severe pressure on the caregivers, particularly on the female members, by and large this is done dutifully. There may be practical disadvantages of loss of privacy or diminution of individual choice, but this is compensated by successfully creating a non-intrusive and non-interventionist environment within the extended family. A self-regulated culture of freedom for individual members or family units generally works for the benefit of all. The unique benefit of effective extended families is the better presence of empathy and compromise, as well as voluntary compliance in sacrificing individual choice or ego. The elders find in the younger children companions to spend time with, which is the best human way to fight loneliness, and children learn to live with their cousins, can play and learn from one another and, most importantly, they receive ready-made wisdom of life from elder members.

A community is made up of people grouped together by common interests. The bond could be due to ethnicity, residence, social status, activities, and so on. Communities can emerge for short-term purposes, for example campaign groups, or long-term purposes, such as faith groups. Individuals may belong to many different communities at the same time – extended family, close family friends and people living nearby that form an immediate community – and their allegiances can change. The individual or group activities, whether informal or formal, are meant to benefit the community. Community spirit demands some 'sacrifice' from individuals for the good of those around them. What we learn from one another, such as fellowship and mutual obligations, strengthens our community spirit. This willingness, and for some, passion, to serve and promote a community through voluntary activities are part of our civic responsibility. Communal gatherings like religious and cultural meetings create opportunities to share life experiences and give a sense of togetherness. Neighbourhood renewal projects, such as removing debris from public places, fixing the street lamps or potholes in the streets, organizing a school fete or a charity event, all enhance community spirit. Formal groups like 'neighbourhood watch' are hugely beneficial to the public interest. Community spirit produces pride in a community and gives it a confidence boost. In a vibrant and well-connected neighbourhood, community spirit is the gel that binds people for the common good.

This community spirit, from an Islamic viewpoint, is essentially about building accord in a locality like an extended family, with mutual rights and responsibilities. It is incumbent on Muslims to maintain family ties: showing politeness, being kind towards and concerned for one's relatives – even if distantly related. Breaking family ties is antithetical to Islamic teachings. The Prophet Muhammad was reported to have said: 'Whoever believes in God and the Last Day, let him maintain the bonds of kinship'. (Hadith narrated by Bukhari) Islam also places a huge emphasis on the duty to one's neighbours – near or far and irrespective of background – it is a unilateral responsibility. Some Muslim scholars were of the view that the definition of neighbours according to Islam is forty houses in each direction, meaning the entire neighbourhood. We have obligations towards our neighbours in Islam, such as helping when in need, passing on good wishes to them for their good fortune, sharing food on special occasions, visiting and helping when they are in distress or ill, and attending their funeral when they die. Neighbours do not deserve to be harmed or harassed in any way, nor should neighbours block the air by erecting walls or barriers without permission or expose others' shortcomings. Many Muslims have maintained these traditional values and have carried them wherever they settled. This ethos of responsibility to near ones and service to wider people has made Muslims well-known as generous givers of charity in Britain.

It is Islam's community spirit and volunteering ethos that inspire the believers – young and old, men and women – to give in the month of Ramadan every year. This was acknowledged by former Prime Minister David Cameron in 2014, when he stated that: 'Charity is one of the things that Islam is all about. Here in Britain, Muslims are our biggest donors – they give more to charity than any other faith group.'[59] The UK regulatory body, the Charity Commission, also appreciated Muslim charitable acts in 2016, commenting that one Muslim charity 'last Ramadan had helped over 1 million people.'[60] According to the Muslim Charities Forum, an umbrella body of big Muslim charities, British Muslims gave approximately £100 million to charitable causes during Ramadan in 2016. This is community spirit at its best!

In the midst of continuous bad press and often discrimination in the job market, many talented young Muslims have decided to work in the voluntary or charity sector. They have brought not only passion and energy but also skills and expertise to raise and manage funds for the benefit of ordinary people in the UK and abroad. This represents a unique community spirit at a time when the number of food banks in a rich country like ours has increased significantly in recent years. Mosques, community groups, youth centres and other voluntary organizations should come up with innovative social and economic enterprises to help and assist people in their primary needs in local communities.

---

59. David Cameron, 'A video message from the Prime Minister to mark the start of Ramadan' (Prime Minister's Office, 27 June 2014).
60. Nick Donaldson, 'Ramadan – making a real difference' (Charity Commission, 14 July 2016).

As followers of a religion that places great importance on the community alongside the individual, Muslims should improve their knowledge capital and contribute significantly to social justice in mainstream society. They should also employ some of their resources in addressing social ills such as drugs, gang violence and other anti-social behaviour problems in their midst that often blight inner cities.

Mosques in many places have the upper hand in preventing or handling a crisis, where traditional community organizations or youth groups might fail. I clearly remember one such case in Tower Hamlets, where the ELM played a very decisive and positive role by helping youth leaders avert a massive clash between two groups of young Bangladeshis in Tower Hamlets in the late 1990s. If it were not for the community spirit, dedication, courage and wisdom of some ELM-linked hard-working young Muslim activists, gangs of Bangladeshi youths from two local neighbourhoods in the western part of the borough would have caused bloodshed. As a trustee of the ELM and teacher in the borough I knew something was going on in the streets of Brick Lane and Cannon Street, but I was not fully aware of the depth of animosity between the two groups. These young boys, some in the same schools and Sixth Form colleges, shared the same religious and ethnic background; they even spoke the same dialect. But dozens of them would roam around their 'turf' intimidating others after school hours and in the evening. Most first-generation parents and local imams had little influence over them, and I was kept informed by youth leaders from the locally-renowned Brick Lane Youth Development Agency (BLYDA) of the sharp deterioration of the situation. We learnt an estimated 2,500 youths were affiliated to one of the many local gangs in the borough.

The turning point, also mentioned later in *The Independent* on 29 August 1998, was 'a violent ambush in an East End park earlier this year. Fifteen members of the Cannon Street gang –

one of the largest in the area – were attacked by an alliance of 50 youths from three smaller groups ... Immediately, the Cannon Street group began plotting revenge.'[61] The availability of hard drugs in the area was also an open secret. When BLYDA's youth leaders learnt that the boys were trying to obtain guns, they became extremely worried. As they knew the main gang leaders from both camps, they spared no time in talking with the ringleaders and then organizing a meeting of the warring gangs. They deliberately chose a religious venue, the East London Mosque. It was a neutral venue and the meeting was on Friday after the Jumu'ah congregation. The choice of venue and timing was a very smart move. Over 300 young gang warriors from opposite camps converged on the big basement hall of the mosque. Of course, a lot of background work had been done beforehand, and seating arrangements were planned wisely.

The BLYDA leaders gave passionate lectures using references from the Qur'an and Prophet Muhammad's teachings to highlight the value of life, the futility of violence, the destruction of their future, the shame they would bring to their families and the indignity to the community and religion. It created a sombre mood in the youthful minds and when the final talk was over very few could control their tears. It was then time to bring the leaders of the opposing gangs together to hug one another, which they did with genuine remorse. The gang leaders then took the microphone and promised, one by one, that they would never again hurt their 'brothers', let alone fight with them for petty reasons. Once the leaders had given their pledge within the sanctity of the mosque they all started hugging one another; the scene was like a mass embracing ceremony that Muslims generally do after the Eid prayer. Some boys were visibly weeping or crying, and having

---

61. Julian Kossoff, 'East London's Bangladeshi street gangs agree to truce' (*The Independent*, 29 August 1998).

brokered the gang truce BLYDA won the respect and trust of the area's disaffected youth. A 'Committee of Youth Against Violence' was formed that started working immediately in the name of *'asha'* (Bengali: hope); this has saved Tower Hamlets from the scourge of gang violence ever since.

Youth crimes in inner cities, such as gang violence and knife crime in London, are costing precious lives. By providing key facilitating roles for all sections of the community, mosques or religious places can not only provide safe spaces, but also provide spiritual solace to local people. With better planning and some financial investment, they can use the social influence of imams and religious leaders to reduce violence in our communities.

* * *

Faith is the inner conviction, feeling and attitude relating a human being to a Supreme Being, or God. Faith includes religious belief and often goes far beyond it. It gives an emotional anchor and attachment to something very dear that gives stability and meaning to many peoples' lives. In most faith traditions, belief and action are intertwined, so a basic knowledge and understanding of faith is a requirement. However, in the modern West increasing numbers of people do not have faith in God and are not affiliated to any religion. Indeed, some have become anti-religious. According to the 2011 census in Britain, Christianity is still a majority religion (59.5 per cent), but a significant proportion of the population responded as having 'No religion' (25.7 per cent). In such a society, this factor of faith or no faith is a social reality. Accepting (or at least tolerating) people's culture, faith or no faith and way of life, is part of living in a pluralist society.

All of Islam's core beliefs and rituals are connected to individual commitment towards God; they are intimately personal and are meant for one's enhanced spirituality and better preparation to work towards public good. They are not that many; most of Islam is about social action, serving others and being useful to the world. In my understanding, all religions have similar teachings in their essence, but followers have contaminated the message and practice in varying degrees over time. Mosques and community institutions, like churches and synagogues, can play a major role in helping believers to be public-minded and integrate positively with others around them. For this, religious institutions need better institutional capacity through professional input and outcome-oriented action. Some Muslim communities began their lives in Britain with members at the lower level end of socio-economic arena. Although youth involvement is still unsatisfactory in some places, the situation in recent times has improved as new generations have emerged.

For historically distinctive reasons, many Europeans and ordinary Muslims have struggled with religious literacy – of their own religions as well as of those of others. In an age when religion has taken centre stage in social and public life because of a resurgence of religious identity, as well as its misuse by extremists and opportunists, this is very unsatisfactory to say the least. Religious literacy is about essential knowledge of, and ability to understand, not only one's own religion but also that of others' in society. Globalization has brought people of different faiths and cultures together; religious literacy is thus all the more important in order to know one another and live together in peace. Although in developed countries religious literacy has become a public policy to improve community cohesion, this has proved too little for the need. In Britain, children receive religious education (RE) in schools, but because overall religious illiteracy is often low and the tabloid media has sensationalized some reporting of and around religions, it is easy to get a skewed picture about religions and their followers.

Religious attachment is profoundly linked with our hearts and could be deemed irrational to some. Religiosity is a human reality, however, and remaining ignorant of religion and people's deeply held religious sentiment or passion is not useful. On the other hand, being ignorant of why people dislike religion or do not subscribe to religion at all is also not helpful. Truth in the unseen is hidden and only arrogant polemicists can claim a monopoly of truth. Irrespective of whether people are religious, irreligious or anti-religious, religious literacy is essential in a pluralist society; illiteracy causes unnecessary social divisions. Given the challenges of misunderstanding and fear about religion in general and Islam in particular, politically- or ideologically-motivated media and think-tanks have the upper hand in being quoted as 'experts' on religious issues. Particularly after 9/11, the religion of Islam has become a victim of media-driven and sometimes politically-stirred imbalanced portrayal and occasional demonization. Embedded, and often problematic, assumptions about Muslims and their faith have contributed to Islamophobia with accompanied prejudice, bigotry, discrimination and often physical violence against the community. Muslim women are at the sharp end of Islamophobia, just because of what they wear by their own choice.

With the arrival of unparalleled numbers of refugees from the Middle East since 2015, as well as from some parts of Africa, Europe hit a new crisis and anti-Muslim rhetoric rose ever higher. During the campaign for the EU Referendum, and in the aftermath of the Brexit vote on 23 June 2016, the surge in anti-immigrant hate crime, especially in areas that voted to leave the EU, became a worry for all. Assumptions such as 'Muslims hate democracy', 'Muslims are anti-Semitic', 'Islam is a violent or misogynistic religion', 'Muslims are taking over Europe', etc. are not only limited to 'Eurabia' fantasists, but are filtering through the psyche of increasing numbers of ordinary people. Ignorance of others creates an 'us and them' mentality, intolerance, fear and hatred. There is no doubt that this is having a huge impact on community relations. The spike in the reported racial violence after Brexit is one example. Muslims should also take some blame in not being able to communicate with their fellow citizens and articulate who they are: their weakness in presenting their case is part of the problem.

Islam demands from Muslims to continuously read, re-read, re-interpret and renew their faith with the context of time and space through the power of *ijtihad* (or reasoning). The strength of scholarship in most areas of life and the reasoning capacity among Muslims everywhere has declined in recent history, due to a dearth of inspirational religious leadership, combined with the socio-economic deprivation of Muslims in many places. As a result, many Muslims are not even familiar with their own scripture and certain terminologies with deeper meaning that are at the core of Islam's social obligation – such as *ijtihad* and jihad (striving or struggling). The root word for these two terms is *jahada*, meaning endeavour, exertion, effort, diligence. Jihad as a personal commitment encourages self-purification through pure intention, patience and determination to achieve one's personal best or excellence (Arabic: *ihsan*). This also means confronting one's personal weaknesses in the best possible manner. Collectively, it means an effort to fight against inequality, injustice and oppression. By extension, this also means engagement in a fight to defend one's life, land and religion but with established rules and Islamic ethics of engagement. There is no room for 'vigilante' jihad in the religion.

* * *

Muslims can be socially conservative on some issues, but they should not be defined by beards and burkas; they are more than capable of being loyal and productive citizens while confidently practising their faith. Religious or social conservatism of a people should not be conflated with radicalism, extremism or terrorism. In fact, most extremists have been seen as ignorant or too relaxed in their religious practice.

Human beings are multi-dimensional and most people are generally happy with their plural identities. I believe that a higher level of religious literacy, with increased human-to-human communication, can equip individuals with the ability to challenge assumptions and scrutinize various intersections of our complex life. Mosques and religious institutions have a vital role to play here, and by becoming more positive and inclusive they can bring people together. More and more mosques have opened up since the tragic events of 9/11 and 7/7, but 'good news is not news', so the positive news from mosques and religious institutions does not always reach people though our powerful media. Thankfully, social media is compensating in this area and many young Muslims and others are able to share the (positive) reality. The Muslim Council of Britain's initiative to initiate mosque open days through its annual 'Visit my Mosque' day in February has drawn a lot of interest from local as well as mainstream national media.

Religious literacy encompasses a better understanding of the core texts and contexts of the world's prominent religious traditions, as well as exploration of their relevance in our time. With reasonable knowledge of the basic tenets of major religious traditions, as well as their diversity and expressions due to differing historical contexts, people can understand religions' role in socio-cultural and political life. One does not have to agree with religion per se, or a certain religious tradition, but with greater background knowledge interaction between those of faith (or none) can become more humane and realistic. For religious literacy to be more widespread, improved induction is needed for more teachers from the wider society; mere pre-service or in-service training cannot provide adequate knowledge and confidence for teachers. This needs more cultural as well as religious knowledge: through interaction, visiting places of worship or cultural centres, keen observation of others and building friendships. As long as training remains non-sectarian and non-proselytising, especially for children in primary and secondary schools, religious literacy could be a game-changer in community relationships. Religious literacy in adults could be improved through formalized education settings in universities, adult education and workplace training schemes. This could also be expanded to out-of-school activities in the local community through lifelong learning, media and literature, and other means. All this will enhance individual confidence, mutual trust and respectful interaction.

With a higher proportion of school-age children from the Muslim community, there is a genuine need for more Muslim role models. A reasonable proportion of Muslim teaching staff or school workforce in places where Muslims have a significant presence will naturally enhance their confidence, which will in turn improve their interaction and engagement with others. Universities, particularly the research-intensive and world-class ones that make up the Russell Group, can also broaden their intake by considering positive actions (not favour) through placement schemes and anonymized CVs as a basis for the first interview.

Interfaith engagement has been a good tool to improve religious literacy, but so far it is limited to a section of already-proactive people. Grass-root social justice groups, like Citizens UK, consisting of civic groups belonging to diverse faith or no faith organizations, have already made a unique contribution to religious literacy. As they normally work on civic issues and with a spirit of learning, they genuinely bring communities together. It is vital that Muslim institutions bring about a sharp renewal of their structure and methodology, and shape themselves to be more inclusive, if they are to succeed in bringing Muslim communities into the heart of our nation's social and cultural life. This will only be achieved if innovative steps are taken and there is a synergy between the older and new generations in this task. In fact, the Muslim community needs a new generation of change-makers to drive this transformation. Muslim groups and communities should thus adopt an inclusive strategy with a vision to be an active part of mainstream civil society.

Over the decades, Britain has become an indisputably pluralist country and its model of pluralism has so far worked well – better than in many developed countries. The metaphor for such a dynamic society is a multi-coloured human garden, where diversity does not lead to parallel lives but seeks to enrich all. The debate as to how religious ethics and not dogma can exist side-by-side with liberal democracy, even enrich one another, has to be carried out with tolerance, respect and objectivity.

* * *

In spite of post-7/7 scrutiny, Britain's Muslim community has been doing relatively well in certain areas, including the charitable sector, the health profession and gradually in education. However, it is important there is similar progress in other areas of public life, such as in the media and communications industries, for the community to defend its reputation as well as to put its case effectively. This will sharply enhance community confidence and minimize misinformation and tension about Muslims in society. What is also needed is empathetic leadership at a grassroots level. Leadership in a family, community, religious group or institution as well as in political organizations gives people a realistic vision and motivates them to achieve. The success of a community or a nation depends on a yearning for excellence, not mediocrity. In Islam, excellence or achieving one's personal best reaches to a higher level if a believer also excels in spirituality. The common term of excellence and deep spirituality in Arabic is *ihsan* (a root word meaning beautification); this broadly means being close to God through love and positive action. 'Only from the heart, can you touch the sky', said Rumi (a thirteenth century Persian poet, Islamic theologian and Sufi mystic).

Over the decades, numerous not-for-profit organizations have been formed by the Muslim community to serve people of faith and no faith, in neighbourhoods and beyond. Most were run by highly dedicated volunteers with financial and professional constraints. Things have improved in recent decades, with a significant section of these voluntary organizations, mosques and other groups now registering with the Charity Commission. With more young professionals now ready to serve the community, local authorities are also taking a greater interest in helping religious institutions with better guidance. A regulatory push via the Charity Commission has seen many of these institutions begin to make good progress in governance, accountability and financial management. However, there is still a tendency towards 'casualness' in some. The tenure of leadership and board membership can still be undefined; the same leadership or leadership style may continue for decades, until stagnation results. This can lead to incompetence, abuse of power, lack of planning, financial irregularities and internal disharmony – all with potential public recriminations. There have even been occasional brawls in mosque-related management bodies, necessitating the involvement of the police, which is hugely embarrassing for our community. There cannot be any compromise on the issues of democratic choice, accountability, succession plans, financial controls and business plans for any organization – public sector or voluntary. Mosques have a huge advantage in engaging their congregation to regenerate the local area –

if they are run effectively. It is vital that Muslim voluntary organizations build their institutional capacity along with individual professionalism through continuous training, as well as review and implementation of good practices. Meritocracy should override any personal or tribal affinity in running an institution.

The collapse of Kids Company in 2015, a renowned charity that supported many deprived inner city children for nearly two decades, has been a high profile wake-up call with lessons to be learnt in running voluntary organizations. In addition to social needs and the law of the land, it is also a religious imperative that voluntary Muslim organizations are run more effectively. This has happened in some cases, where the wide experience of older Muslims has merged with the vigour and professionalism of younger ones. Unfortunately, this has yet to be the case in many places. A hybrid leadership structure with a well-defined vision and strategy, clarity of governance and well-formulated business plan, combined with a deep volunteering ethos, are essential. It is also vital for Muslim voluntary organizations to plan for continuity and renewal of the board, with a clearly agreed upper limit in the tenure of leadership for the Chair, director or board member. In recent times, the practice of limiting this to eight or ten years for the Chair and limiting the number of board members to between 7–12, with election or renewal of leadership every two, three or four years, has started to bear positive results. There should also be a maximum age-limit of active leadership or directorship: the convention now is one should retire on one's seventy-fifth birthday.

The British Muslim community (made up of many 'communities') is still relatively new and going through a phase of teething problems and challenges. Various Muslim organizations that I knew as pioneering in the 1970s and 1980s have either disappeared or are struggling to relate with current reality. For Muslims to become a full part of meritocratic

Britain, our community has to invest heavily in its youth. The community as a whole must also improve its capacity through continuous strengthening of its institutions, improvements to its social and spiritual intelligence and increasing its political literacy. For many reasons already outlined, Muslims in Britain have historically been underachievers. They need to see the big picture, with a healthy reconnection and contextualisation of the past. Only then will the community's position be secure and normalized within wider British society.

Young Muslims should be at the heart of this strenuous effort (or, jihad) of creating a vision of a common good. Our physical belonging to society must include our emotional attachment to it, with effective engagement with its people. Being part of wider society brings with it inclusive participation: in community work, social and civic activities, economic exchanges, arts, sports, culture and politics. We must bring our heads and hearts together to make this civic engagement effective and enduring. The community needs to aim high and equip itself with better character and determined action. In fact, it is better the community sometimes steps back, freeing itself from the habits of doing things casually and starting afresh. The legacy of the Andalusian Muslim era, which encouraged inclusion and pluralism, can be inspirational to many of our young people engaged in social activism. However, this 'looking back' should also be forward-thinking, as the world has moved on. We must belong with the people we are living amongst and ourselves be a catalyst for positive change. We must also ask ourselves some hard questions: how can we rise above the current challenges that we are facing today; how do we maximize the potential of our institutions that our predecessors built; and, how do we move into the next phase of a confident society living as equal citizens?

To answer these questions, we must also ask how best we can invest in our real future, i.e. the human resources that we possess, namely the disproportionately higher number of youth in our community. Our first generations wisely created essential 'hardware' in the form of buildings, institutions and businesses. It is absolutely essential that we now create the human 'software' and harness their potential to lift up the community and together (with others) become a force for good in the wider society. Success in this area will fend off the challenges of apathy, demotivation and extremism that we see in some sections of our youth. This clear and visionary approach is in line with the spirit of Islam's universalism, which can defeat narrow 'tribalism' or the 'my people, right or wrong' attitude as well as insularity. Our religion is ever vibrant by the fact that it gives unmatched importance on acquiring and using knowledge and education, thoughtfulness and reasoning, faith and action. British Muslims need to challenge the status quo of the recent struggles and take colossal steps in not only raising their economic prosperity, but in enhancing social regeneration, contributing to academia and scientific research, engaging in local communities beyond their own borders, and accelerating public engagement.

With Islam's inherent community spirit and ethos of inclusion, we can perform better with our multiple identities. We don't only have to hold a singular identity, we can be British and Muslim, an East Ender and Muslim, a Bradfordian and Muslim, a Glaswegian who is Muslim, and so on and so forth. This will be the best way to defeat extremism and bigotry. Our religion teaches that our duty towards others and our planet is unconditional and unilateral. At the end it is in the people that we need to invest.

Conclusion

Striving for the Middle Way

MY CHILDHOOD MEMORIES remind me of how my family members would always lend a helping hand to others, especially to those who were not well-off. This included the local Hindu families of a lower-caste background. To us, we were all equal. This may have been the established practice just in our village, but it was the only way we knew.

During adolescence I saw amazing examples of community activism in my own elder brother. Moniruddin Sikder was ten years older than me, a boisterous young man well-known for his loud voice and laughter. His dream was to join the Pakistan Air Force and when an opportunity arose he applied straight away and went through the rigorous physical and mental tests of the selection process. Our mother was not happy about this, but she kept quiet. However, once the news was out that my brother was selected she could not take it anymore: 'No, he cannot go,' she simply told my father, and that was it. I was old enough to understand the dilemma in the family. I saw my father as a great problem solver and he tried his best to convince my mum, but she would not budge;

other family members tried, but had no luck. After a few days of drama, my brother grudgingly decided to forego his career in the Air Force and instead became a primary school teacher in a nearby village.

He was a young man with creative ideas and unlimited energy. Beyond his teaching job, during the day he spent much of his free time solving other people's grievances on issues such as loans or land disputes. With his organizing skills and commanding personality, he gathered a few friends of his own age to repair or build unpaved roads to better connect our area with nearby villages and the local town. The time the elders came up with an ambitious plan of setting up a high school in our village, he took charge and drove it forward. When he found his teaching job too demanding for all this work, he left teaching and joined a local council with a community-related job a few miles away from our village. With increased flexibility and free time he then single-handedly led the school project to completion in 1973. It soon became registered with the central education board in Dhaka and became one of the best schools in the region. The school project would change the life of ordinary people in the area, and open the lives of their children to many more opportunities.

I looked at my brother as a role model. He selflessly served others and the local community. After my 'O' level equivalent exam, I left my village for higher education – first to the capital Dhaka and then to Chittagong – but whenever I returned to my village I was fascinated by his drive and passion for community work. He loved his calling and would run around tirelessly, but in doing so he ignored the basic disciplines of life: eating regularly and taking rest, until he suddenly caught bowel cancer in his fifties. Within three months of diagnosis, he passed away. Whether his lifestyle was one of the reasons for his cancer was a different matter, but living an undisciplined life was not a wise practice. It was a great loss to our family and for the community, too. Nature is a silent teacher and I learnt the importance of maintaining balance or moderation, of pursuing a path of self-discipline and control as well as time for relaxation.

The community activism that I began in the late 1980s in east London was of course different in many ways. Britain, particularly London, has always been diverse. This diversity multiplied after the Second World War with the arrival of many newcomers, my own people among them. The burgeoning British Muslim community also became phenomenally varied in terms of its religious practices, social and political views, cultures and lifestyles. Working with these communities and navigating through changing social dynamics has been a huge learning curve for me. For social activists inspired by the values and teachings of faith, the experience of working in post-religious Britain is indeed amazing and often challenging, especially after 9/11 and 7/7! As I became busier with Tower Hamlets' various communities, and later busy on the national stage too, it was a struggle to balance my job, family, community work and social life, while treading the social and religious middle way.

* * *

Staying on the middle path or centre ground of life's journey is a social and religious requirement for Muslims. We are reminded in the Qur'an and by the Prophet Muhammad to keep away from the lure of extremism. Believers are supposed to live a life of 'the middle way' and adopt moderation in what they do. They seek guidance from God to stay on the 'straight path', *sirat al-mustaqim* (*al-Fatihah* 1: 5), and are expected to remain 'justly balanced' (*al-Baqarah* 2: 143). However, keeping to the middle path on life's highway does not mean walking a thin line of 'dos and don'ts'. In my understanding, life it is about making a conscious effort to remain around the centre and avoid the two extremes while making decisions. This is at the core of individual and public life in Islam. Losing direction from the middle way for whatever reason is a deviation from Islam's core teachings. Muslims should be aware that life's middle path may not be seen as 'cool' by the people around you, but this is the best way for a believer of any background to remain consistently steadfast. Islam is known as a 'natural way', so any people at any time and space can navigate through the complexities of life and stay in the middle. Those who are reasonably knowledgeable of Islamic texts and the Prophet's life teachings, as well as having some understanding of contemporary society, know well that they should keep away from the cliffs of extremism.

The religious middle way is often related to a believer's individual and social attitudes. In my observation, people choose the middle way in personal and social dealings most of the time. We may have occasional bouts of extremism, especially in our emotional behaviour, but often bounce back once we see the value in leading a balanced life. Of course, there will always be some people – maverick or whatever – who will make the world more challenging. However, preference for the middle path can also be seen in politics, where the majority of citizens or electorates in developed and stable democracies such as Britain would generally expect their political leaders to be not far away from the centre ground of politics. Common sense says that far left or far right politics and over-regulation or under-regulation in an economy does not help a country or a nation in the long run. Nevertheless, there has been extremism for as long as human beings have been on this planet. This can flourish in an unstable or violent family and socio-political environment and is often vented in the form of destructive ideas and actions. Hidden behind self-righteousness or dogma, extremism exists within religious as well as non-religious ways of life. For too many people it is easier to adopt extremism and let their ego dictate them.

For a long time, Muslims in general have lost the equilibrium in personal and social life; this is perhaps the key to why some young people resort to criminal acts. However, a community should not be solely responsible for the criminality of a few. There may be some other factors – such as socio-economic deprivation and prejudice – that fuel the reasons why a higher proportion of the prison population in Britain are Muslims, and the community should always reflect on why this is the case. Most importantly, why do some young people, however small in number, lose connection with their roots to such an extent that they join overseas terrorist groups? Self-reflection is vital for any people and Muslims should look around themselves, their mosques and community institutions to assess if they are welcoming and inclusive enough, and if their governance and accountability need serious improvement. They need fresh ideas for the present and an effective plan for the future to secure their position as successful and well-integrated minorities in the West. Their sense of belonging and emotional attachment to the land must be followed by a deep commitment to their neighbours around them. Through their actions they should prove they are as ordinary as others and have the will and ability to bring good for all. The only way they can do this is to remain true to the religious middle ground and engage in civic action for the benefit of all.

While there are core beliefs and rituals of worship that are immutable, much of religious scripture needs interpretation and explanation by knowledgeable scholars taking into account context and the times. This is the tradition of *ijtihad* (reasoning) that has enabled believers to live their faith on Islam's middle path in changing circumstances since the early period of Islam. It has led to diverse schools of thought, all authentic in their belief and practices. The rediscovery of that spirit of accepting differences in good faith is the best route to a middle way and an antidote to any harmful extreme views or actions.

* * *

Human diversity is an asset for a society, as it makes life colourful and often constructively challenging. Some of history's greatest achievements came about through the diverse ideas that people brought to the table. I firmly believe that diversity should not bring isolation, suspicion, intolerance or animosity. Rather, it should enhance creativity and healthy competition amongst people. Diversity and inclusion together are at the core of a civilized society. There is a misplaced assertion that religions are unable to accommodate diversity and thus foster hatred and sow discord. On the contrary, the core message of major faiths is balance, harmony and cooperation, which can never be achieved through extremism. Religious and sectarian violence is extremism at their worst, as they are rooted to de-contextualized texts or criminal misuse of theology for political opportunism or power-grabbing purposes. The differences in doctrine and rituals among various religions should be seen as an expression of diversity, not division. The Qur'an states that diversity is in the spirit of human creation on Earth and for people to know (to understand and respect) one another (*al-Hujurat* 49: 14).

In an increasingly interconnected and interdependent world, there will always be some bumps along the way – but bumps should not be a barrier. Although some, opportunists at best and Islamophobes at worst, are constantly attempting to put the entire Muslim community in the dock for the criminality of a few deranged individuals, the shadow of ignorance and misinformation appears to be gradually clearing up – albeit slowly. It is heartening that following every atrocity carried out by any terrorist, ordinary people from all walks of life have stood together shoulder-to-shoulder, determined not to let society fall into the hands of those extremists and criminals who want division.

Globalization has been a great benefit to humanity, but it has also given rise to insecure employment, low wages and inequality with often stateless corporations shirking their social and financial responsibilities. The result is frustration and anger among people who genuinely feel left out. Far-right political groups, backed by sections of the media, are capitalizing on this by using immigration, refugees and lone-wolf attacks as political pawns to score points. People are living in echo chambers, fears are often exaggerated for political purposes and the media and newer 'fake news' sites amplify them to such an extent that ordinary people are tempted to believe this narrative of doom.

However, we must see the glass half full. In spite of pockets of segregation in some inner city conurbations, community relationships in Britain are still far better compared to many other European countries. In Britain, the political left enjoyed a limited success in the 'snap election' of June 2017, when they campaigned on a positive message of 'for the many, not the few'. More of us are living near those of a different ethnicity or culture than ever before. Young people who intermingle across communities have less of a problem with diversity. However, more needs to be done to promote interaction, engagement and positive integration, especially in rural communities.

* * *

We now live in a post-truth, uncertain world that has witnessed a sharp decline in its moral compass. The social and political meltdown in many places across the globe has made us feel less safe and the post-9/11 mistrust and erosion of democratic values is still haunting us. People are anxious, worried and unhappy, and unless handled carefully, the rise of authoritarian populism on both sides of the Atlantic may lead the modern West to slide backward in history. Mavericks or demagogues from the political left or right who play with people's raw emotions should be seen as problems; their rhetoric or anger cannot bring about solutions to complex, modern problems. There are reasons for people to get angry, but anger is not a plan! Only being united can we take over the reins of destiny in our own hands. People of all faiths and none should wake up and unite to work together. In the midst of uncertainty and worry there is a need for a renewal of values and applied ethics. We need a new generation of middle-of-the-road or centrist (Arabic: *wasati*) leaders who, with their integrity and competence, can bring realistic optimism and help inspire our citizens. We need to instil a sense of realistic hope and optimism for our future, particularly among our young people. The multi-faceted works carried out by the third sector and voluntary groups in Britain need further strengthening.

From faith or non-faith teachings we all have an obligation towards one another and to our planet. We have the obligation to tolerate, respect, care, live-and-let-live and agree to disagree. We also have 'fundamental British values' such as democracy, the rule of law, individual liberty, mutual respect and tolerance of others. These values are universal, inclusive and non-negotiable in any society. They are Islamic too! Faith is tied with a moral code of action, and a properly understood faith can be a strong anchor and healer in this turbulent time of laissez-faire life, where yearning for spiritual solace has risen sharply. The hammer of individualism and consumerism is crippling many minds and souls that only demand and seek their own rights. Needless to say, in human society one's right is another's obligation. It is binding on Muslims to recognize and practise these values wherever they live or settle; more so in a diverse and complex society such as the UK. Some Muslims today see the concept of an *ummah* through exclusivist eyes, but the Prophet of Islam prepared the 'Charter of Madinah', for the Muslims to be able to live a pluralist and inclusive life alongside the Jewish people of various tribes and the pagans of Madinah, immediately after he migrated to the city in 622 CE. All the people in the city-state constituted 'one nation' or *ummah*. The Charter is recognized as one of the earliest written 'Constitutions' in history.

The best way forward for Muslims is to go the extra mile to build trust among those around them and work harder to prove to wider society that they truly care for Britain and have its best interests at heart. Muslims should be at the centre of an already existing robust and vibrant civic society. They should enthusiastically engage in broader civic movements to fight for social justice and inclusion and against intolerance, discrimination and social division. This can only be possible when they develop strong social leadership from within. They need to think 'outside the box'.

The Muslim community needs change-makers with a transformational character, who see the bigger picture. They need creative dynamism and determination to participate in intellectual jihad to acquire knowledge, and the skills to navigate through the challenges with required humility and spirituality. For too long it is others, mainly right-wing detractors, who have portrayed them as uncivilized or claiming that their faith is not compatible with modernity. It is time Muslims challenge this status quo, and do so with strength of knowledge and dignity. Young people, the asset of any nation, can be the backbone of our new struggle to build trust and reduce intolerance. When young and old from all backgrounds join hands they become change-makers in a society; a people-power for good. Needless to say, young people need a safe public space; they cannot be treated using a top-down diktat. In life they will pick and mix, they will make mistakes – and then they will learn. With their energy and innovative qualities, they will also be able to advance in areas which we have only just begun to think and explore.

I started my community work without any inkling of the future challenges that we as a community, and the world at large, are now facing. This activism gave me an opportunity to get to know people of my ethnic and religious background as well as many others in wider society. The expanding sphere of my activism drove me to work hard. I learnt, made mistakes and learnt more with every step. The rough and tumble of our lives are full of temptations and challenges. We need to make a consistent and conscious effort in order to remain on the middle way. This needs, in my opinion, pure intentions, determination and persistence. I tried my best in life, as I understood it, in my thoughts, ideas and activism. Irrespective of whether this personal struggle or jihad has brought any intended change in anyone's life, surely this has enriched me. At the end of the day, each person needs to leave this life with some contentment that they tried their best to create a better world.

Index

A Long Jihad

Association of Teachers and
  Lecturers (ATL), 126
Awami League (AL), 47
Awwal, Maulana Abdul, 96

Balham Mosque, 78
Bangladesh Air Force (BAF), 17,
  19, 35, 190
Bangladesh High Commission,
  18
Bangladesh Nationalist party
  (BNP), 47
Bangladeshi diaspora, 45, 48
Barber, Brendan, 125
Barelwis, 107
Base Commander, 27, 34-5
Bedey Community, 234
Begum, Shamima, 218
Bengali men, in Britain, 168
Biggs, John, 173
Bigley, Kenneth, 139
Blair, Tony, 12, 62, 89, 113-4,
  118, 120-1, 124, 135, 137,
  149, 156
'blame-game,' 244
BME (black and minority
  ethnic) communities, 202,
  239
Bosnia and Herzegovina (BiH),
  83, 85-7
Bosniak Muslims, 82, 84
in Srebrenica, 83, 86
bottom-up approach, 109
Bouazizi, Mohamed, 186
Boyle, Danny, 200
Bradford Muslims, 81
breaking family, 250
Breivik, Anders Behring, 186,
  227
Brexit, 174, 234, 236, 256-7
Brick Lane Great Mosque. See
  Brick Lane mosque
Brick Lane Jamme Masjid. See
  Brick Lane mosque

Brick Lane mosque, 24-5, 160-1
Brick Lane Youth Development
  Agency (BLYDA), 252-4
Britain's Islamic Republic, 163
British East India Company.
  See East India Company
British model of dealing with
  pluralism, 168
British Muslim community,
  77, 84, 88, 103, 106-7, 151,
  176-7, 228, 262, 267
history of, 103
British Muslim Forum, 138
British Muslims, 71, 88, 91
British Sikh Consultative
  Forum, 209
Brocke, Edna, 147
Brown, Gordon, 120, 137-8, 211
'Building Families' parenting
  course, 184
Bunglawala, Inayat, 131, 136,
  164-5
Bush, George W., 118, 120
Butler, Tom, 209

Caldicott, Dame Fiona, 147
Callaghan, Jim, 25
Cameron, David, 218-9, 225,
  234, 251
Cantle, Ted, 116
caricature of Islam, 232
Carter, Jimmy, 80
Celsius 7/7, 123
Central Working Committee
  (CWC), 101, 111, 139, 151,
  153
Cerić, Mustafa, 86
Charity Commission, 95, 251,
  261
Charles, Prince, 10, 96, 191
Chelsea's Dielectric Group, 37
Chief Fire Officer, 177
Chief of Air Staff (CoAS), 33
Chilcot, John, 120

276